WOMEN
AFTER
HIS OWN HEART

Sister Lois Curry, O.P.

WOMEN
AFTER
HIS OWN HEART

**The Sisters of Saint Dominic
of the American Congregation
of the Sacred Heart of Jesus,
Caldwell, New Jersey
1881–1981**

**Graphics by
Sister Gerarda Panek, O.P.**

new city press, new york

ACKNOWLEDGEMENTS

*The author is grateful to the following publishers
for permission to use quoted materials:
Alba House (Society of St. Paul), Staten Island, New York;
Glencoe, Inc., Encino, California; Priory Press, Dubuque, Iowa;
The Seabury Press, New York City; Sheed, Andrews
and McMeel, Inc., Mission, Kansas; and Southern
Illinois University Press, Carbondale, Illinois.
The author would like to thank Reverend Carl
Hinrichson and Reverend John Catoir for permission
to quote from unpublished materials.
Scripture texts used in this work are taken from* The New
American Bible *© 1970 by The Confraternity of
Christian Doctrine, Washington, D.C., and are used by
permission of the copyright owner. All rights reserved.
Brief quotations from* The Documents of Vatican II,
*Abbott-Gallagher edition, are used with permission of
American Press, Inc., 106 W. 56 Street, New York, N.Y. 10019.
© 1966. All rights reserved.*

*Published in the United States by New City Press,
the Publishing House of the Focolare Movement, Inc.,
206 Skillman Avenue, Brooklyn, N.Y. 11211*
*© 1981 by the Sisters of Saint Dominic of the American Congregation
of the Sacred Heart of Jesus, Caldwell, N.J.
Printed in the United States of America
Library of Congress Catalog Card Number 81-82149
ISBN 0-911782-37-0*

*To all those Dominican women
who have instilled in me a thirst for learning,
a reverence for reflective study,
and the desire to share the fruits of contemplation.*

FOREWORD

It was in September, 1913, that the Dominican Sisters of Caldwell first entered my life. At the age of nine and following my mother's death, I was entrusted to their care and direction. At the Mount Saint Dominic boarding school for boys, I came to appreciate at a most impressionable period of life what a treasure was left to the Church in the religious congregation founded centuries ago by Saint Dominic. From these truly dedicated women I learned by example as well as by precept. These Sisters came to our area a century ago. For sixty-eight of those hundred years I have known and admired them.

At this writing a veritable litany of names crosses my memory. Some are associated with the classroom; others with various ministries. At all hours we were directed and supervised wisely and lovingly. The overall result is a lasting impression of reverence. The Sisters of Saint Dominic, like their founder, have lived and labored for the precious souls placed in their path by Divine Providence.

I refrain from stating particular names in deference to the myriad of those blessed ones whose identities have gone un-recorded or have been forgotten in the relentless passing of decades. They were not desirous of the world's acclaim. When they embraced the religious life they sacrificed many precious associations. Before their God, however, they are true heroines. A loving God never forgets and their names are recorded in the divine book of life. They were generous to the point of giving their very lives in service to the great High Priest and His Mother Mary.

Our tribute must fall far short of the mark. We are, nonetheless, consoled in the realization that God will never be outdone in generosity. The written record is presented with justifiable pride in this masterful work of Sister Lois Curry. Who of us can ever estimate the unwritten record of these hundreds of religious women bound by sacred vows? How nobly they have served the fellow members of their community as well as the uncounted thousands who have come to them over the years for inspiration and guidance!

May we who have been privileged to observe this centennial be moved to catch the torch from these loyal members of the family of Saint Dominic and pass it on to generations yet unborn.

Msgr. Walter G. Jarvais
Immaculate Conception Seminary
Mahwah, New Jersey

PREFACE

This survey of the history of the Congregation of the Sacred Heart of Jesus is the work of many Sisters. It was my momentous centenary task to act like the scribe who went to the storehouse and found a treasury of things old and new.

The early records of the Community, written by Mother M. Catherine, Mother M. Alacoque, Sister M. Amanda, Sister M. Josephine, Sister M. Dominica, and Sister M. Rose, are preserved in beautiful Spencerian Script ledgers.

In 1892, Sister Rose prepared the earliest history and compiled the document which was placed in the cornerstone of the Motherhouse at the Mount.

In 1923 she passed the torch of research to Mother Joseph who was ably assisted by Sister M. Clementine and Sister M. Aloysius. Translations of German records from Ratisbon and Brooklyn were compiled by 1932.

Once a sufficient amount of raw data had been obtained from the various Congregational and Diocesan archives, Mother Joseph had hoped to have a history published by Monsignor James Crawford, whose classic work, *Daughters of Saint Dominic on Long Island,* is evaluated highly. Nothing came of the initial correspondence (1945).

Sister Vivien commissioned Sister Marie to make a readable compilation of all available materials. This writer is deeply indebted to Sister Marie for her earlier work, her continued support, and her valuable criticism during the present research.

It is impossible to convey the depth of spirit and the vast panoply of significant events which lie at the heart of the past one hundred years. Within the time allotted and limited by the available resources, this topical history is written as an initial effort to inform the present generation about our glorious past, to inspire them to bring it to contemporary fruition, and to serve as a catalyst to encourage a deep bond of unity of heart even amid a diversity of expression.

The history would still be in the mind and heart of the author if she had not had the encouragement of the Council and the valuable assistance of Sister Irene Marie who combed the archives for its many hidden treasures and who updated the oral history; Sister Gerarda whose graphics punctuate so beautifully the traditional yet contemporary thrust of the narrative; Sisters Marie, Rita Margaret, Brigid Brady, Suzanne McCaffrey, Nancy Bourk, Inez, and Mary Agatha for editorial assistance; Sister Beverly Cardino and Ms. Cindy Ciangio for their help in proofreading; and last but not least Ms. Ruthann Williams and Mrs. Marilyn Christy for endless hours of transcription and typing. Further I must acknowledge the generosity of Claude Blanc from New City Press, Peter Wosh from the Diocesan archives at Seton Hall, and the many Dominican archivists and historians who opened their hearts and materials to me.

May this first published history be a beginning word which finds resonance in the heart of each reader so that later works may provide a fuller, richer revelation of both the spirit and fact of this Dominican Community of women who struggle to be faithful to their Founder and to be effective in building up the Kingdom.

Sister Lois Curry. O.P.
April 15, 1981

CONTENTS

PROLOGUE

The history of the Sisters of Saint Dominic of Caldwell, New Jersey, known in the Order as the American Congregation of the Sacred Heart of Jesus, illustrates the continuous struggle to adapt the spirit and life-style of Saint Dominic Guzman (1160–1221) to the needs of the Church in every age. Each of the significant periods surveyed in this story develops a recurring theme. First there is a dream, then an articulated vision, and finally a plan to balance the tension between the active-contemplative dimensions. The constructive regenerating changes are brought about through discerned reflection on the past with an eye towards appropriate adaptations to present needs.

The story is told so that everyone who reads it can enter wholeheartedly into the love story between God and His faithful ones and receive new hope and new life.

Dare then to enter the past dreams in order to understand the dreamers of today. Look deeply at the past visions to criticize constructively the visionaries of the day as they struggle to adapt the traditional ways to present times. Study past plans for life and mission and dare to construct vital plans for a hope-filled future.

1

To dare, to dream, to envision, to plan, and to have the courage to change—this is the Caldwell Dominican heritage. The women and men who begin and fashion the heritage simply continue the life and mission of Jesus in their own day. They are always leading others to the Father through the Son in the power of the Spirit. They are usually spinning their dreams amidst stark, non-accepting environments. They continue to formulate plans to meet the real needs of ordinary people and confront the unjust spirit in their times. Their plans never intend to destroy any law or structure that is life-giving. These dreamers and visionaries are rebuilders according to the promise of Isaias: "Your people will rebuild what has long been in ruins; building again on the old foundations, You will be known as people who rebuild the walls. . ." (Isaias 58:12).

The prophetic vision began in the heart of God the Father who so loved the world that He sent His Son so that we would not die in our sin but live. It was enfleshed in the human heart of Jesus who is the Way, the Truth, and the Life. It continued to be manifest in the Middle Ages which gave birth to the hearts of Dominic and the founding Sisters from the Convents of Prouille, Rome, and Ratisbon.

Four women of deep faith and courage, Mother Benedicta Bauer, Mother Josepha Witzlhofer, Mother Augustine Neuhierl, and Mother Catherine Muth, thrust the story from the cloisters of old-world Europe into the heart of the emerging Catholic Church in America.

Within twenty-two years three independent American congregations could trace their foundation to the cloistered Convent of the Holy Cross in Ratisbon, Germany. On December 16, 1881, Winand Michael Wigger, the third Bishop of Newark, wrote the declaration of independence for the Sisters of Saint Dominic of Jersey City without their knowledge or consent. The letter was addressed to the pastor of St. Boniface Church where the Sisters staffed the school.

Dear Father Kraus:

> In answer to your letter of inquiry, after having well considered
> all the reasons advanced by you, I beg leave to state that I am
> quite willing that the house of Dominican Sisters of Jersey City
> should be detached from that of New York. I the more willingly
> give the consent, as the Rules and Constitutions of the Domini-
> can Sisters favor the independence of every one of their houses.
> With kind regards to yourself and the good Sisters I am
>
> Your servant in Christ,
W.M. Wigger
Bp. of Newark

The Sisters did separate from New York and, since that
time, the Community has been determining its role in the
Church and this archdiocese. The Preamble of the Constitutions
approved and distributed February 23, 1980 expresses succinctly the ultimate goal.

> Our Congregation is entitled: The Sisters of St. Dominic of the
> American Congregation of the Sacred Heart of Jesus. We are an
> institute approved by the Church which provides a way of life for
> its members to achieve the deepening of their baptismal commit-
> ment to Christ through the joyful living in community of the
> evangelical counsels of chastity, poverty, and obedience. The end
> and purpose of our congregation, as of all religious life, is to
> bring about the full flourishing of charity and to affirm our
> dedication to this goal. Since our congregation is dedicated to the
> Sacred Heart, the evidence of Christian love should be our sign
> among the people.

The Community defines itself as *Women After His Own Heart.*

IN THE STILLNESS

"Be restless with
tremendous desire for
God's glory . . . Seek
to pursue truth and clothe
yourself in it."

Saint Catherine of Siena

1,2,4–Holy Cross Convent, Regensburg, Germany
3–St. Dominic, Mt. St. Dominic, Caldwell

The Caldwell heritage did not begin with the letter of separation written by Bishop Wigger in 1881, and it has not yet reached its perfection in the present Constitutions. It is always in the process of becoming; therefore, it seems fitting to look back on the dreams, visions, and plans of the Founding Father and Mothers which directly influence both the present and future.

In the stillness of the Cloisters of Osma, Prouille, Rome, and Ratisbon, a spirit was born and came to fullness of life. Enter the stillness and come to grips with the glorious heritage. In the silence and between the lines, listen and you will surely hear and see the mysterious plan of God at work in and through the lives of the women and man whom the Church recognizes as Founder and co-foundresses.

It is usually quoted that, behind every great man, there is a great woman. This story is reversed; behind each of the very great women there is a great man: Dominic Guzman.

Saint Dominic lived in an age of rapid change and turmoil. The European world of the twelfth and early thirteenth centuries was experiencing the death of one culture and the birth pangs of another. The former culture, rooted in the land and supported by tottering feudalism, was yielding to an urban commercial pattern of life. It was a time of critical, unprecedented social, political, and economic change. It was an age of changing values which forced people to clarify convictions and identify roots.

The Church was faced with the need to articulate its Judaeo-Christian heritage boldly and to witness to the timeless relevance of the Christian values and lifestyle. Dominic Guzman knew the faith and loved it. Dominic believed in its relevance and fruitfulness for all times. While he recognized the creative and progressive elements of his age, he looked with serious concern at its conflicting and destructive aspects. His central compulsion was to preach the Gospel. His dream was to create a dynamic religious lifestyle capable of giving witness to a simple life and of providing the environment to form contemplative apostles.

In 1184 Dominic was ordained a canon regular for the Cathedral Church at Osma in Spain. In the stillness of his cloister and through the liturgical life of the church, he discovered the centrality of the Incarnation and life, death, and resurrection of Jesus in salvation history and on-going liberation. Study of the Scriptures, reception of the Sacraments, and the prayers and service of his Community revealed to him a deeper understanding of who God is and His plan for us. Contemplative solitude implanted the Truth so deeply in his heart that, when Dominic was confronted by the devastation wrought by the untruths of the heresy of his day, he abandoned the cloister for an apostolic life.

Dominic and his bishop, Diego, felt called to preach the Gospel to the Tartars. When they approached Pope Innocent III with this request, the pope became God's spokesman. Dominic's mission field was to be France, not Russia; his weapon, preaching, not martyrdom. In accepting the will of Innocent, Dominic discovered the need of the Church for a world-wide order of preachers to be defenders of the faith and lights for the world in every age. Support of the papacy and obedience to the call of the Church would be part of the Dominican spirit for all time.

Dominic is the spiritual Father. He transmits to his sons and daughters a spirit of life and a lifestyle which he believed should be flexible, open to dispensation and judicious change. To create a contemplative environment and a community steeped in the study of theology and Scripture, so that its members can preach by word and example that Jesus Christ is the Lord who continues to liberate his people through the events of life, is the ultimate purpose for the Dominican life. The Dominican Family of Priests, Brothers, Contemplative Nuns, active Sisters, and lay women and men share a life of prayer, study, and service. In the spirit of the Dominican quest for truth and human liberation, all members of the Family strive to understand the wondrous ways of God at work in their lives. A deepened contemplative response leads each person to question history and to accept responsibility for co-founding a new and dynamic religious social order for the times.

Women of deep faith, constant trust, and life-giving courage fashioned the dreams, visions, and plans which influence the present. In the stillness of the contemplative monasteries of Saint Mary's (Prouille), Saint Sixtus (Rome), and Holy Cross (Ratisbon), the spirit of the Third Order Conventual life of the present Congregation of the Sacred Heart of Jesus is rooted.

Saint Dominic conceived the idea of the contemplative monastic life for women, formerly called the Second Order lifestyle, as a response to the heresy of his day. The foundation of the first monastery in Saint Mary's, Prouille, is intimately connected with the spread of the Albigensian heresy throughout southern France.

About 1022, Albi, a town in southern France, became the European birthplace of Catharism, later called Albigensianism after the town from which it spread. The leaders of the heretical sect taught that there were two gods: one good and one evil. They denied the doctrines of the Blessed Trinity, Incarnation, and Resurrection which formed the heart of Christianity. Since they taught that the body was the creation of the god of evil, they believed it would die at death and there would be no resurrection on the last day. Suicide was justified because the body was evil and to kill it was a way to free the spirit trapped within. Severe penances which brought about sickness and death were encouraged, not in order to place oneself under the control of the spirit, but rather, to bring on death.

This heresy ravaged the plains of the Languedoc in France. Dominic became acquainted with the heresy early in the thirteenth century. He noted with great pain its chief effects: confusion, division, sin, and death. When he was commissioned by the Pope to combat the heretics, Dominic recognized that he could best overcome the heretics by using their own methods: powerful preaching and disputation, simplicity and austerity of lifestyle, and availability to all who would seek them out with sincere hearts.

His availability to nine heretical women is key to the story. One evening after an open air sermon, Dominic entered a near-by church to pray for an hour. As he knelt, the door opened. A group of women approached him with the cry, "Sir, we would see Jesus." They fell on their knees begging him to guide them. "Servant of God, help us. If what you say be true, we have long been deceived by the spirit of error, for until now we have always believed those whom you call heretics, and we have obeyed them and looked upon them as holy men. We adhered to their doctrines, and now your sermon leaves us in cruel uncertainty. Servant of God, we beseech you, pray the Lord will make known to us the true faith, because in it we wish to live, to die, and to be saved."[1]

These wealthy women were believers who had been declared perfect in the heretical sect. They were placed in charge of colleges, places for preaching and teaching, as well as hospices for heretical retreatants. In these houses the women led a life that was poor, austere, and chaste. They also received children of heretics and reared them in the faith.

Dominic realized that the Catholic Church would have to offer an alternative community and a similar role if he were to remain faithful to his conversion. He decided to found a house which would be a refuge for converts and a place where religious education could be given to these new converts and through them to others. The importance of a thorough knowledge of the faith, which leads to a deeper penetration of its mysteries and to intimacy with God, would be the heart of the matter for Dominican women and men in every age.

Once the dream had been articulated, like the patriarchs of old, Dominic abandoned himself to Divine Providence and asked for a sign from heaven. At a lonely spot outside of Fanjeau, on July 22, 1206, he knelt in prayer. Suddenly a globe of fire darted downward and rested upon the deserted church of Notre Dame de Prouille. Later this property was donated to St. Dominic by the Bishop of Toulouse. It was converted into a monastery and revenues to sustain the cloistered life were provided by Berenger of Narbonne.

On November 22 of the same year the nine converts, as well as two Catholic penitents from Fanjeau, became the first contemplative Sisters of Saint Dominic. With the authorization of Bishop Foulques, Dominic invested them in the habit on December 27. Their dress consisted of a white habit, black veil, and black woolen mantle to which a scapular was added after Blessed Reginald's vision.[2] A primitive rule embracing poverty, chastity, and obedience, silence, abstinence, fasting, and choral recitation of the Divine Office was practiced and then codified by 1220. "The life of the monastery was strictly contemplative. The Sisters engaged in educational and apostolic work only by exception in individual cases. The Priory of Friars connected with Prouille consisted of at least four priests and some lay brothers."[3]

The simple lifestyle, including by 1212 strict enclosure, became the norm for all later contemplative foundations.

The roots of the contemplative life for Dominican women can also be traced to Italy. In 1220 Pope Honorius III imposed on Dominic the task of uniting six small communities in Rome into a single large reformed community. The Sisters were to follow the rule of Prouille. Saint Dominic brought a Prioress,

Sister Blanche, from Prouille to preside over the new community. The new foundation moved into the Priory of Saint Sixtus which the Friars had vacated on February 15. This ancient convent is now occupied by a community of Irish Dominicans.

The rule of Saint Sixtus became the model for all later monasteries founded by the Dominican Friars.

Under the direction of Blessed Jordan, the second Master General of the Order, Friars established monasteries in Spain and Germany. The monasteries established at Strassburg and Althemhohenau preceded the foundation at Ratisbon which is the European Motherhouse for the Congregation of the Sacred Heart.

Since it is from the Convent of the Holy Cross, Ratisbon,[4] that the four courageous women would come to America in 1853, a survey of its history seems timely.

There were pious women, who had dedicated their lives of prayer and penance for the success of the Crusades, living on the outskirts of Ratisbon.[5] Though history is somewhat ambivalent, it appears that they practiced no specific rule, until the Dominicans petitioned Bishop Siegfried to found a Dominican monastery for them in 1233.

The ancient chronicle of the Convent records that the Town Council, advised by the Bishop, offered the "Steingrube," located on the west side of the city, as a fitting building site. Work progressed slowly since the good women could not guarantee the necessary revenues for building or sustaining a strictly cloistered life. Bishop Siegfried again assisted. He appealed to Count Henry von Ortenburg who allotted the tithes of the parish at Schwarzhofen for this worthy cause. Once the funds were secured, construction continued and the Convent was dedicated on November 12, 1244.[6]

On February 13, 1245, the Convent was formally approved by Pope Innocent IV who placed it under the protection of the papacy and the direction of the Dominican Order. Though its status as an episcopal or pontifical community changed periodically, since 1803 it has been under the jurisdiction of the Bishop of Ratisbon.

The years 1244 to 1260 witnessed the growth of the monastery. Whether the "Albert, Ordinis Praedicatorum," who signed the document of transfer of property from Count von Ortenburg to Holy Cross Convent, was Saint Albert the Great is uncertain. It is certain, however, that the convent was given special attention during the episcopacy of Albert in that city, 1260–1262.

Though the convent remained financially solvent and grew in numbers, its spirit and discipline suffered greatly throughout the fourteenth century.

Its numbers were decimated during the Great Plague (1348–1359), and divisions and a break-down of regular observance accompanied the other ravages caused by the Great Western Schism (1379–1418).

As early as 1406, Thomas di Fermio, Master General of the Order, began to reform the Convent. This arduous task was completed by 1476 when the enclosure was enforced strictly, and exemplary nuns were placed in leadership.

This reformed spirit and life of regular observance continued to strengthen the nuns in succeeding generations. "Holy Cross Convent was a fortress in the struggle against the Lutheran Revolution (1517ff), the Thirty Years War (1618–1648), and the Napoleonic confiscations (1802ff). It was a unique example of survival through adversity and upheaval, a convent that rose with new life from the remains of its own decline, that stood firm upon trembling ground—faithful if not always at maximum fervor, in the life of the Second Order of St. Dominic."[7] It is the only German convent to have a continuous history without suppression or secularization.

In 1799 Maximillan IV ascended the throne of Bavaria, the kingdom in which Ratisbon was located. Since he had twice married Protestants, it came as no surprise when he advanced not only the cause of toleration for Lutherans but also launched a persecution against Catholics. During his reign religious foundations were secularized. Four hundred convents were closed, their lands ceded to others, and their nuns disbanded or forced to live in central convents with subsistant pensions.[8]

Until 1803 Holy Cross escaped suppression. In that year,
the Commissar of Napoleon, who had established control over
Bavaria, assembled the nuns in their refectory. Each nun was
questioned: "Will you return to the world (with a pension) or
remain in the convent subject to Prince Bishop von Dalburg, to
whom your land has been ceded?"[9] All the nuns chose to
remain.

Prince Bishop Karl von Dalburg issued a decree that the
nuns must teach in the city school or be suppressed. The nuns
were bewildered. Like Mary, another perplexed virgin, they
thought to themselves, "How can this be? What of the enclosure?" The irate bishop settled the dilemma. He arranged for
suitable teaching rooms within the enclosure, provided for the
education of the faculty, and decreed the opening of the
school.[10]

The contemplative nuns of Holy Cross Monastery were
forced to integrate the active and contemplative lifestyles in a
new way. Survival, and their desire to remain religious in the
Church, dictated change. The fusion of faith and trust in
Providence, and reliance on a common sense decision, had
provided a novel response to a new challenge. This courage to
dare to do the different, untried thing would be a heritage at the
heart of many similar decisions which would face their daughter
convents in the twentieth century American Catholic Church.

The continuous period of secularization was marked not
only by religious persecution and financial oppression by the
state, but also by actual military conflict in Ratisbon. Holy
Cross Convent was in the direct fire between the French and
Austrian lines during the later Napoleonic wars. Preserved from
physical destruction by Divine Providence, the Convent did not
remain preserved from internal laxity and sloth. "Holy Cross
Chronicle records the general deterioration which began to
disorganize community life. The Dominican Prior, Father
Brunner, had played the role of true prophet in predicting a
school in connection with the Rule of the Second Order.
Irregularities, such as individual Sisters keeping private bank

accounts, disposing of money, giving presents, became pre-
valent. Each Sister received a certain amount of spending
money which she could use as she liked."[11]

Life in the convent took a new direction in 1836 when
Bishop Schwaebl of Ratisbon placed the convent under diocesan jurisdiction and mandated reform. By 1845 Mother
Benedicta Bauer had been elected prioress and, with the assistance of Franz Joseph Schiml, confessor of the convent, the
reform was realized.

Mother Benedicta had never sought leadership in Ratisbon. On the contrary, as early as 1827, she was among the
Sisters who volunteered to go to America and found a convent
in the diocese of Cincinnati under the jurisdiction of Edward
Fenwick, O.P. The plan did not materialize then, but the
missionary spirit remained dormant in the heart of the eminent
prioress.

Having accomplished the internal reform, Mother turned
her energies toward the establishment of new foundations in
Germany at Niederviehbach and Mintraching. She was a woman of deep faith who heard the word of God and acted with
daring to accomplish his apparent will in spite of risks demanded in personnel or financial resources.

Mother's zeal for spreading the faith and the lifestyle of the
Second Order would not be satisfied until both were extended
to America. Since she could count on the financial support of
the Bavarian mission society, she continued to search out a
viable opportunity to send Sisters to the new world.

The occasion which came in 1851 centered around the visit
of Reverend Dom Wimmer, O.S.B., an American missionary,
to his cousin, Sister Elizabeth Wissel, in the Holy Cross
Convent. Though Dom Wimmer's precise intentions at best
seem visionary rather than practical, Mother Benedicta acted on
his request. By 1853 four Sisters had volunteered to go to
America, and Mother wrote for the customary decree of
dismissal.

Mother wrote to the Bishop in the spring of 1853.

My Lord:

During his visit to Ratisbon, two years ago, the Rt. Rev. Abbot Wimmer of St. Vincent's Abbey, Pennsylvania, U.S.A., called upon us and during the course of his conversations frequently expressed the wish that some of our Nuns would found a convent and missions in America in order that they, following the example of our Holy Father, St. Dominic, might labor in that vineyard of our Lord for their own salvation and for the salvation of the neglected Catholic children, particularly those of German immigrants. He offered his service most earnestly in furthering this project as a token of gratitude to St. Dominic.

In January of 1853, he wrote again stating that, since his return to America, the thought of this plan was constantly in his mind and that, during the meeting of the Council of Baltimore, he had discussed the matter with the Dominican Fathers present. The superior had graciously declared that he and his brethren would be greatly pleased to have German Dominican nuns nearby; he also promised to provide for their spiritual welfare and assist them in temporal affairs. This letter was read to the Sisters and the volunteers renewed their applications to be permitted to accept the invitation and prepare to leave for America as soon as possible.

Thereupon we notified the Abbot of the perseverance and persistence of the Sisters and besought his advice in regard to the steps to be taken in executing this plan.

In his reply of April 4th, the Abbot declared that the Sisters could start for America and St. Vincent's College as soon as all the preliminaries had been attended to. They could stop at the college for a time to study the English language, continuing, at the same time, all their religious exercises. He, himself, would attend to everything else. He advised us to obtain a "dismissorial" from your Lordship testifying that the Sisters had come to America with your Lordship's sanction and the permission of their prioress and that she had asked him, Abbot Wimmer, to be their director and protector. At the same time he advised us to seek the aid of the Reverend Court Chaplain, Father Mueller, who is the director of the King Louis Mission Society. We are enclosing the reply Reverend Father Mueller sent us on May

11th, 1853. Therefore, we most humbly beseech your Lordship to grant the aforesaid "dismissorial" to the choir nuns, Josepha Witzlhofer and Augustine Neuhierl, and the lay Sisters, Francesca Retter and Jacobina Riederer. A gracious reply to the humble petition of your obedient servants is hoped for by

Your Lordship's most humble servant,

M. Benedicta Bauer, Prioress.[12]

A copy of Father Mueller's letter, mentioned above, has not come down to us, but the Bishop must have been pleased with the arrangements since he sent the "dismissorial" on May 29, 1853:

We, Valentine, by Divine Mercy and Grace of the Apostolic See, Bishop of Ratisbon...

Since for some time the Reverend Dom Boniface, Superior of the Order of Saint Benedict of North America, has desired that we should send nuns of the Order of Saint Dominic of the monastery of the Holy Cross of Ratisbon, who are especially fit for the educating of girls; most willing assenting to his pleas, after having conferred with the prioress and council of the said monastery and after previous serious examination of the Sisters who, with the consent of their Superioress, offered themselves for the afore-said mission, we dismiss, in the Lord, the Sisters beloved in Christ: Mary Josepha Witzlhofer and Mary Augustine Neuhierl with the lay Sisters Mary Francesca Retter and Mary Jacobina Riederer, on the condition that they should remain in the same congregation to which by vows they were joined under the jurisdiction of the Prioress of Holy Cross (and if necessity should demand it, it is permitted to them to return to the said monastery of the Holy Cross), until a new monastery in America can be permanently erected. Moreover, we have confirmed as Superior with ordinary authority, Mary Josepha Witzlhofer, to whom the Prioress gave the government of the new congregation of Sisters. Therefore we earnestly commend these Religious whose fervor for promoting of the greater glory of God and the salvation of souls, we have well known, to the most Reverend and Illustrious Excellency, the Ordinary of that Diocese to whose jurisdiction they will be subject, requesting that he will deign to

receive them in his paternal heart as daughters, encourage them
with apostolic charity.

Given at Ratisbon, in the Kingdom of Bavaria, on the 29th of
May 1853.

Valentine, Bishop of Ratisbon
Painter, Secretary[13]

The following July the unsuspecting Abbot Wimmer confided to his friend his understanding of this missionary venture.

Latrobe, Westmoreland Co.
July 29, 1853

In the near future I shall have to go to New York again to meet
six Dominican Sisters that the Convent of the Holy Cross of
Ratisbon is sending me as a cross (as if I did not as yet have
enough crosses). I am to look for a suitable place for them.
Already letters for that purpose have been sent East and West.
Perhaps I shall be able to locate them in Williamsburg, a suburb
of New York City, where the German pastor and Vicar General
Raffeiner is disposed to take them if the Archbishop permits it.
Otherwise, I must, for the time being, send my people out of the
city to the farm and give the Sisters the house in Indiana,
Pennsylvania, until such a time that I can find a suitable place
for them.

I really should not have burdened myself with this affair; but
the Prioress did not cease to beg me and so I agreed, or rather
promised, to help as much as I could to find a place for them
outside our diocese. I hoped thereby that Saint Dominic would
put in a good word for me when I needed it.[14]

The four Sisters sailed for America on the *Germania*
July 25, 1853, and reached New York on August 28. In
Crawford's history a column from the German newspaper
announced their first awakening in America.

August 2, 1853, this article appeared in the foreign news
column of *Katholische-Zeitung* of New York. "A new order has
followed the orders of the Bavarian Sisterhoods, who are
interesting themselves in the welfare of poor German Ameri-

cans. Yesterday four women departed from the Convent of Holy Cross here, for a mission in North America provided with everything which the establishment of such a convent requires, and followed by the heartfelt good wishes of their companions in religion. The Reverend Court Chaplain Mueller, who is at the head of the Mission Society of Saint Ludwig, came especially to provide the travellers with the necessary papers. Then he accompanied them as far as Leipzig. They will begin their work of teaching under the superintendence of Boniface Wimmer."[15]

The journey of the four took them to the docks on Fulton Street in New York. The awakenings of faith in the hearts of the German immigrants began in confusion and apprehension since they were left stranded, but the journey reached the desired end through their adamant spirit to dare, to dream, to envision, and to plan for a new life in the new world and to help build something that would endure.

2.

"We go, we travel constantly, for our life is nothing but a pilgrimage."

Mother Benedicta Bauer

AWAKENINGS

2

1.

2

3.

4.

5.

Early in the morning of August 28, 1853, four women dressed in European peasant garb rather than in their usual Dominican habit, unable to speak English, uncertain of their destination, surrounded by twenty chests of goods from their ancestral convent, disembarked from the *Germania.* They faced the stark reality that Abbot Wimmer had not arrived to meet them. Eventually Mother Josepha pulled out a letter from Father Mueller and sought help to find the Redemptorist Fathers mentioned in its contents. Some workers on the dock called a coach and gave the necessary directions. The women vanished carrying with them only four small carpet bags which contained the white habits, black veils, and Rule books which identified them as Second Order Dominicans of the Holy Cross Convent in Ratisbon.[1]

Reverend Mother Seraphine, the second Mother Prioress of the American Congregation of the Holy Cross, records the event according to her remembrances of conversations with Mother Josepha. "In the beginning God allowed the first Sisters to be tried in the furnace of tribulation. The Abbot Wimmer who was to have met the Sisters on their arrival in New York

and taken them to Carrolltown did not appear. It was certain in
the special providence of God that the Sisters stood neglected in
a strange land and did not know what to do. Happily the Court
Chaplain Mueller had given the Sisters letters of introduction to
the Redemptorist Fathers in New York. The Sisters were
directed there to take counsel. Reverend Father Kleineidam and
a lay Brother, Nicholas, took the forsaken Sisters in and cared
for them. Through their kind offices, Mother Josepha and
Mother Augustine—and the two lay Sisters—were taken to
Newark to a family named Blaggi.[2] You can imagine the feelings
of the poor Sisters to be transferred from the peaceful cloister
where they had been sheltered and cared for, to a strange world
where they had no friends—not even to know where they would
be sheltered."[3]

Further investigation exonerates Abbot Wimmer and illustrates the behind-the-scenes direction of the Sisters' future by
the clergy. In a letter written to Mother Benedicta Bauer, the
Abbot explains why he was unable to meet the Sisters at the
dock; and he outlines the arrangements he had made for their
future in the new country.

September 18, 1853

Venerable dear Mother Prioress:
That your daughters arrived safely in America, you already
know. As well as I could, I provided that they should be
immediately received by my co-frater, P. Nicholas Balleis, in New
York. I could come to see them and provide for them only the
fifth day after their arrival. Because for the time being I knew of
no place for them in the country, I agreed with the Reverend
Vicar General of New York, Father Raffeiner, that he take the
Sisters to his parish church in Williamsburg, a suburb of New
York, which numbers 30,000 inhabitants, nearly 15,000 of whom
are German Catholics. The place is excellent in location as a field
of activity. Oh, how the girls and mothers rejoiced as they heard
they had Sisters and especially when they saw them! Also the
Right Reverend Arch-Bishop gladly received them. Because no
convent is there, we were obliged to lodge the Sisters in the
rectory which adjoins the old church. Do not be alarmed at this.

The pastor, the above named Vicar General, is an old father, a holy priest, and has only one curate. The rectory is spacious. I remained for four days with him to arrange everything. The four Sisters already after the first week have a complete enclosure as regards the outside—the people; and also interiorly with regards to the priest. Naturally, they are in considerably close quarters, but it is satisfactory. They have a kitchen; next to it a study room; on the other side is a dormitory large enough for four. At the same time I bought four iron, very comfortable, bedsteads, so that I might see whether there was sufficient room; we found that there was additional space for a table and a chest or bureau. The pastor who lives on the upper floor has access only to the kitchen. I arranged to make even this part of the enclosure, by locking the quarters. I had a partition made near the outside door so that now they receive there only mail and no one has access to their house.

Thus, I succeeded in making an uninterrupted or strictly private passage way which leads to the church and also to a large room under the church where the Sisters may store their clothes, or if they wish, they may use it for sleeping quarters. A large garden surrounds the church which gives them space in which to recreate and to work. The school adjoins the church. Their future convent will either be built on the same spot, if the old pastor so desires, or on the west side of the large new church which would still be better. Here, the pastor has three lots or places for buildings; between these, however, in the center, there are two small houses which would have to be purchased. They would cost from $5,000 to $6,000. This amount must not alarm you or frighten you. $6,000 is a trifle. By means of school activities and institute, that amount would soon be paid—the real burden for your children is this: that they must cook for both priests, *i.e.,* that they will share the food with them.

We have arranged that the Sisters will send the meals upstairs by means of a dumbwaiter as they do in the convent. Nevertheless, this, we realize, is somewhat annoying and troublesome. Alas, nothing else could be done. The old priest purposely took the Sisters so that he would not be obliged to have a cook and also to save money. He is rich, but he is very close. Perhaps in turn he will some day will the Sisters his money. If he grants them only the lot for the building as he promised, he will be donating the equivalent of $1,000. I assure you that everything is all right, *i.e.,* if the old priest does change his mind, and if he keeps his word. I hope he will, because he realizes that he is at an advantage, and he likes his parish and he knows that his parishioners are eager for and need the services of the Sisters; and lastly because he depends or relies considerably on me. I impressed sharply upon the Sisters this fact; viz., that they should not be seriously concerned if they suffered somewhat financially—but I urged them to get in touch with me if they were in want so that I might personally fight it out with Father. In order that the Sisters will not be obliged to arrange the beds and rooms of the priests, the Father engaged the services of a pious widow and I told the Sisters to pay the salary to her for this service because they too, would often be in need of her services; in this way the old priest may more easily be satisfied. He is at the time their ordinary confessor. I begged a Capuchin Father from New York to be the extraordinary confessor. Pray with your children at home that the original spirit of charity, union, resignation, and patience may continue to flourish among the Sisters here and that the Lord may direct everything for the best.

The two exchangeable notes of $6,000 gulden and $1,000 gulden, $4,000 of which was in my name, I collected. The reverend old gentleman wonders if the Sisters could not lend him the money until they need it. He would give them five per cent interest. I urged the Sisters to accept the offer. The old Father does not need the money personally but he will re-invest it in a so-called Savings Bank which will give him six per cent interest; thus he will gain one per cent.

Thereby the Sisters will be worth more to him materially; at the same time the Sisters will benefit for they do not need the money now. When I left, they still had 250 schillings on hand wherewith to buy chests, storage cabinets, etc., this money soon will be used up. The money earned by teaching will support them otherwise. Naturally, I am not yet in a position to discuss the building of a new convent. We must see how everything develops—at any rate just now there is no need therefore.

But there is something which needs immediate attention; you must admit one or two postulants who are well versed in English. You may not object to this because the nature of the case demands such.

"One who endeavors to attain the object must of necessity use the means." One who has not from youth been brought up in the use of the English language will never be able to master the English sufficiently well to teach it. You are at liberty to send us German teachers or postulants but we ourselves must admit and train English postulants here. That is what the other teaching Sisters do—so do my Benedictines—so your Dominicans must do likewise. Since you yourself confided your daughters to me, and also the Rt. Rev. Bishop in his testimonials, and Rt. Rev. Archbishop of New York, also his Vicar General, consider me the spiritual director of your Sisters, I have, therefore, assumed a definite responsibility for them. I believe I have the necessary authority to direct the Sisters in this matter—hence I have ordered Mother Josepha to admit promptly any worthy English postulant who might apply for admission. I told her I would be responsible to you for I am better acquainted in America and I know better what must be done here, than you at Holy Cross, in Regensburg. I certainly mean well in your regard and that of your Sisters.

Now something else—had I known it sooner your Sisters would have been assigned to a very fine place in the City of New York affiliated with the Capuchin Church. The pastor, Father Ambrose, scolded me sternly because I did not tell him about the Dominican nuns because he would have taken them. Well for the present that plan is spoiled, but I would like to know whether you could send him four Sisters. He is about to purchase a house next to the Church which may be adapted for a cloistered convent; he is not certain that he will be able to buy the house. If he does he would want German nuns for his girls. If you have four more Sisters (two postulants and two Sisters) to spare, (remember—good and industrious) you may write to me, so that in the fall, if he is able to use them, he need only to write to you for them. This must remain a secret just now. I did tell your Sisters in Williamsburg about it—but I did not tell them the place. They too, must not further mention the fact—still less if the enterprise fails.

Whether I have performed my task well or badly I do not know— I certainly meant well—of that I am certain. I cannot often travel to Williamsburg because it is 400 miles from here and requires at least 60 florins. But if there is a need, I will come in spite of that fact.

Furthermore, I wish to keep in touch with my adopted children by letter-writing and wish to direct them until they are better acquainted and can direct themselves. Every beginning is hard. Much must be endured. But whoever means well with God and possesses good will, God will be helpful in the end. The Sisters were all very well; they served me well, entertained me as long as they could. Please reprove them because they would not accept anything from me for the chest or trunk which cost thirty-four florins. At the beginning they were full of hope and courage (Sept. 7) and I hope all will be well. Everything was so well ordered that one cannot help feeling that the will of God is being done. Pray for me and write an answer soon. I greet you all in the Lord and remain with utmost respect.

Yours sincerely,
P. Boniface Wimmer, O.S.B.[4]

Dom Wimmer's letter indicates that the confusion of August 28 gave way to the orderly settling-in process which culminated on September 2 when one hundred pupils began school in the basement of the church. Mother Josepha and Sister Augustine taught all the children in German.

Mother Josepha Witzlhofer continued the fine tradition of religious spirit and education of youth which she had learned in Ratisbon. According to two students of Holy Trinity who later became Prioresses of the American Congregation of the Holy Cross, Sisters Catherine Herbert and Philomena Frey, "Mother Josepha was tall and slender, with a very pale face and hands like wax. She was refined and lady-like, almost ethereal so that the children considered her a superior being."[5]

Monsignor Crawford enhances this perception. "She had her limitations and the defects of her virtues. Her gentle and retiring disposition probably made her at times too docile and pliant.... Her sterling worth makes her limitations very small indeed. By her example she bequeathed to her spiritual daughters the following great virtues:

1) Obedience to the Bishop and his representatives as the voice of the vicar of Christ.

2) A wonderful perseverance in the face of disheartening obstacles....

3) A proper technical training for the various works of the Community....

4) The embodiment of refinement and religious decorum, a spirit of prayer and sacrifice. Although she tolerated a canonical loose-ness of administration because conditions made it necessary, she held the observance of her holy rule and the holy traditions of the Dominican Order most zealously."[6]

Mother Josepha exerted a benign spiritual influence on nuns and students alike. By 1854 enrollment soared from one hundred forty students to two hundred twenty. To meet increased enrollment and a projected increase in the number of Sisters, the school and convent were moved to larger quarters. A second missionary band consisting of Sister Michaela Braun, who returned to Ratisbon by 1857, Sister Seraphine Steimer, and Sister Emilia Barth arrived from Ratisbon in 1855. The death of Sister Francesca, from tuberculosis two weeks after their arrival, was very moving and significant.

The Sisters entered a new stage of growth in numbers and property. They had suffered greatly because of inadequate housing which aggravated the harshness of winter. For two years the Sisters sold art works in order to save money to build an appropriate convent. With the savings of the Sisters, the continuing donations of the Missionverein, and the gift of the Most Reverend John O'Loughlin, the newly consecrated Bishop of the recently erected diocese of Brooklyn, the Convent of the Holy Cross on the Southwest corner of Graham Street and Montrose Avenue in the heart of German Williamsburg was dedicated on November 9, 1857, the feast of All Saints of the Dominican Order. The Sisters established an academy for girls in the west wing of the convent.

Mother Josepha made many judicious decisions with the verbal consent of the Ordinaries of the diocese. Her acceptance of American postulants and the establishment of a mission-house in New York City brought about independence from the European Motherhouse.

Although the story of the gradual independence is a complex one, replete with threats of Mother Josepha's excommunication and very angry feelings on both sides of the Atlantic, the details are unnecessary to this history. According to Crawford who has done the most extensive research: "Although both Williamsburg and Ratisbon disputed until about 1863 or 1864 concerning the actual time of the incardination of the Williamsburg Community as a Brooklyn Diocesan Community, and although there is regrettable absence of documents confirming the change of canonical status, November 9, 1857 may be considered the birthday of the Brooklyn Dominicans and the granting of full authority to Mother Josepha as the Mother Prioress."[7]

Prior to that date on April 3, 1857, Mother Josepha wrote to Ratisbon: "We have four hundred children taught only in three divisions, send us therefore more Sisters." In reply Mother Benedicta Bauer, who had been forced to resign as prioress by the new Bishop of Ratisbon, Sister Thomasina Ginker, and Sister Cunegund Schell as well as a postulant, Cresentia Traubinger, arrived at Williamsburg on October 2, 1858.

By June of 1860, Mother Benedicta and Sister Thomasina left for the midwest and finally founded the American Congregation of Saint Catherine of Siena in Racine, Wisconsin. The following October, Bishop von Synestry of Ratisbon sent his formal decree of separation. Sisters Josepha, Seraphine, Augustine, Cunegund, Emilia, and Rosa as well as several postulants constituted the newly founded American Congregation of the Holy Cross.

Even before this formal decree had been received, Mother Josepha, with the consent of Bishop O'Loughlin, approved the founding of the mission proposed in 1853 by Abbot Wimmer. Sisters Augustine, Cunegund, and Rosa founded the missionhouse attached to Saint Nicholas Church, Second Street, New York City. This foundation is the direct geographic root of the Caldwell Community.[8]

The newly established community mission found itself, once again, in inadequate housing. After five years the Sisters had saved enough to build a suitable Convent. Sister Augustine promptly made the most beautiful and largest room the Chapel. The Sisters had yearned to have a chapel where the Blessed Sacrament could be reserved. The chapel and convent were dedicated on November 9, 1864, by Reverend Felician Krebetz, the new pastor who succeeded the benevolent Capuchin, Ambrose Buchmeier. The convent was placed under the protection of the Holy Rosary.

At this time, the Second Street community included Sisters Augustine Neuhierl, Cunegund Schell, Ambrosia Mannes, Hyacinth Scheininger, and lay Sister Antonia as well as the novices Sisters Theresia Hoffman, Aquinata Fiegler, and Magdalena who had been sent from the Motherhouse to help relieve the Sisters whose school was over-filled.[9]

In 1865 Father John Danter of Saint John's Church, 30th Street, New York City, requested Dominican Sisters. Sister Augustine negotiated with the Motherhouse. Sisters were promised. When the Motherhouse reneged on the commitment, Sister Augustine, presumably with the permission of both her religious superior and her ecclesiastical superior, sent her choir nuns, Sisters Ambrosia and Theresia, and lay Sister Magdalena, to 30th Street. This action seems to have precipitated a move toward gradual independence from Williamsburg.

A letter written by Mother Augustine to Mother Hyacinth Oberbrunner of Racine in 1866 offers some insights: "Formerly we secured Sisters from Williamsburg, but not of recent date. I sent back to Williamsburg several troublesome Sisters which displeased the Superior and who forthwith determined that in the future we should admit our own candidates which we could easily do, but just at the present moment that I shall have to arrange for five classes puts me in a great predicament...."[10]

Mother Augustine did not receive Sisters from any other American source. American postulants applied to her community in August of 1866; and, by 1869, formal separation from Williamsburg was completed. At that time, "the convent at Williamsburg demanded $8,000, which sum was paid them by Mother Augustine. The deed for the two houses on Second

Street was transferred to the convent there, the Sisters formed a corporation of their own, and separated in peace and friend-liness."[11]

At the time of separation, the archives of the American Congregation of the Holy Rosary, then the Community of the Sisters of Saint Dominic of New York, record the following members: Mother M. Augustine (Prioress), Sister M. Hyacinth (Sub-prioress), Sister Alberta (Novice-Mistress, 1869–1872), Sister M. Rose (Kitchen Mistress), Sister Aquinata (teacher, higher grades), Sister Catherine Muth (teacher, lower grades and Novice Mistress, 1872–1874), Sister Josepha (Mistress of children), Sister Agnes (music teacher), and Sisters Michael, Dominica, Barbara, Seraphine, Antonia, and Aloysia as well as two postulants, Barbara Reichart and Sophia Winkler. Sisters Cunegund, Ambrosia, and Theresia opted to return to the Williamsburg Community.

The dynamic spiritual personality and tremendous mis-sionary vision of Mother Augustine had a profound effect on the new Congregation and its daughter foundations.

Mother Augustine, Maria Joseph Neuhierl, was born on June 13, 1819, the oldest of the seven children of Joseph and Barbara Stadlerine Neuhierl. Maria proved to be a gifted, diligent, responsible member of her educated middle-class fam-ily. Having completed her teacher training in 1838, she entered the Monastery of the Holy Cross at Ratisbon, seven miles from her home village of Walderach, and made profession as Sister Augustine of the Infant Jesus on June 1, 1840.

Though she labored zealously in parochial education, her superiors recognized her desire to be a missionary and sent her to the "Institute of Englische Fraulein" at Altotting for the purpose of mastering English. When the American missionary venture was finalized, she volunteered.

Her dedication as teacher in both Holy Trinity and Saint Nicholas Schools was outstanding. As Superior in Second Street, and even more so as Prioress General of the infant American Congregation of the Holy Rosary, she "never swerved in the smallest degree from the discipline or the conventual practices which she had learned in the cloister of the Second Order at Ratisbon."[12]

Her love of education and for strict observance was complemented by her compassion for the poor. During a prolonged strike for better wages in New York City in the late 1860's, women and children came to the Second Street Convent to beg. Mother Augustine sent Sisters to bakeries and markets to ask for provisions to give to the needy.[13]

The quality of her saintly life reached its perfection in the patient acceptance of a painful death. On her deathbed she bequeathed this spirit to her spiritual daughters: "Be fervent and good; hold fast to your holy Rule and Constitutions. Practice obedience.... Practice holy poverty. Up to the present, this virtue has had a meager regard, for the poor of the world practice it more than we have done. Love chastity.... Give your hearts to God alone. Strive to do all you can to spread the good of the Holy Order.... This is not a human labor; it is God's work."[14]

Though Mother Augustine spoke of life in religion and labor for the Church as God's work on her deathbed, during her life she labored and challenged others to labor zealously as cooperators in the work. Conscious that her small community had grown to twenty-seven members by 1872, Mother Augustine lived in the spirit of Saint Dominic who said, "The seed will fructify if sown, it will but moulder if hoarded," and sent her Sisters forth to Jersey City, New Jersey. This foundation represents the direct geographic root of the Caldwell Community.

"On September 10, 1872, Mother Augustine sent five Sisters, Aquinata (Superioress), Josepha, Michaela, Clara, and a lay Sister, Theresia, to Father Kraus in Jersey City. Here the parish gave the Sisters a little house which was attached to the Church. One of the rooms which served as an oratory for the Sisters was located in such a way as to make it possible for them to see the high altar wherein reposed the Blessed Sacrament."[15]

Sister Aquinata was well-suited to carry on the work of the Holy Order in Jersey City. Her life gives testimony to the

Scripture that "People must think of us only as Christ's servants, stewards entrusted with the mysteries of God." She lived the truth, "what is expected of stewards is that each one should be found worthy of trust." (1 Cor. 4:1-2)

The youthful Superior embraced life with enthusiasm and experience far beyond her years. Even as a child, her parents, Aloys and Barbara Iffland Fiegler, recognized her sterling qualities. A teacher, Miss Striker remarked, "Our little Appolonia will be a leader someday."[16] Another quoted to Mrs. Fiegler, "Your daughter is most remarkable. She is an example of diligence, obedience, self-control, and piety. God surely must have something good in store for her."[17]

How God revealed the something good to be a vocation to the Dominican Order and the gift of leadership is a remarkable story.

In the 1850s depression had hit her homeland of Saxony. Mr. Fiegler and his son Arnold left for America in search of a better life for the family. Mrs. Fiegler and her sister, Anna Hartleb, worked to support their daughters, Appolonia and Wilhemina Hartleb (later Sister Boniface, O.S.D.). By 1860 the women came to America. Four years later, Appolonia, much to the chagrin of her father, decided to enter the American Congregation of the Holy Cross in Williamsburg where she made profession as Sister Mary Aquinata in 1865.

She had distinguished herself as an excellent teacher of the higher grades in Saint Nicholas School and showed remarkable talent in music, art, sewing, and administration.

This gifted religious was now called to create a sense of unity and purpose among the multi-national community at Saint Boniface. Sister Mary Philip Roche recalled that Sister Aquinata was sensitive and compassionate; always ready to serve. Because of her personal charism and spirit of observance, joy and dedication were hallmarks of the Jersey City Convent. The Sisters lived close together in the small building for which they had paid $838.37 in cash, half the cost of the building. The rest was to be paid by the Sisters taking care of the church for a number of years.[18]

On September 17, 1872, classes opened in Saint Boniface School with an enrollment of sixty-five children. The parents were overjoyed, and Father Dominic Kraus never failed to encourage the Sisters in matters of the school.

The first convent was too small to provide for the needs of the Sisters. They obtained permission to collect funds for an extension. "When not collecting, they were busily engaged with the needle as means of income. Sacrifice was indeed the slogan of these holy women."[19] During Holy Week of 1874, the first brick addition was added. The annex cost $2,000 and was dedicated on the feast of St. Vincent de Paul, July 19th.

Sister Aquinata, the astute administrator and visionary, recognized the need for a larger building that could serve as both an Academy and Convent. Having received the necessary permission from Mother Augustine, Sister purchased four lots adjacent to the church. Though the $16,000 seemed prohibitive, she believed, "It was God's work she was doing and it was to Him that she looked directly for help in carrying it on."[20] Help also came from three generous parishioners: George A. Brock, Mr. Joseph Severding, and Mr. John Miller. The balance was borrowed from the Motherhouse in New York and was returned with interest when the Jersey City Community became independent.[21]

This letter to Bishop Corrigan on June 26, 1877, sheds additional light on the timeliness of this daring venture:

> Since my Sisters have fair prospects of obtaining a loan for $15,000 under favorable circumstances, they will contract to build a convent as soon as the thing is made sure, provided your Lordship is satisfied. There are four lots to the church which cost $16,000. Eight thousand was paid in the beginning 4 years ago by the Motherhouse of New York as a dowry to this community. The rest was furnished last year by our Sisters. They have besides 5,000D in hand and are expecting a few thousand—say 2,000D— more from their Sisters in New York. They will have 7,000D to start with.
>
> The cost of the building will probably amount to 20,000– 25,000D. It is intended to become besides its original purpose a

boarding school to which part of the pupils of New York will be transferred. At the same time I completed arrangements for a new school house—the present accomodations do not deserve the name—they are worse than bad.... Although the job would be separated from that of the Sisters, it might nevertheless be united in one plan with the Sisters' building....

Your humble servant,[22]

D. Kraus

Mother Augustine died on May 24, 1877. She was succeeded by Sister Hyacinth Scheininger who did not discontinue the project, but transferred Sister Aquinata to Traverse, Michigan. Sister Baptista, a member of the Congregation of the Holy Rosary, places this transfer in its time-bound context. "There was a question as to who would succeed Mother Augustine. Mother Hyacinth got the appointment, though many thought Sister Aquinata the more able. In the course of time, the work of the Sisters in Jersey City had proved very successful and the urge to independence from the Motherhouse in Second Street strongly manifested itself again, presumably as a result of the appointment in which Mother Hyacinth was appointed Mother Prioress. This proposed separation was looked upon with much disapproval by the Sisters of New York and very probably by Bishop Corrigan who, it is believed, was instrumental in having Sister Aquinata removed to Michigan where she was to act in the capacity of Visitator to the only mission in Traverse City, Michigan."[23]

Correspondence between Father Kraus and the Bishop develops similar themes. Father Kraus accused Monsignor Quinn of unwarrantable interference in the election and infers that the vicar general had a negative attitude toward the six houses of the community in New Jersey. Kraus, a close friend of Mother Augustine and a pastor who had a good relationship with his own Sisters, insists that Mother Augustine had recommended Sister Aquinata as her successor. He further asserts that, if the Sisters could have voted, they would have affirmed Aquinata. [24]

Sister Marie Thomasine Blum cites a different opinion:

Since the Constitutions of the Order in those days prescribed that none but Sisters twelve years professed could vote in the election, the only Sisters eligible were Sister M. Hyacinth Scheininger and Sister M. Aquinata Fiegler, for it must be remembered that the community was still very young. An election thus being impossible, appointment became necessary. Consequently, Monsignor William Quinn, Vicar General and our ecclesiastical superior at the time, at the almost unanimous request of the Sisters appointed Sister Hyacinth, the senior by profession.[25]

The conflict of interpretation indicates the role of the ecclesiastical authorities in early critical decisions. Regardless of the true significance of opinions, it does seem that Sister Aquinata may have envisioned Saint Dominic's, Jersey City, as an independent house more on a Third Order model. Her move west precluded that in 1878, but Sister Aquinata did not relinquish her dream of directing the construction of the new building. After the nuns were settled in Michigan, Sister Aquinata returned to supervise construction.

On April 1, 1878, ground was broken. The cornerstone of the very monastic structure was laid on May 24, 1878, just one year after the death of Mother Augustine. The official Bishop's Registry enriches the account. On November 17, 1878:

the new convent and academy of St. Dominic adjoining Saint Boniface Church, Jersey City, was blessed by the Rt. Rev. Msgr. Seton. The solemn Mass was sung by the Very Reverend Bonaventure with F. Masechal and F. Shadler assisting.

The new structure is 100 ft. by 56 ft. deep and a chapel extension of 96 ft. and is built of brick with prestone trimming. It is divided into a cellar basement and four stories. The east wing was set apart as an academy for girls, and the west wing will be the convent proper. The furniture and stalls of the Chapel are of butternut and very handsomely arranged. Entire cost $36,000.[26]

In May of 1879, Sister Pia was sent formally to replace Sister Aquinata. Father Kraus offers his sentiments on this occasion. In a letter to Bishop Corrigan, Father Kraus proposed that Sister Aquinata's removal would cripple the school and had already distrubed the harmony of the Jersey City Community. He insisted that Mother Hyacinth would never find another Superior to coordinate the multi-national community since Sister Aquinata was the favorite of the Irish members. A visit to Mother Hyacinth, in which he pleaded for an explanation of the move and advanced reasons why it seemed advantageous to change the Second Order Rule to that of one more appropriate to active Sisterhoods, proved fruitless. Mother was implacable on both decisions.[27]

Regardless of the accuracy of Father Kraus's perceptions and the possible human reasons for Sister Aquinata's removal, it is obvious that she was not destined to become the founding Mother of the Jersey City community. She founded the American Congregation of Our Lady of the Sacred Heart, Grand Rapids, Michigan. By 1887 that congregation had begun application for affiliation with the Third Order. Sister Aquinata believed "that the rigors of pioneer life would be better endured and applicants encouraged under the Third Order Rule, without the choir sister distinctions."[28]

Back in Jersey City Sister Catherine Muth had been appointed Superior in October, 1879. Though she understood the stance of her pastor, Sister Catherine agreed wholeheartedly with Mother Hyacinth that independence should not be taken seriously. In fact, it seems that Sister Catherine had "promised her superior that she would never allow the Convent to be separated from the Motherhouse in New York."[29]

Like most questions which produce tension and bring to the surface existing divisions, the question of independence surfaced periodically and would not be left unanswered. From correspondence in the files of Bishop Corrigan, it is apparent that the formation of a New Jersey province had been considered as a compromise but was never adopted.[30]

The final steps to independence involved the battle of two strong wills. The earliest annals of the Jersey City Community reveal the exchange between Mother Hyacinth and Father Dominic Kraus:

> The Convent of Saint Dominic, Jersey City, remained subject to that of Holy Rosary, New York, until the year 1881, nine years after its foundation. It then became independent of the New York province for the following reasons.
>
> The deceased Mother M. Augustine had promised that, at the completion of the new Convent, a reception and profession of novices might take place therein. It thus happened that in November, 1881, a Novice (Sister M. Josephine) who had been baptized by Rev. D. Kraus and brought up in his parish was ready to make her vows, and a postulant who had been a boarder with the Sisters for many years (Sr. M. Avelline) was ready to receive the holy habit. Consequently the Rev. Father considered this a most opportune time to hold the Reception and Profession in the new Convent Chapel, thus realizing the promise made by the Reverend Mother Augustine. Accordingly the Rev. Father Kraus applied personally to the Rev. Mother Hyacinth (New York) who had been appointed to succeed Rev. Mother Augustine as Prioress by the Rt. Rev. Msgr. Quinn, V.G. of New York, to fullfill the much desired wish and promised permission of her predecessor. This request was, however, positively refused by the Rev. Mother Hyacinth, claiming that the Senior Sisters of the Community, were strongly opposed to the proposition. Mother Catherine consequently besought and pleaded earnestly with Mother Hyacinth to grant the permission for the above named novice to make her profession and the postulant to receive the holy habit in the Jersey City chapel; so as to avoid the serious unpleasantness of a separation from the Motherhouse.... However, all pleadings and entreaties proved useless and the profession and reception took place in New York on November 26, 1881.[31]

Father Kraus made a final plea to the newly consecrated Bishop of Newark. Since Bishop Wigger had been consecreted

only one month his decision might appear to be premature, but
Mother Jordan of New York recalls that Msgr. Doane, who had
been the Administrator of the diocese for eight months, approved of the separation.[32] With the approval of Msgr. Doane
and the verbal consent of Bishop Corrigan, the coadjutor
bishop of New York, Bishop Wigger believed he was making an
enlightened decision.

There are no letters or records of any kind on file that
indicate that Mother Catherine had anything to do with the
negotiations. The letter confirming independence was sent to
Father Kraus.

Newark, Dec. 16, 1881

Dear Father Kraus,
   In answer to your letter of inquiry, after having well considered
all the reasons advanced by you, I beg leave to state that I am
quite willing that the house of the Dominican Sisters of Jersey
City should be detached from that of New York. I the more
willingly give the consent as the rules and constitutions of the
Dominican Sisters favor the independence of their houses.[33]

A thorough search of several archives failed to provide an
extant copy of the letter mentioned above, so the nature of "all
the reasons" is unknown. There is also no clue as to how the
Sisters, whose life was to be so seriously altered, were apprised
of the change of status. A brief sentence says it all, "Mother
Catherine reluctantly accepted the accomplished fact."[34]

The legal separation is recorded from December 16, 1881,
but the incorporation into the state of New Jersey dates from
September 20, 1882.

The newly formed community numbered twelve professed
Sisters: Mother Catherine Muth (Prioress), Sisters Josepha
Klein, Dominica Sander, Pia Schneider, Clara Bittel, Joanna
Schuttinger, Mechtilde Ostendarp, Thomasine Buhlmeier, Ser-
aphica Lang, Angelica Schlutter, Alacoque Wertel, and Mary
Philip Roche, as well as two novices and four postulants.

The document of incorporation states simply:

II. The corporate name adopted by us is "The Community of the Sisters of Saint Dominic of Jersey City"

IV. The proposed name of said institute is "The Community of the Sisters of Saint Dominic"

V. The general purpose of said institution is the religious and secular education of the young and the promotion of learning.

VI. The number of trustees for the managing of affairs of said institution shall be seven. . . .[35]

2.

3.

1.

3

SOMETHING THAT WILL ENDURE

"Women of hope see in the circumstances of today the seeds of tomorrow's life."

Sister Vivien Jennings, O.P.

1-*St. Dominic Convent Chapel, Jersey City, New Jersey*
2-*Cornerstone, St. Dominic Convent, Jersey City, N.J.*
3-*Sister Aquinata Fiegler*
4-*Mother Catherine Muth*
5-*Stained Glass Window, St. Dominic Convent, Jersey City, New Jersey*

The Diocese of Newark into which the Sisters of Saint Dominic were incardinated has a history which parallels their own. The diocese began July 29, 1853, three days after the four nuns left Ratisbon. The second Bishop was consecrated May 24, 1873, just eight months after the Sisters came to Jersey City. Bishop Wigger, the third Bishop, was consecrated October 11, 1881, two months before he issued the decree of separation from New York. Their beginnings, as well as their mutual growth and development, were intimately connected.

What was happening in the Catholic Church in New Jersey between 1853 and 1881 was only a microcosm of the situation throughout the Catholic Church in America. In 1850 there were 1,606,000 Catholics in the United States as opposed to 663,000 ten years earlier.[1] Heightened birthrates and a new wave of immigration from Ireland, Germany, France, and the Netherlands had significantly altered the Catholic census. The First Council of Baltimore attempted to meet pastoral needs by the creation of new dioceses. The State of New Jersey, which had been a suffragan diocese of the Archdiocese of New York, became the independent diocese of Newark by the decree of Piux XI, *Apostolici Ministerii.*

The first Bishop, James Bayley, convoked a diocesan synod, August 22-24, 1856. He was most anxious to implement the spirit and letter of the decree on Catholic education issued by the episcopal convention.[2] He encouraged the Sisters of Charity to start a New Jersey foundation at Convent Station; and, by 1872 when the Sisters of Saint Dominic came to Jersey City, there were fifty-seven parochial schools with an estimated enrollment of 13,500 students.[3]

When Bishop Bayley was appointed Bishop of Baltimore, Michael Augustine Corrigan was named his successor in Newark. This learned, saintly man led the diocese through the economic boom of 1872 into the bust of Black Friday, September 1873. In his diocesan report of 1876, the prelate noted four main areas of concern: the need to divide the burgeoning diocese, the fostering of efficient Christian education, the recruitment and proper formation of priests, and the continuous struggle against the vice of drunkenness. By 1880 the number of schools had increased substantially, and there were 199 priests (132 secular, 67 religious) serving 190 churches.[4]

October, 1880, Bishop Corrigan was named the coadjutor with the right of succession to the Cardinal Archbishop of New York. Since there was no clear arrangement for succession in the Newark diocese, Monsignor Doane, the Vicar General, was appointed administrator during the eight-month hiatus. By August of 1881, Doctor Winand Michael Wigger, pastor of Saint Vincent's Church in Madison, New Jersey, received his appointment as the third Bishop of Newark.

Bishop Wigger continued the work of his predecessors with special concern for the advancement of Catholic education on every level. He strove "to better prevailing conditions by requiring the examination of teachers and by appointing inspectors to visit the schools and examine the children. He likewise declared that absolution should be refused both to parents and children when the latter attended the public schools without permission."[5] This sanction was removed by 1893. Bishop Corrigan paid tribute to his successor. "Bishop Wigger is a man of untiring zeal, perhaps the most extraordinary bishop in the country in that respect."[6]

This zealous bishop and the new community of the Sisters of Saint Dominic of Jersey City entered the year 1882 with apprehensions. For the Sisters the year went very quickly. August 4 marked the first ceremony of religious reception and profession into the new community. *Leslie's Illustrated Newspaper* of August 19, 1882, published this account:

A RECEPTION OF DOMINICAN NUNS

On the 4th of August, the day set apart in the Roman Catholic Church to honor St. Dominic de Guzman, the founder of the white-clothed Friars and Sisters, an interesting ceremony took place in the chapel of St. Dominic's Academy, Jersey City. The Bishop of Newark, Rt. Rev. W.M. Wigger, D.D., gave the white veil to four young ladies, Misses Rose Kunz, Margaret Dolan, Mary Starzinger, and Mary Johnson, who thus became novices in the Order of St. Dominic. He also bestowed the black veil on Sister Josephine and Sister DeChantal, who having completed the term of novitiate, had persevered in their intention of renouncing the world and devoting themselves perpetually in the Order.

The aspirants to the white veil entered the highly adorned chapel in bridal dress, and crowned with myrtle, and attended by bridesmaids. The bishop, as each knelt before him, removed the myrtle crown and cut some locks of the hair, the woman's glory, now to be no longer a pride. The white veil was then, with appropriate ceremonies, blessed and laid upon the head thus consecrated to the Lord; and each received the habit she was henceforth to wear in place of the mundane robes in which she came to the altar.

The two young ladies who passed their novitiate then approached. They renewed their resolution to die to the world, and each was crowned with a crown of thorns before she pronounced the vows which made her a cloistered nun.

The convent contains a community of twenty-five Sisters, the prioress being Mother Catherine. Attached to it is a well-conducted academy, attended by more than a hundred young ladies.

The year 1883 began a unique chapter in the history of the Jersey City community, the decade of recruiting postulants from Germany. The annals of the Convent record:

> Until this time all the postulants were native-born Americans with the exception of Sister Mary Basil who came from Germany. As it was found necessary to have German postulants, an appeal was made to the Rt. Rev. Father Bonaventure, O.S.B., who had gone to Europe to perfect himself in the art of painting, to secure some good postulants for the community. Accordingly on his return to this country the Rev. Father brought two young ladies with him who had been recommended by the Rev. Father Paul, O.S.B., subprior in Sheyern, Bavaria.
>
> Father Bonaventure and the two postulants arrived in America, Sept. 17, 1883. On the occasion of their reception, the postulants received the names Sisters M. Benedicta and M. Magdalene.
>
> From 1883-1893 about one hundred and forty girls from Germany were received into the community. Twenty of whom had been sent by Rev. Father Paul, O.S.B., of Sheyern and the remaining by Rev. Father Horn of Freisling, Bavaria.[7]

This visit of Father Bonaventure had been preceded by the recruitment visit of Abbot Wimmer. The abbot had attended the Vatican Council and remained in Italy for the fourteenth centenary celebration of the death of St. Benedict in 1880. He travelled to Salzburg, Regensburg, Metten, and Munich in Bavaria. His message to the Order and to his friends was to encourage young men and women to work among the immigrants in America. This decade was to be one of growth and development. There was always more work.[8] The Benedictines began a program of recruitment amid cultural turmoil.

Germany, and in particular Catholic Bavaria, had been stunned by the Kulturkampf of Bismarck. Bismarck saw it simply as time to redefine the age-old struggle between Church and State. "To him it was essentially a political not a philosophical struggle; but in the quest for state supremacy, he was unable to confine it to the political arena."[9]

Catholic workers and their families were struggling to overcome religious confusion, economic depression, and widespread pessimism. Programs to strengthen the faith and encourage vocations were sponsored by the Benedictines, 1881-1894. Enthusiastic youth were attracted to the dedication involved in missionary work, and parents were relieved to have daughters and sons leave the hard times for a better life.

The testimony of some of the pioneer Sisters provides additional details. Sister Thomasina Primmer, a member of the American Congregation of the Holy Rosary, recorded her remembrances after her retirement. Her story is most enlightening.

> I had always wanted to do something for God. Now that I was finishing my schooling I had decided to join the Community of the Sisters of Notre Dame who staffed my school. One day a Dominican Father came to school and gave a stirring talk on the religious life and the need for vocations in America. He encouraged us to become religious teachers in a country where religion is included. I confided my desire to Father Anton, my pastor, who told me about the Benedictine Fathers who helped girls go to America.[10]

In another place in her diary, Sister Thomasina describes the role of the missionverein in the journey to the New World.

> The Catholics of Bavaria, Germany, established a Foreign Mission Society to encourage young people for their purpose. (Extension of the faith among Germans in foreign lands.) King Louis of Bavaria was deeply interested in the missions, and he contributed the necessary funds for those who had not the means of travelling. There were 15 girls to come to America in 1884. Four of us were destined by our pastors for Holy Rosary Convent, New York City. There were three for Jersey City, First Street, which was the newly established Motherhouse for the Sisters who had separated from Second Street, New York,

headed by Sisters Catherine and Mechtilde.... Five were to go
to Williamsburg now Brooklyn, but there was no one to meet them
at the steamer and so our Sister who had waited for us brought
them to Second Street where they were called for later in the day.

Three Benedictines were appointed to interest themselves in
vocations for foreign missions. They provided for initial preparation and then the pastors took care of the young girls who had
applied for final direction and aid in this venture. Father
Boniface was my director.[11]

Sister Alexandrine Kalb of the Caldwell community told a
similar tale. Mr. and Mrs. Kalb had attended a mission in the
parish church. The Benedictine priest encouraged them to consider sending a child as a missionary to America. He reminded
them that God is not outdone in generosity and would certainly
reward them and the fatherland in this difficult time. When the
Kalbs went home, they lined up their seven daughters, slightly
reminiscent of Jesse offering one of his six sons to be the King of
Israel after Saul. The father looked lovingly at each and then
said, "Catherine, you are the best suited. You are religious and
compassionate." Young Catherine, who was working in the hospital, gave up her position, was presented to her pastor, and
then went on retreat with the Benedictine Fathers responsible
for recruitment. Her confessor gave her a final word, "If you
ever want to come home, just ask to write to me. They cannot
refuse." He gave her a nonsense verse to include in the letter.
The note would indicate her desire to return to Germany, and he
would send the necessary funds. Sister Alexandrine remarked
that she was often very lonely and discouraged, but she could
not turn her back on God. The nonsense note had no place in
her life.[12]

The most familiar story is told by Sister Beda Schmid, who
entered the Jersey City Community and later became the first
Mother General of their daughter foundation, the American
Congregation of the Immaculate Heart of Mary. Anna Schmid
had always wanted to be a Sister. At that time there were many
missionaries who appealed to the Benedictine, Father Paul, for

candidates for foreign missions. Anna had heard that a call to America was a call to convert Indians. Shortly after a retreat Mother Beda came to America. Though she was surprised that there were no Indians, she plunged into the life of the Sisters of Saint Dominic with generosity, enthusiasm, and unmistakable trust in the Master who had called her to these foreign shores. She, like so many others who left Germany, simply believed it was the Lord who had shown the way.[13]

Personal desire to serve God as a missionary was complemented by the meaningful support of the Ludwig Missionverein and other groups dedicated to the propagation of the faith.

> The Catholics of the United States often point with pride to the grand structure of the Church that was built up in this country within a short period of 150 years. And well they may, for this growth is rightly considered a prodigious accomplishment, which, indeed, often extracted the last ounce of energy from pioneer bishops, priests, religious, and lay people. . . . They turned to the Europe from which they had come to obtain whatever assistance they could. In this quest they were successful in having three mission societies organized, which were to help them in part or in whole over a period of ten decades. (1822-1922)[14]

By 1844 the Ludwig Missionverein became independent from the Society of the Propagation of the Faith in Lyons and the Leopoldville Society in Austria. The Bavarian group sponsored the establishment of national parish schools to promote religious education and provide incentive to youth to achieve responsible positions in their local communities.

The Society also made great efforts to staff these schools with German-speaking Sisters. They supplied funds for travel expenses and assisted the Sisters of Notre Dame, Saint Dominic, Saint Ursula, and Saint Benedict to lay firm foundations in the New World. Between 1854 and 1866, the diocese of Newark received $23,680.00 in aid,[15] while communities of religious women throughout the country accumulated $23,880.00.[16]

The candidates sponsored by the Missionverein"...as a rule were talented and, as they received a good education in their native language, it was not found difficult for them to study and acquire the English language."[17] Those candidates who came to America, who had had little formal education, generally became lay Sisters involved in domestic service.

The decade of recruitment was brought to an abrupt end in 1893 by a change in attitude and policy concerning the appropriateness of accepting German candidates without a more definite plan for their acceptance and training. The annals state, "The majority of the German Sisters have been pious God-fearing souls; but, through the fault of the few among them, who did not know how to thank God for their holy vocation, we have been forbidden to receive any German girls. This prohibition took place on October 15, 1893, after a disturbance that had been going on for years."[18]

Though there is no further clarification of the nature of the disturbance mentioned above, it is clear that the prohibition was issued by Monsignor Januarius deConcilio, the appointed spiritual director. He was greatly concerned about candidates who came from Germany without proper application, especially those who were very young.[19]

A detailed program for application and acceptance was established for both native-born and foreign candidates. Mother Catherine wrote to the pastors and to Germany: "No applicants should be sent in the future until they have been notified that they were received."[20]

The decade 1883 to 1893 was significant in other ways. In the beginning of this period of turmoil marked by economic hardship and recurring disease, a mission was founded in Caldwell to provide health care for tubercular Sisters; at its conclusion a new governing structure was adapted under diocesan director.

The year 1883 ushered in a time of economic crisis for many urban centers on the eastern seaboard. Jersey City was particularly hard hit since the Great American Sugar Refinery, as well as the Pennsylvania and Central Railroads of New

Jersey, were forced to lay off the majority of their skilled and unskilled immigrant employees who populated the city's ethnic neighborhoods.

As if unemployment were not scourge enough, disease in epidemic proportions ravaged the urban ethnic ghettos. Death stalked their many overcrowded, poorly-ventilated, and unsanitary double-decker tenements. In 1882 the polluted water of the Passaic River had been identified as a contributing factor in the spread of both tuberculosis and typhoid fever, and a new water supply was sought.

Since a large portion of Lower Jersey City had been built upon land reclaimed from the marshes, scientists believed that the land below the surface was swarming with disease produced by decaying organic matter. Tuberculosis, which was taking thousands of lives annually in New Jersey, found its breeding ground beneath the surface of the land, spread its venom like wild fire, and claimed its victims with little regard to nationality or age.

Since the dread disease had only recently been diagnosed as communicable and not simply controlled by quarantine or immunization, the city seemed powerless to prevent its spread or to assist with the cure since tubercular patients required long convalescence in a healthy country environment.[21]

The strain of economic depression and the wave of despair and pessimism in its wake surrounded the struggling, new community. Their own membership was seriously affected as the disease claimed many of the younger Sisters.[22] In spite of their own hardships the Sisters continued to beg food for the poor and to take care of children left orphaned by the disease.

By 1884, the proper care of tubercular Sisters was a serious concern. Mother Catherine sought permission to found a mission which would serve as a Convent and a convalescent home. When Father Kraus heard of the plan, he objected strenuously to Bishop Wigger. He proposed that the Sisters rent a house rather than begin a new mission, since they were already in debt and did not have sufficient personnel.[23]

This time, Father Kraus did not convince the Bishop. The

Sisters received permission to purchase the Harrison Estate on Roseland Avenue in the borough of Caldwell which was called the "Denver of the East."

On May 26, 1884, Mother Catherine, Sister Basil, two novices (Sister Benvenuta and Benedicta), and two boarders from St. Dominic Academy (later Sisters Mercedes and Catherine de Ricci) were taken to Caldwell in a horse and carriage driven by Joseph Muth, Mother Catherine's brother. The trip took all day, but the passengers were overjoyed when they finally arrived at the Harrison Estate with its small house and well-kept garden.

Whether Mother had always intended to include a boarding school in the new mission is a moot question, but one was advertised by the following September. Sister Basil was placed in charge of the children, and Sister Thomasine was appointed the superior. Mother Catherine assigned small groups of Sisters to the convalescent home for two or three weeks' rest depending on their need.

Arrangements were made by Bishop Wigger to have Reverend Walter Purcell, the brother of Sister Amanda, say Mass and minister to the Sisters and the people in the area, since there was no Catholic parish in the vicinity.

By 1886 this house, which later was destroyed by fire, proved to be too small and a larger house at the west end of the village was purchased. The school enrollment soon necessitated another move. On January 10, 1888, Mother purchased the old seventy-six room Beach House[24] and surrounding acreage to serve as a temporary school, infirmary, and Convent. At the same time she bought thirty-one and a half acres of land on the other side of Bloomfield Avenue because "she had hopes of transferring the Novitiate to Caldwell, of providing an adequate Infirmary, of providing for orphans, and establishing Perpetual Adoration of the Blessed Sacrament where young and old could pray ceaselessly that the blessings of God might rest on the labors of the Sisters."[25] This tract was far enough removed from the village to provide the perfect contemplative setting.

The Sisters set up a fine boarding school, infirmary, and

Convent on the Beach House property. Its farmlands furnished fresh fruits and vegetables and provided space for chickens and a cow. Joseph Muth moved into one of the two houses located on the other site and served as caretaker until 1897.

Mother Catherine showed great daring and resourcefulness both in purchasing the property and in having the foresight to lease a small tract to the Erie Railroad so that there would be convenient transportation for the Sisters, boarders, and visitors.

In the Fall of 1891, Mother Catherine sought permission to erect a Convent, very similar in design to the European Mother-house at Ratisbon, on the knoll property. After lengthy deliberations in regard to costs, the Bishop approved. On the feast of Saint Joseph, 1892, the Sisters missioned in Caldwell proceeded to the future site of their "motherhouse-to-be" and broke ground.

Since the building was to be erected on the crest of the knoll, the architect planned a very deep foundation. The specified stones for the foundation were transported by rail to the foot of the property; but since there were no paved roads, they were carried in relays to the site by the postulants and lay Sisters. Sister Alexandrine remarked on one occasion that "it was back-breaking work, but they were proud to help build the building in which minds would be built for God." To her and to the many other sainted souls, those stones were more than symbols of stability and fidelity.

On May 22, 1893, the cornerstone was laid for Mt. St. Dominic. The following document was placed in the cornerstone:

The Second Order of Saint Dominic was established in this country by four Dominican nuns, from the Convent in Ratisbon, Germany. Sometime in the year 1853 they left their cloister with the permission of their Bishop and at the expressed desire of Abbot Wimmer of Saint Vincent's Abbey, Pennsylvania. Owing to the wilderness of the country, they were not able to settle in Pennsylvania but made their first establishment in Williamsburg, the Ven. Sr. M. Josepha being the superior. Some time later, the Venerable Sister M. Augustine, one of the four, took charge of the School and Convent in connection with St. Nicholas Church in Second Street, New York City.

After a time the two places became independent of each other and in the course of the same years, Sister M. Augustine became Prioress of many different branch houses, of which the Convent of St. Dominic in First Street—Jersey City was the first. In the year 1881, the Rt. Rev. Bishop Wigger D.D. took under his own jurisdiction the Sisters who were stationed at the Convent in First Street—Jersey City and they became independent of the Convent in New York.

At the same time the Ven. Sr. M. Catherine was superior and she subsequently became Prioress of that Convent and the present fifteen missions, which sprung from it, of which Caldwell was the first.

By the grace and bounty of God and the unceasing efforts of the good and prudent Mother a sufficient sum has been collected together, to commence the building of the convent on the beautiful property in Caldwell destined to be the future Novitiate of the rapidly increasing Community.

At this present day on which the cornerstone is being laid Monday, May 22, 1893, the Rev. Mother Catherine O.S.D. is still superior of the community of 150 Sisters and twenty-three postulants, scattered among the different missions.

The Rt. Rev. Bishop W. Wigger of Newark, a most worthy and zealous bishop who has always been most kind and fatherly to our Community, is expected to honor us by presiding at the ceremony of the laying of the cornerstone of this our new convent. The first year of the establishment in Caldwell was one of intense suffering to the Community but, as the time for building approached and during the time of its erection, the suffering and affliction had increased so that at the present time it has reached a point of exterior persecution for some and it would appear as if the evil spirit has placed all his powers in motion, to prevent the completion of the undertaking. The situation of the new building is entirely suited to the contemplative life, being so far away from the public road and will, we trust, be used for this purpose with the help of God and the approval of the Rt. Rev. Bishop, in accordance with the earnest desire of the present Prioress, Ven. Mother M. Catherine. The adoration during the day was begun on the feast of Saint Joseph 1892. The Sisters and children took turns two at-a-time, saying the rosary for the necessities of the whole community.

From the beginning the chapel in the convent was used as a church for the Catholics, who were scattered over the various suburbs of Caldwell. In 1892 a piece of land facing Bloomfield Ave., belonging to the Sisters, was offered to the Rt. Rev. Bishop for the church. The offer was accepted and a small church was accordingly built in honor of St. Aloysius. It was dedicated on November 17, 1892, by Rt. Rev. Bishop Wigger. The chaplains who attended Caldwell, previous to the erection of the church were Rt. Rev. W.A. Purcell, Rev. J. Duffy, Rev. W. Marshall, Rev. J.J. Shaughnessey, Rev. T. McGuire, Rev. J. Dolan, Rev. H. Kruze, and Rev. J.J. Boylan, who was the first appointed pastor of the Caldwell Church named St. Aloysius.

Rev. Father Nolan, a most zealous and pious young priest, who had been chaplain for a very short time, died in Caldwell, December 27, 1892. He was a very delicate constitution and having contracted typhoid fever, succumbed to the illness.

During the slow progress of the building of the convent in Caldwell, Reverend Mother Catherine continued to govern the community of both professed and novices, assisted by Sister M. Emmanuel in the care of the latter. Rev. Mother Catherine having divided her attention to both Caldwell and Jersey City was necessasarily often in Caldwell, consequently Sister M. Alacoque and Sister M. Basil aided in the care and took charge of Jersey City during her absence. Besides the novices there were also sixteen lay Sisters and eight boarders.[26]

The year 1893 found Mother Catherine supervising the workers at the Mount and creating the contemplative atmosphere she felt so necessary for religious life. The same year was marked by the beginnings of greater diocesan direction. Ecclesiastical superiors throughout the country were assuming greater control over the Institutes of women under their jurisdiction.[27] They had a vision for the future; and accurate information concerning the finances, personnel resources, and general spiritual and temporal stability of each group was imperative. In order to ascertain the desired report, Rt. Reverend Januarius de Concilio, the pastor of St. Michael's Church,

Jersey City, was appointed the spiritual director of the Jersey City Dominican Community.

His first action was to approve the community leaders: Mother Catherine (prioress) and Sister Mechtilde (sub-prioress). Then he established a Board of Consultors with the power to vote on all transactions regarding finances, appointments, and assignments. It included the spiritual director as president and the prioress and sub-prioress (ex-officio) as well as six appointees of the president after consultation with the Pioress: Sisters Joanna, Seraphica, Avelline, Dominic, Alacoque (bursar) and Josephine (secretary).

In the spring of 1894, the Monsignor made his report to the Bishop. Though there is no written record of its contents, according to the annals "disagreements between Monsignor de Concilio and Mother Catherine, as well as misunderstanding and misinterpretation of some of Mother's actions on the part of some members of the Community," caused the Bishop to replace her.

On April 25, 1894, a letter was sent to Sister Mechtilde:

> For various and grave reasons in the interests of your community I have decided to appoint you, and I hereby appoint you the Prioress of the Dominican Sisters in place of Mother Catherine. When you receive this letter, please go at once to the Convent in Jersey City, and take possession of the Office of Prioress. I have written to Mother Catherine that you will be there today or tomorrow, and have asked her to give you all the necessary information, the keys, books, money, etc. belonging to the community. I would suggest that she be appointed Superioress in some other house outside of Jersey City, and that you treat her with great kindness and consideration.[28]

Sister Mechtilde did as directed; Mother Catherine obeyed reluctantly.

It is difficult to understand why a woman whose appointment had been approved recently should have been replaced so summarily. Though there is no copy of specific reports or the letter of the Bishop to Mother Catherine, some background information is available.

By 1894 both the Bishop and the spiritual director were anxious to see the Community change its ecclesiastical status to that of Third Order. The demands of the parochial school and the complaints on the part of the Sisters, concerning the burdensome character of the Second Order Rule in relation to active life, had brought them to this conclusion. As early as 1890, Mother Catherine had been advised to inquire about possible affiliation with the Third Order, but it was well known that she was opposed to any change of lifestyle. Her insistence on perpetual Adoration and other strictly monastic exercises annoyed the spiritual director who tried to make her understand the plight of the Sisters.

Monsignor deConcilio, who had worked with Sister Mechtilde on the Board, saw her as a woman who could move the community toward affiliation and stability. The needs of the diocese and the need for openness in the leadership of the Community could certainly be one interpretation of the "grave and serious reasons" clause in the letter of appointment to Sister Mechtilde.

Information obtained from personal letters found in the archdiocesan archives, as well as general statements made in the *Minutes*, support objective speculation concerning the misunderstanding and misinterpretation of the Sisters.

Since Mother Catherine was then forty-seven years old and had borne the burden of authority throughout her religious life, she was certainly under strain at this time. Along with the physical strain associated with mid-life crisis and its accompanying mood swings and personality change from time to time, she also suffered acute psychological strain, since it was apparent that many Sisters were living the Second Order Rule indifferently.[29]

Mother Catherine's zeal for regular observance led her to correct even the smallest infractions of the rule. Her strict interpretation and harsh discipline, in the face of what she con-

sidered flagrant abuse, was easily interpreted by others as
fanatical, deranged behavior. It also must be remembered that
the buying of property from 1884 placed considerable strain on
community finances. Some felt she was obsessed with the building project and had overlooked the normal needs of the many.[30]

Though there were valid reasons for her replacement, the
bishop's recommendation that she be appointed superior, some-
where outside of Jersey City, certainly indicates that he believed
she was mentally and physically competent to exercise leadership on the local level.

The community annals state that letters of the change of
administration were read at all the mission houses, but there is
no record of the community response except that "after the
reading of the letters the question arose as to the disposition of
Sister Catherine, ex-prioress. Caldwell was suggested, but when
a vote was taken, it was found that six stood against, to one for
Caldwell. Lawrence, Massachusetts, was suggested, and the suggestion was acted on favorably."[31]

The Community assignments seem to indicate, however,
that she spent the rest of her life in Caldwell and was never again
in any position of authority.

It seems fitting to offer some words of tribute to this noble,
steadfast, misunderstood woman of faith, Founding Mother
Catherine, before continuing the narrative about the change of
status.

Mother Catherine, Mary Muth, was born August 15, 1847,
in Kirshenhausen, Wurttemburg. When she was five years old,
her parents emigrated to the United States and settled in the
vicinity of Holy Redeemer Church, Third Street, New York
City. Mary was a pious girl and wanted to become a religious.
After having completed what was the equivalent of normal
school, Mary approached her confessor, Reverend Father Brand-
statter, C.S.S.R. Since he was familiar with the Sisters of the
Holy Rosary Convent and knew they were just beginning to
accept postulants, he recommended Mary to them. Thus Mary
Muth became the first postulant. She received the habit on

August 12, 1866, and made profession as Sister Mary Catherine, January 18, 1868.

Sister Catherine distinguished herself as a teacher of the lower grades at St. Nicholas School. Then, since she possessed a depth of spirit and great understanding and appreciation of the common life and cloistral observances, she was made Novice Mistress, 1872–1874. Her health began to fail so she was assigned to Gloucester, then to Greenville, and finally to Jersey City in 1879.

She accepted her role, first as Superior and then as Mother Prioress. With maternal solicitude, she created a structure which provided for the professional as well as spiritual formation of the Sisters. During the difficult years, 1883–1893, she was solicitous for the health of the Sisters and encouraged them to be concerned for others.

During her administration, convents and schools were opened at Mt. St. Dominic (1884); St. John's, Jersey City; St. Mary's, Boonton; and St. Venantius, Orange (1887); St. Ann's, Newark, and St. Mary's, Rahway, (1888); St. Rose of Lima in Ohio (1885); and Assumption in Lawrence, Massachusetts (1889).[32]

During her visitations to each convent, Mother fostered a concern for the development of an atmosphere that was conducive to contemplative living. She was quoted as saying, "Build a cell within your heart, where you can converse continually with the beloved of your souls."[33]

Her personal ability to integrate the active-contemplative dimensions of Dominican life, as well as her concern for social needs outside of the school, mark her as a contemporary model.

Most of the Sisters, whose remembrances of Mother have been recorded, knew her at the end of her life when she was already showing signs of the mental illness which occasioned hallucinations and bizarre, erratic behavior. They recall, however, that she was a good friend to Sister Amanda and would often tell the novices stories of the Dominican saints and remind them to be faithful to the Beloved who is always faithful.

The Sisters who cared for Mother Catherine did so with utmost tenderness and concern. Though they understood well that she dreaded leaving the Mount, her condition had become so severe that she was placed in Overbrook Hospital, September 22, 1916.

There is little information available from the early days of that institution, but the Master Card released upon request offers a poignant picture of Mary Muth, the patient:

> Mary Muth, Catholic, member of the Sisters of Saint Dominic, resident of Mt. St. Dominic, Caldwell. The patient is 69 years old, 5 ft. 2½ inches tall and approximately 170 pounds. She was admitted after having suffered from acute depression and periodic hallucinations for two years. Mary Muth died on October 2, 1916, of vascular heart disease which was aggravated by the chronic brain deterioration and related side effects.[34]

The Master Card is somber and must be complemented by a list of accomplishments if an adequate picture of Mother Catherine is to be preserved. The contemplative setting of the Mount is a credit to her foresight and daring. When funds were scarce, she determined to risk using all available resources to insure the proper atmosphere for religious formation and adequate health care for the sick and aged. Her fidelity to the Second Order rule offers a paradigm for a spirit of observance in any age, and her constant concern for the poor and the families and benefactors of the Sisters remains as a hallmark throughout the history of the community.

Sister Marie, who was a novice at the time of Mother's death and funeral, recalls that the Mass was impressive and solemn. There is no written eulogy. Mother Catherine was buried in the Montclair cemetery, and her body was later transferred to Gethsemane, Caldwell. Its placement directly in front of the Crucifix is truly symbolic of Catherine, the silent, suffering servant.

Mother Mechtilde was appointed Prioress in 1894 and again in 1897. She provided for the spiritual and temporal needs

of the community and continued to dialogue about the change
of ecclesiastical status.

One grave concern was the indebtedness of the Community. The Bishop allowed the Sisters to collect in any parish,
where the pastor approved, in order to decrease the debts. The
local missions were also assessed $5.00 per Sister each month.

By 1900 there was a sufficient number of Final Professed
Sisters to hold a direct election of the Prioress. On July 13,
twenty-six Sisters assembled in the chapel of the Jersey City
Motherhouse to vote. Sister Mechtilde received twenty votes on
the first ballot. She and the president of the Board appointed
Sisters Basil (Sub-prioress), Hyacinth (Novice Mistress), Josephine (Secretary), Dominica (Bursar), Joanna, Seraphica,
Alacoque, Avelline, and Augustine as members of the Board of
Consultors. By the election of 1903, Mother was re-elected and
the Community adopted the Third Order Conventual Constitutions as an experiment.[35]

The events from 1881 through 1906, which culminated in
the affiliation of the Community as the American Congregation
of the Sacred Heart of Jesus, are most poignant and offer
insights into the human pain associated with change.

Sister Aloysius Amann in her *Extracts* traces the tensions
of mindset back to before the move to Jersey City. "Even before
we first came to Jersey the young Sisters, mostly American
born, did not have deep devotion and attachment to the old
cloister." She also cites the opinion of two Masters General who
advocated a change of status.

Père Jandel in a letter to Father Haas, the spiritual director
of the Wisconsin community, stated:

> It seems to be a sheer impossibility, for the Sisters to take on
> themselves the strenuous burdens of the cloistered life to which
> the Sisters of the Second Order are obliged, together with the
> labors of the active life to which the American Sisters devote
> themselves. It seem sufficient if the Sisters content themselves
> with the labors of the active life to which the American Sisters

devote themselves. It seems sufficient if the Sisters content themselves with the obligations and duties of the Third Order, as do many congregations of the order here in Europe who devote themselves to education and works of mercy.

His successor, Pére La Rocca, made a more definite plea during a visit with the leaders of the American communities in 1881. He recommended the need for a general government and the foundation of motherhouses with dependent missions as necessary to the American Church. La Rocca encouraged them, "to adapt the life of the Third Order Conventuals for it blends the life of prayer and action, of Martha and Mary both. It would be excellent for you." He concluded, "Remove anything that might impede the success of the apostolic labors."

Whether Mother Catherine heard these words or not is not clear, but certainly their spirit was alive in the heart of Sister Thomasina Bulhmeier, who repeatedly spoke to Mother Catherine of the many inconsistencies which impeded effective apostolic labors.

Sister Thomasina was a postulant when the Jersey City community began at St. Boniface. In 1881 she was teaching at St. Dominic Academy and decided to remain with the new community. Since she showed remarkable prudence and an aptitude for administration, she was made superior first in Caldwell (1884), and again in St. Rose, Lima, Ohio, (1885).

Before Sister left for Ohio, she again dialogued with Mother, "We are struggling under the Constitutions intended for the cloister, but we are really doing the work of the Third Order."[36] Mother did recognize the validity of her point of view but, as the prioress, felt that she had to speak for all those who desired to remain faithful to the life in which they had made profession until death. Mother replied flatly but with compassion toward those who felt differently, "Two can never be Three."[37] She gave Sister Thomasina her blessing and hoped that the new school and responsibility for the first Ohio mission would distract her from the novel ideas that were sources of great frustration and Community disturbance.[38]

In order to understand the inconsistencies which seemed so real to the young Sister Thomasina, it would be well to take a cursory look at the lifestyle which was in question.

What was life in the cloister like? The Sisters took solemn vows and were bound to episcopal enclosure. All visitors saw them through an iron grille, and they left the cloister only for reasons of apostolate or health.

A day in the life of a nun is exhausting to read about, and it is not very hard to believe that intense fidelity was necessary to endure its rigors with joy.

They rose at 4:30 all year round except on Monday when the call came considerably earlier—three o'clock. During the seasons of Advent and Lent the rising hour was 4:15. Then came Morning Office, Meditation, Holy Mass, followed by breakfast. The Sisters at that time were privileged to receive Holy Communion in their convent but three times a week, Sunday, Tuesday, and Friday only.... This was followed by Rosary at times. Preparation for class and study lasted from 6:15, immediately after breakfast, until 7:45.... The morning school session lasted from 8:30 to 11:15. Then came the particular examen in the chapel followed by dinner at 11:30. Vespers were said after dinner by the choir Sisters and at two o'clock by the lay Sisters, the latter substituting the required number of Our Fathers, Hail Marys, and Glorias for the Divine Office. These Sisters wore the white veil and black scapular and did not join the choir Sisters during the recitation of the Divine Office. At the end of Compline the chapel bell rang, summoning all the lay Sisters to the chapel where the beautiful *Salve* Procession was held for all.... One half hour's recreation followed after which the Sisters returned for the afternoon session lasting 1 to 3 o'clock.

After school the novices studied and the Professed teaching Sisters returned to the classroom where they gave instruction in the arts of sewing, knitting, crocheting, until 5 p.m., at which time they were called to the chapel for Matins and Lauds followed by supper. This was followed by the community visit to the Blessed Sacrament when litanies and other long prayers were said. Recreation followed immediately thereafter, lasting until 8 o'clock. Then came Rosary, if it had not already been said, night prayer, hymn, followed by the profound silence bell after which the Sisters retired for the night. All lights were expected to be out by 9 p.m.[39]

The Sisters ate rather sparingly. Breakfast consisted of bread and coffee. Dinner was the main meal of meat, potatoes, vegetables, and gravy. Supper was a light meal of a boiled potato with no salt, bread, soup, or tea.

Abstinence from meat was part of the rigorous life. Meat was allowed three days of the week, except during Lent, when a fourth day of abstinence was added; and during Passiontide no meat was permitted at all. On the days meat was provided, a kind of satisfaction was offered by reciting extra prescribed prayers.

Though the Sisters retired early, they did not sleep in great comfort. There were no springs for their beds, and the husk mattresses were filled only once each year.[40]

Sister Thomasina, who had tried to be faithful to this rigorous routine for some years, had come to believe that its rigors were detrimental to health and to the apostolic effectiveness of the teaching Sister. She pleaded with Mother Catherine to consider the adoption of the Third Order lifestyle which was meant to assist the active Dominican sister.

When Sisters Thomasina, de Chantal, and Aloysius arrived at Lima, Ohio, on August 30, 1885, they were met by the Reverend Father O'Leary who ultimately became their spiritual director. He noted the difficulties involved in combining "two lifestyles," so proceeded to dispense the Sisters from any inconsistent observances of prayer, penance, or work in order to foster better health for the Sisters and excellence for his school.

Sister Thomasina accepted the dispensations without referring the matter to Mother Catherine and, by May of 1886, she decided to ask Bishop Wigger for a dispensation from the Second Order Rule in its entirety.

Reverend Bishop,
    ...Relying entirely upon your good judgment and charity we submit the justice of our case, for our souls' salvation and that of

many whom we expect, if God should be pleased to prosper us and designs to unite with or join us as we make our appeal.

The difficulties great and small which disturb the peace of conscience and the happiness of the many Sisters of our community are not unknown to you and are alas, only too real! The Rules and Constitutions which at our profession we vowed to keep are not and cannot be observed. In our home in Jersey City some are indifferently kept; here, they are entirely ignored. Here we have no enclosure or pretense of such form of life....

We deem it unnecessary to give your Lordship a detailed account of our mode of life, as we feel you are aware of the inconsistencies and irregularities underwhich we struggle.

Sister went on to remind the Bishop of his conversation with her a year before and assured him that they had tried to live out his admonition to reconcile their consciences, but now they seemed irreconcilable. She pleaded:

We simply plead for consistency—plead that we be permitted to harmonize our daily lives with the rule of the Third Order which we are intended to apply to the practice of active teaching religious.... Please act quickly as it has come to our knowledge that the Rector in charge will not continue our services unless our rules are made to harmonize with our work.[41]

Though Bishop Wigger offered no personal opinion at this point, he consulted with Mother Catherine but no action was determined.

On May 30, 1886, the Bishop received a second letter from Sister Thomasina:

Rt. Rev. Bishop Wigger, D.D.

Please pardon the anxiety which prompts us to ask if you received our letter of the 10th, begging you to dispense us from the Second Order Rules and Constitutions and to adopt those of the Third Order of St. Dominic...

Our letter to you was written as you know after long deliberation and whatever may seem to your Lordship as weak in our appeal we trust you will attribute to the difficulty and dis-

advantage arising from presenting our case in writing.... Our
vocation and our holy habit are both dear to us, and our gratitude to God for his bestowing both upon us makes our desire to
serve him with as much perfection as our weakness will permit.
This is the leading motive in our hearts when we ask you to free
us from the encumbrance of Rules which it is not to be pretended
we should observe.[42]

In the meantime Mother Catherine had received a letter
from Father O'Leary about the possibility of having the Sisters
transferred to the Ohio diocese as Third Order Conventuals if
she would give her permission. Though Mother mentioned in a
letter to the Bishop that she had forwarded Father O'Leary's
letter to him, there is no copy of O'Leary's letter. The bishop
advised Mother to make a visitation of the convent and, if
conditions required it, she should simply change the Sisters.

Upon her return from Ohio, she wrote a detailed account of
her findings:

July 17, 1888

Rt. Rev. Bishop Wigger,
    After a long and wearisome journey to the West I have again
returned home and hasten to inform your Lordship of the result
thereof. The condition of the houses in Ravenna and Defiance
was most favorable and resembled Convents as the discipline
observed in the same was as good as could be expected in missions; but in Lima there was little or no discipline as the order
observed there was not according to the Rule of St. Augustine or
the Constitutions of St. Dominic but rather according to the
priest's (Rev. Father O'Leary's) dictates who as I have already
informed your Lordship dispensed Sister M. Thomasina from the
Breviary which she has not said for almost two years although
she reads six different papers which they receive and has taught
up until July. Besides the Rev. Gentlemen has compelled all the
Sisters there including in the house to break the abstinence on
Wednesday and Saturday and eat meat not only once but three
times on the above mentioned days and that since the beginning
of last September. To abolish this I thought it necessary to
change Sister Thomasina who was superioress of that Convent

and replace her by another more observant and conscientious
Sister, but Sister Thomasina would not obey my orders... As
neither Sister Thomasina or Sister de Chantal would submit to
obedience and be changed I sent the other five Sisters home leaving only one Sister who wished to stay with them, in Lima. When
leaving Lima I told Sister Thomasina that I would await her
submission until retreat....[43]

In a later correspondence Mother informed the Bishop that
the Sisters, Thomasina, de Chantal, and Aloysius, had obeyed
his command and were now missioned in Defiance, Ohio; but
that they still hoped that their dispensation would be forth-
coming. Later Mother Catherine told him that the Sisters and
Father O'Leary had persuaded the archbishop of Ohio and the
bishop of Oregon to consider accepting the three Sisters as soon
as they were dispensed.

All final arrangements were made through the respective
prelates. Bishop Wigger had the final word to say: "I have
written to Bishop Junger (Nesqueally Diocese, Oregon) tran-
ferring to him my jurisdiction over you and the other Sisters, as
you are about to separate from the Motherhouse in Jersey City
and establish one of your own in the Nesqueally Diocese.
Mother Catherine said, 'You are on your own.'"[44]

After three years Sister Thomasina had received permission
to follow her heart. She and Sisters Aloysius and de Chantal
were not defiant women of little religious spirit and practical
experience. They were women of hope who saw in the inconsistencies of today the possibility of change and a different
tomorrow. They dared to leave the familiar ways and risk the
unknown because they felt as long as they stayed "no decision
would be made; for one thing, too many were against changes,
willing to make small changes, but hoping always that some day
those would not be needed and the old stringent life of the
cloister could be fully resumed."[45]

Mother Catherine's insistence was not based on ignorance
or lacking in compassion. She understood the process by which
the change was possible, but she believed that the larger com-

munity had "a love for the life they had lived from the time they entered the convent, and they considered it a betrayal to alter the course."[46]

Each woman heard the Spirit and responded as her faith-hearing demanded. On April 11, 1890, the Master General approved the American Congregation of St. Thomas Aquinas, Tacoma, Washington. In the same year Mother Catherine was told by Bishop Wigger to inquire concerning possible affiliation. The Reverend J.V. Reisdorf, O.P., contacted Rome concerning Mother Catherine's community's status.

September 21, 1891

Reverend Dear Mother,

I have received news from Rome concerning your Order. These are the answers to my questions.

1. As your convent in Germany was not a congregation, all your foundations, in the United States needed to be affiliated expressly by the Master General. Mother Catherine could not maintain indefinite control over the missions if they were to remain Second Order but rather, each should seek to get enough members to become a separate Second Order Community.

2. To be Sisters of the Second Order, you must have episcopal or papal canonical enclosure, as Father Smith explained to you.

3. You must besides take the solemn vows, as far as you can do it in the United States.

4. To become a Congregation, you must have a Mother General, to be elected by all the Convent Prioreses, and have your Con-stitutions purposely arranged to that effect. But if I understand the Procurator General, the Second Order cannot become a Congregation as a Congregation holds General Chapters and transfers often Sisters from Convent to Convent. I suppose this is not in harmony with the spirit of the enclosure of the Second Order. As soon as I shall have the opportunity, I shall pay you a visit to Jersey City and bring the letter of the Procurator General....[47]

There is no evidence concerning any further dialogue between Father Reisdorf and Mother Catherine. Nor is there any clear evidence objectively to define Mother Catherine's plans for the future. Since she did not seek to give independence to the missions and did not move to affiliate, perhaps this hesitation also occasioned her replacement.

Mother Mechtilde continued to pursue the inevitable change. On July 13, 1903, forty-one Sisters assembled in the Motherhouse chapel to re-elect Mother Mechtilde. "On this occasion the Rt. Rev. Bishop O'Connor (who succeeded Bishop Wigger in 1903), having approved that in the future the Sisters adapt the Constitutions of the Third Order of the Sisters of St. Dominic of St. Mary's of the Springs, Ohio, he accordingly called for the votes of the electors, for the approval of the same. After casting their votes, it was found that the vast majority approved of the adoption of said constitutions, whereupon the Rt. Rev. Bishop declared that the observance of said Constitutions go into effect at once and accordingly, on this date, the Sisters began the recital of the Little Office of the Blessed Virgin Mary." On August 4, 1903 the lay Sisters received the black veil which henceforth was worn in place of their white one.[48]

Sister Petronella, now a member of the Akron Community, is the only surviving member of the Jersey City Community who lived under the Second Order Rule. She remarked that the change meant there was no grille, there was a new office book, the lay Sisters wore a different color veil, but their works still kept them rather separated, and all the Sisters took simple vows. The daily life did not change all that much, at first.

Shortly after the election and adoption of the Constitutions, Father Wahl was appointed the Community Spiritual Director. Since he was very familiar with the Community, he did not hesitate to direct the Board of Consultors to discontinue the title lay Sister and advised that the former lay Sisters, who prior to that date had no official standing in the Registry of the Community, take their places not from their profession as did everyone else at that time, but from the time that the Community adopted the new Constitutions. The Board voted that "the present lay Sisters would take their places before Sister Ferrer and companions."[49]

Father reminded the community that a change in veil and a

change in the status according to the registry would not necessarily change the work of the Sisters, "since the community
would still need members to be involved in the type of work associated with the role of the 'former lay Sister.' Such work, however, should be considered essential to the well-being of the
community and church, and those engaged in it should be considered of equal rank with only those limitations brought about
by the time of their labors."[50]

April 28, 1906, marks the exact date of the affiliation. In his
letter of confirmation, Hyacinth Cormier, the Master General,
directed the community to choose a title. Mother Prioress consulted the majority of the members of the Board, and the Congregation was to be called the American Congregation of the
Sacred Heart.

There is no record of the discussion which led to the name.

On July 13, 1906, Mother Mechtilde was re-elected as the
Prioress and, after lengthy discussion, it was resolved that all
members of the present Board would continue to hold office
until the new constitutions were written.

4

"The agony of decision is a form of abandonment to the Lord's plan."

Sister Lois Curry, O.P.

DIVIDE
AND
MULTIPLY

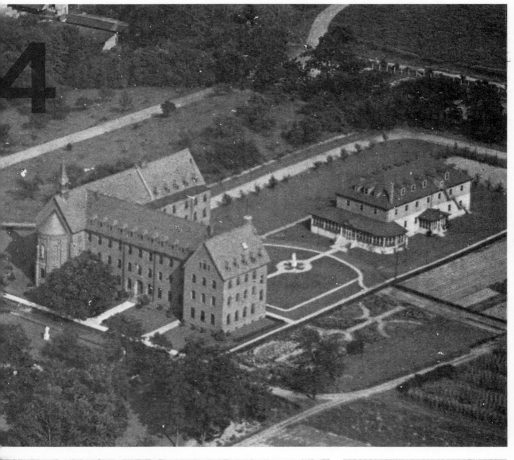

The years 1906–1929 ushered in a time of greater self-direction which included the adoption of Constitutions well-suited to apostolic experience, the creation of a new government structure, and the formation of a new congregation in Akron, Ohio.

The first three years after the affiliation were a time for experimentation. Changes in lifestyle came gradually and the community experienced a sense of spiritual and temporal well-being. Financial matters occupied a great deal of time, and properties were mortgaged to meet legal debts. By 1909 Mother Mechtilde and the members of the Board held a lengthy discussion concerning the adoption of the experimental Constitutions. They were adopted with the exclusion of the chapter relating to the lay Sisters.

In July the election of the Prioress was held in the chapel of the Motherhouse. The Right Reverend Monsignor Stafford presided while Fathers Wahl and Kelly acted as scrutineers. Seventy-four Sisters voted. Mother Mechtilde received thirty-nine votes; Sister Avelline, fourteen; Sister Alacoque, nine; Sister Pia, six; Sister Josephine, six; and Sisters Irene and

Christine each received one vote. The Councillors remained the same.

In the next year it was decided to purchase additional Caldwell properties "so as to avoid the possibility of strangers locating so near the convent."[1] Thirty thousand dollars were allotted for the purchase of eight acres from Mr. Slayback, four lots from T.C. Provost, and the Ryerson Estate.

The former Ryerson Estate included a building that had been used as a private sanitorium. It was decided to renovate the structure and open it as a rest home for professional women. This year-round residence, which proved to be a popular summer resort and convalescent home, was called the Villa of the Sacred Heart.

Marie Seuffert, who lived in the Villa, describes the atmosphere as most pleasant. "The nuns did a wonderful job. We had very comfortable rooms and the dining room and parlor, as they called it in those days, were very nicely decorated and well-kept. The food was delicious. Fresh fruits and vegetables and homemade bread were always part of the fare. The nuns were so gracious and concerned about us. There was a beautiful chapel on the second floor and Masses and other religious services were held there. I remember fondly Pen, a Saint Bernard, that had been given to them by one of the employees of the nearby penitentiary. Life in Caldwell was peaceful."[2]

This interest in expanding properties and extending services was complememted by a concern to conform all facets of community life to the approved Constitutions. An area of special interest was the program of religious formation.

As early as 1896 the Community had initiated formal application procedures for postulants, those young women seeking admission as candidates to religious life.

December 30, 1896
APPLICANTS TO THE ORDER OF ST. DOMINIC ARE REQUIRED TO ANSWER THE FOLLOWING:
Those cannot be admitted who are bound by the following impediments: marriage, illegitimate birth, expulsion from an-

other community, any contagious malady, or defamation by judicial sentence. Do any of these exist in your case? State your name and surname; those of your father and mother; your age; the place of your birth; your residence; your profession or employment, as also that of your parents, and whether or not they are in need of you.

State the condition of your constitution and health, your natural disposition.

State your proficiency in point of education; where you acquired it and how long you pursued your studies. Were you born and baptized in the true faith? Have you your certificate of baptism, and what recommendations can you bring?

...Do you feel sincerely disposed to bind yourself to a life of poverty, chastity and obedience, and are you willing to be tried by the regular novitiate without any dispensation from any Rule of the Order? Can you depend upon the firmness of your determination to save your soul in religion?

What means have you to defray the expenses of your novitiate, and can you bring the outfit of clothing required?

Should you leave or be dismissed, will you be satisfied to receive such of your effects as are not worn out or lost, and the money that remains over your expenses in the house?[3]

The completed form was forwarded to the Mother Prioress along with a certificate of health, a transcript of educational credits, and a letter of recommendation from the confessor and/or pastor. No personal interview was required. Applications were reviewed by the Board at the monthly meeting, and the candidate was advised of its decision through the secretary. Having been accepted, the candidate received her list of required articles and a date for admission.[4]

Sister Hildegarde recalls her experiences as a postulant in 1911. On January 3, 1911, her sister Eleanor and her brother Valentine walked her to the convent. As they approached the Motherhouse, the walk up the staircase seemed endless. She rang the bell; and Sister Rose, the novice mistress, brought them upstairs. She was struck by the stillness of the place and the warmth of the Sisters. This atmosphere contrasted vividly with the noise and busy-ness of life at Newark Avenue, the shopping center for lower Jersey City.

Twelve postulants entered in 1911.[5] They lived the regular schedule of prayer, study, and manual work. During the day each received advanced education from the professed Sisters and were taught German, painting, and needlework as well.

All activities of the convent seemed ordered. In the refectory the Sisters sat and were served according to seniority in religion. The tables were u-shaped with benches built into the walls. There was a beautiful fireplace at the end of the room. Next to it was the scullery, the room where meats and vegetables were prepared.

One custom which was totally new to the postulants was begging. The professed Sisters frequently took the postulants to New York City to beg for food. Though the postulants enjoyed the ride on the Erie Ferry, begging was difficult.[6] The merchants were very generous, and it was a good feeling to know that many would be fed because of their work.

The postulants from Jersey City had another embarrassment with which to contend. Since the German Sisters were accustomed to having beer served with their main meal, the postulants accompanied by a professed Sister went daily to the local tavern to fill the beer tins for meals.

At the end of the postulate the twelve young women knelt before the Board and asked to be admitted to Reception. The Reception ceremony initiated them into a deeper stillness and called them to greater concern for the Dominican spiritual life.

The Community was most anxious to keep the Congregation one in spirit and in practice. Therefore, the formation of the novices was a prime concern.

Dominicans in general, and Caldwell Dominicans in particular, strive to develop a common spirit without crushing individuality. "The school of St. Dominic professes respect for man and individuality. No legitimate aspirations or natural aptitudes are crushed; and it will never be said of Dominican souls that to see one is to see them all. Certainly, all must go through that spiritual and religious formation which makes them die to themselves in order to live in God, but in this plan, with its well-defined outlines, each physiognomy is free to remain distinct, preserving its special features."[7]

From 1881 until 1912 the Novitiate was located in the Motherhouse in Jersey City. Only mature experienced religious, steeped in Dominican spirituality and capable of communicating it to others, were assigned to train the novices.[8] The canonical year stressed the deepening of a personal relationship with God and proper understanding of the vows and common life in relation to contemplation and effective activity. The appropriate practice of Dominican customs and observances was also emphasized. Recreation often centered around music and art. Needlework was done and sold as a source of increased revenue.

The novice was invited to know and to experience the fruits of the Dominican way of perfection. The primary call was to develop a holy desire for God's presence. In the spirit of Catherine of Siena, the fourteenth-century Dominican mystic, the novice was urged to create an inner cell wherein one can find knowledge of the self in God. Then prayer, the vows, penance, and study can be seen as aids to growth in awareness of that Presence in and through all the situations of daily life. The heart of Dominican spirituality and the novitiate experience was first, the appreciation of silence and solitude as the milieu for contemplation; and second, the development of meaningful ways of sharing the fruits of contemplation with others. Another essential Dominican attitude concerned the centrality of liturgy, the Eucharist, and the choral recitation of the Office. Novices throughout the decades struggled to learn Latin and master the chant and rubrics to offer fitting praise to God. They also studied the lives of Dominican saints, and each class can relate stories about the plays and songs written to celebrate the particular saint's sanctity and to demonstrate the novice's grasp of that spirit as it was applicable to the times.

The Masters General of the Order continually encouraged communities to develop programs for doctrinal and biblical study during the Novitiate. "There is no question of filling the convents with intellectuals, nor pretending that in religious life knowledge is superior to love. This would be disastrous. Intellectuals, no; but educated religious, yes; in other words, religious who desire to know God better in order to love Him better; to love Him better in order to know Him better; and to know and love Him better in order to serve Him better."[9]

Great care was taken concerning adequate interpretation of the new canons for religious.[10] Accordingly, Reverend Father Stanislaus, O.F.M., author of the translation of the new code, advised a flexible schedule for novices. They were permitted to attend regular classes three hours per week and devote one hour each day to secular study. All other time was to be allotted for classes in religious and spiritual life, private reflection, and prayer. Domestic chores were curtailed: laundry on Mondays and dishwashing every evening and Sunday afternoons.[11]

Novitiate lasted usually for twelve months and culminated in the profession of vows. Vows were pronounced for three years. On March 25, 1907, the Board unanimously agreed that the Sisters would renew vows twice, each time for a three-year period, before making final vows.[12]

When the newly professed member left the Novitiate for her first mission assignment, she was introduced into an ordered life which made a valiant effort to integrate prayer and common life with the pressing demands of parochial education.

The daily horarium did not differ from one mission to the next. The Sisters rose at 5:40 a.m. and were in chapel for recitation of the Little Hours (Prime, Terce, Sext and None), followed by meditation and Holy Mass. During breakfast common spiritual reading was shared. The school day began at 8:00 a.m. and ended at 11:45 a.m. All Sisters assembled in the chapel for particular examen and the Angelus before going to the refectory for the main meal. They then went to the Chapel to chant Vespers and Compline which ended with the traditional *Salve* Procession and the singing of the *O Lumen*, a hymn to St. Dominic. The afternoon school session lasted from 1:00 p.m. until 3:15 p.m. After school the new teachers spent time preparing classes with a master teacher. Lessons in art, music, and needlework were also given. The Community again assembled to chant Matins and Lauds and to recite the rosary. Supper was followed by a common study hour and recreation. Night prayer was at 8:30 p.m. and lights were to be out by 9:30 p.m. Profound silence was enforced until after breakfast.[13]

The year 1912 was a momentous one for the Community which had grown in membership and excellence of reputation. On July 13, the election of Prioress was held in Jersey City. Reverend Wahl presided while Fathers P.W. Smith and J. Dawenhauer acted as scrutineers (those who count the votes). Seventy-seven Sisters voted. Since Sister Avelline had not received enough votes on the first ballot, a second ballotting was necessary. She then received forty-one votes and became the third Mother Prioress of the Community. A few hours after the election, Mother Avelline and the Board met. "There was a short discussion about the advisability of transferring the Motherhouse and the Novitiate to Caldwell, New Jersey. Votes were cast and all were in favor."[14] Thus in twenty minutes the community became the Sisters of Saint Dominic of Caldwell, New Jersey.

Before continuing the narrative, it seems advisable to take a serious look at Mother Mechtilde who had served as Prioress since 1894. The archives state that she was a religious of very firm and upright character, a true devoted daughter of Dominic.

Louise Ostendarp was born in Cincinnati, Ohio, on January 27, 1859. All the children of her family entered religion. Father Bonaventure Ostendarp, O.S.B., played a significant role in the early story. He celebrated the first Mass in the new St. Dominic Convent chapel, he recruited the first German postulants, and he did the cartoons and paintings of the Dominican Saints on the side panels of the Jersey City Chapel. Her sisters, Sister Gertrude, Sister Celestine, and Sister Bonaventure, were members of the Congregation of the Most Holy Rosary.

Louise Ostendarp entered the Congregation of the Holy Rosary from Covington, Ohio, July 12, 1872; received the Holy Habit June 26, 1873; and made profession April 3, 1875, as

Sister Mechtilde of the Most Blessed Sacrament. In 1881 she volunteered to stay with the new Jersey City Community. She was first missioned at Saint Boniface School, then appointed the directress of music at St. Dominic Academy and, at the time of her appointment as prioress, had been the superior of St. John's, Jersey City.

No one can really begin to imagine the feelings of this thirty-three-year-old woman who was called overnight to replace the venerable Mother Catherine under whom she had served as sub-prioress. She left no written record of any misgivings, and her deeds recorded from 1894–1906 show her determination to mold the Community "fast-knit to Christ" and at the service of the Church.

It is difficult to find a record of her constant deeds of charity because she was adamant that the good done to the poor should remain anonymous in order to guard their dignity. Mother Mechtilde was particularly solicitous about children left orphaned. Some waifs were old enough to attend the Academy; but, for those who were too young, she purchased a residence on Second Street where they could be cared for.[15]

Mother Mechtilde is described by many as an exacting superior who knew what needed to be done and made others want to do it. Like Mother Catherine, she frequently visited the missions in order to encourage each Sister to greater observance and fidelity. She was very concerned about vocation recruitment and often made personal contacts with potential candidates during her visitation.[16]

It is no wonder that Mother is remembered for her firmness and authoritative stance. From 1894 she served the community in some leadership capacity. In 1923, Mother Mechtilde was appointed the superior of Our Lady of the Elms in Akron and suffered personally and most keenly at the time of the separation. Beginning in the 30s, she was either a member of the Council or a local superior until her retirement to the Mount in 1941.

Since there is no recorded eulogy for this valiant woman, it seems fitting to recall the words spoken to her on the occasion of her Golden Jubilee, 1925:

Venerable Jubilarian:

Our own dear Mother Mechtilde:

It is indeed a great honor to be allowed to address you thus on such an auspicious occasion—a Golden Jubilee! Looking back through the vista of fifty years, how far away seem the Golden Arrows shot by Apollo, the sun-god on the western horizon of life. And yet we know what happens to vistas as we approach their leafy bowers and pass under their green foliage—the distance recedes and so hardly before we realize it, their verdant length is traversed and the panorama of sky and earth lies before us.

Thus we find our Mother Mechtilde has travelled serenely on towards the shining gold of half a century spent in God's service, unperturbed by the brightness of successful achievements; nor unduly cast down by the darkness of failures. Like the little child looking for the pot of gold at the end of the rainbow, so have you, dear Mother, sought clearly and steadfastly the golden grades that come with the fulfilling of God's will. That is why our beloved Community has assembled here today to congratulate you...

The same speaker extolled her as "'Moses-like' for you led us into the land of promise."[17] The image seems most apt. Mother Mechtilde did not seek leadership; she was called and spent her entire religious life in that role. She led her Sisters from the burdensome life of the cloistered-active way to the Third Order lifestyle. Though she was firm and unbending in demanding obedience, she was equally strict with herself and created a strong bond of understanding among the Sisters under her care. Prayer was the breath of her life. She loved silence and spent many hours with her Lord before the Blessed Sacrament. During her administration, four schools were opened in the Diocese of Newark and eight in the diocese of Cleveland.[18]

After serving as superior in Rutherford and at St. Dominic Academy, Mother Mechtilde returned to the Motherhouse in 1941 to celebrate her Diamond Jubilee. Her final illness was of short duration but her suffering was extreme. Perhaps words penned to her in 1942 made the suffering more bearable: "Self-oblation means offering oneself to God, even to the point of sacrifice. Abandonment means losing yourself to God for anything He wants to do with you. When properly used they do not differ greatly."[19] Mother Mechtilde died on January 11, 1944.

Mother Avelline and her councillors made the change to Caldwell with ease and efficiency. The postulants and novices were told to get their things ready and were given fifteen cents for the trolley fares. The first night away from the noisy crowded city was spent on army cots since no permanent residence had yet been determined.

The Sisters had barely settled into the new Motherhouse when the Board initiated another change which had great impact on many. On September 28, 1912, "there was a lengthy discussion regarding the advisability of changing the present style of gimp. Finally votes were cast, which were found nine in favor and one against. Hence it was resolved to adopt the plain coif and said change to go into effect November 1, 1912."[20]

Though there is no record of the precise content of the discussion, it is not difficult to imagine. The gimp with its pleated five points symbolized the five wounds of Jesus. It had significance to many Sisters who had worn it their entire religious life so the change was not welcomed. Surely the amount of time it took to prepare the gimp was one factor in favor of the change. Sister Amabilis remarked that it usually took three attempts to get it perfect.[21] The Sisters began to wear the plain coif with a starched white collar that was worn over the scapular on November 1.

That same month the Board attempted to establish a uniform rite for the choral recitation of the Office. The *Domine in Unione* was to be recited before the Office of the Dead and the antiphon, *O Sacrum Convivium*, was to be used before the regular hours of Office when they were recited in the presence of the Blessed Sacrament. Cloaks were to be worn at all hours of Office.[22]

The chapel in the Motherhouse was redecorated and frescoed by Mr. Ragghe in 1913.

Mother Avelline and the Council had encouraged a new

sense of unity, direction, and purpose. When they learned that Sisters Yolanda, Bernadette, and De Ricci, three of the pioneer Sisters to Ohio, had applied to Bishop Kudelka of the Superior Diocese in Wisconsin to be received into his diocese as an independent foundation, they were shocked.

Mother first was informed of the movement during her visitation of the Ohio missions. Some Sisters told her that they had been approached to support the founding of a separate congregation for the German Sisters. After investigating, Mother discovered that the Sisters involved were very few, and she sought the advice of Bishop Schrembs of Cleveland. He informed her that the Sisters had approached him and he had declined.

At the same time Mother received a significant letter from the Apostolic Delegate concerning the formation of novices and the state of fervor and observance throughout the community. It appears that seven unnamed Sisters had requested separation from the community "precisely because the discipline was not observed."[23]

Mother Avelline was shocked by the contents and replied immediately. She informed the Delegate that, upon her election, July 1912, she immediately removed the young and inexperienced Sister Assumpta from her role of Novice Mistress and had replaced her with the more mature, experienced Sister Rose Kunz. This move, she felt, would take care of any laxity or deficiency in the formation of the novices.

As to the religious spirit of the Congregation, Mother denied the charges and raised questions concerning the motives of the Sisters. She stated quite honestly that she felt Sisters De Ricci and Yolanda were more concerned with attaining superiorship than with regular discipline, and concluded: "since only Sisters who have a good religious spirit should be sent to make a new foundation and not such as have an independent spirit,"[24] these Sisters should not be released.

In June of 1914 Bishop Kudelka wrote to Mother personally. "There is a great future in the North-West for our Church. Everywhere new congregations are springing up and I

am in great need of Sisters. I would be happy to receive the
Sisters who approached me in Bucyrus if you and your council
approve since this approval is required by the apostolic delegate."[25] It is evident that Mother and her council resented the
way the Sisters had gone about the initial request. It is equally
clear that they voted unanimously against the new foundation.
Sisters Yolanda, De Ricci, and Bernadette were recalled to the
Motherhouse.

In order to make some response to Bishop Kudelka the
Council decided to open a mission in Hurley, Wisconsin,
September of that same year. Sisters Basil, Yolanda, Aquinata,
Matthew, Ignatia, and Alexandrine were sent to staff the school
and house.

As the time for the election of prioress approached, Bishop
O'Connor, who had been in continual consultation with the
Council, encouraged the Congregation to assume the new
government structure prescribed by Canon Law for Third Order
Conventuals. On June 5, 1915, he ordered the convocation of
the First General Chapter.[26] The houses of the Community were
grouped according to size and delegates were elected.

On Monday, July 12, the first General Chapter was
opened. There were four ex-officio members: Mother Avelline,
Mother Alacoque, and the ex-prioresses Mothers Catherine and
Mechtilde; as well as twenty-three elected delegates: Sisters
Joanna, Angelica, Philip, Basil, Josephine, Augustine, Pia,
Magdalene, Antoninus, Rose, Irene, Paula, Bernadine, Adal-
bert, Ignatia, Antonia, Clementine, Veronica, Beda, Clarissa,
Luitgardis, Edward, and Adelaide.

On July 13 Very Reverend R. Meagher, the Dominican
Provincial, presided at the election. Reverend Mother Avelline
received twenty votes on the first ballot. The bell was rung, and
all the Sisters came to the chapel to offer prayers and a promise
of obedience to the first Reverend Mother General of the Congregation. Mother and her Council (Mother Alacoque, Vicaress; Sister Irene; Sister Josephine, Secretary General; and
Sister Clementine) were elected for six years. Sister Imelda, the
elected Bursar General, was not a member of the Council.

The next day the delegates assembled to discuss suggestions sent by the Sisters to the Chapter for its deliberation. After lengthy discussion, it was unanimously resolved to adopt regulations to be observed throughout the Congregation.[27]

Mother Avelline promptly turned her attention to the improvement of the Community-owned institutions and the printing of the Community Constitutions which were to be distributed to each Sister.

The year 1916 began with the diocesan authorities issuing a salary scale for Sisters. The community immediately re-evaluated its assessments. If the salary were two-hundred fifty dollars a month, the Sister was assessed five dollars; if the salary were three hundred dollars, the assessment was seven dollars. Since music lessions provided additional revenues, it was decided that a teacher with forty pupils would be assessed twenty-five dollars per month, while one with fifty would send thrity dollars.[28]

Since there was a great concern about the excellence of the schools, by September the Council decided that the Inspectress and principals of the parochial schools would hold a meeting once a month, alternately in Caldwell or Jersey City, to discuss matters of vital concern to the advancement of education. Every first Saturday Sister Felix conducted the meetings.

The Community's reputation for excellence in education was well-deserved. Saint John's School in Jersey City served as a model school and many "novice-teachers" were molded in its classrooms.

Once the United States had formally entered World War I, the Sisters supported the war effort and promoted prayer for peace. Letters from the Motherhouse exhorted the local houses and individuals to be careful of spending unnecessary money and to be especially mindful of the families of soldiers and those who had special needs during these strained times. If annals had been kept, they would have included for each convent endless stories of continuous generosity to the poor and afflicted.

The Second General Chapter was convened July, 1921. Reverend Mother Avelline was elected for a second term. Sisters Veronica, Mechtilde, Joseph, and Mary Philip served as her councillors. Their deliberations bore fruit in several areas: Sister Joseph was named the Directress of Studies and assigned to contact Sisters who would pursue advanced studies at Catholic University; the graves of the Sisters who were buried in Montclair were to be exhumed and brought to Gethsemane, and the Dominican Fathers were to become the annual retreat masters.[29]

The first notable event of Mother's second administration was the opening of a Normal School accredited to the New Jersey Department of Public Institution. Four of their best teachers came from Trenton to conduct Saturday and summer school classes. At the end of the second summer, several Sisters received elementary and secondary certificates. Within three years qualified Sisters from the Community taught the classes. By 1927 thirty-three Sisters had obtained advanced degrees from Catholic University, Fordham University, and Villanova College.

In 1924 a report of the status of the Congregation was forwarded to Rome:

Personal report: Professed members   294
                    Novices   16
                    Postulants   12
                    Total   322

Spiritual report: Our Constitutions have been faithfully observed and offer no serious difficulty. Material and financial report: The Congregation is involved in teaching Catholic youth in 22 schools in the diocese of Newark and 10 in the diocese of Cleveland. No dowry is required for our candidates and income is sufficient for the maintenance of our members and any surplus is used to sustain our institutions.[30]

Since much of the significant data for the years 1923 through 1929 is concerned with the separation of the Ohio missions, the chronological flow of the narrative will be interrupted in order to concentrate on the Community relationship with the diocese of Cleveland.[31]

For almost fifty years the foundations in the diocese of Cleveland had made significant contributions to the spirit and mission of the Caldwell Community. In 1885 Reverend Father Henry, Pastor of St. Rose's Church in Lima, Ohio, asked for Sisters to teach in his school. "The request was hailed with joy mingled with sorrow. Joy, because it meant the spread of God's kingdom; sorrow, for the Sisters realized that the pioneers would have to leave their loved Sisters to live at a great distance from them."[32] This mixture of emotions would be felt again on March 9, 1929, when sixty professed Sisters and seven novices, who belonged to the Caldwell Community, affiliated themselves to the new community of the Sisters of St. Dominic of Akron, Ohio.

The intervening forty-four years tell a story of courage and commitment. The Dominican missioner, Dominic Fenwick, began a fruitful apostolate in the new state of Ohio in 1808. By 1921 the Catholic population warranted the formation of a diocese. Cincinnati was chosen as the site and Fenwick became the Bishop. By 1850 the diocese was raised to an archdiocese with suffran sees in Cleveland (1847), Columbus (1868), Toledo (1910), and Youngstown (1943). The Sisters of Caldwell staffed schools in each of these sees with the exception of Columbus.

Even though these missions no longer form a part of the Caldwell story, it seems fitting to muse for a while over the beginnings since the formative character of this community was clearly stamped on the West.

Reverend Mother Catherine selected Sisters Clara, Benvenuta, deChantal, Thomasina, Aloysius, and Lucy as the pioneers to Ohio. Reverend Mother accompanied them on the journey. At eight o'clock the community assembled in Jersey City to bid farewell to the pioneers. Coaches conveyed the heavily veiled Sisters to the station. The Sisters spent a long, uncomfortable night on the dirty, jolting train. People watched the Sisters cautiously. After twenty-four hours they arrived at Lima where they were met by the kindly Pastor Henry. The early history and lifestyle in Lima (1885-1887) have been considered previously.

A second application was made in that very year by
Reverend Father J. Cahill of Immaculate Conception Parish,
Ravenna, Ohio. Sisters Lucy, Dominica, and Stanislaus arrived
and discovered that no convent was readied. Housed in the
rectory one night, they finally moved into the house of Mrs.
Lupfer. The two upper and lower rooms were poorly furnished
and did not meet even the simple needs of the Sisters. In the
kitchen there was a stove and a chair, cupboards containing
four cups and saucers, a knife, a wooden bucket of potatoes,
some bread, coffee, and eggs. Upstairs there were four beds
without mattresses. The Sisters struggled to maintain the cloistered life in these bleak surroundings. Finally, since the parish
could no longer support the church, school, and a suitable
convent, the school was closed, though it reopened later in 1891.

The third formation was made at Sacred Heart Shelby Settlement, Ohio. On September 29, 1890, Sisters Benvenuta, Yolanda, and Bernadette were met at the depot by a Councilman.
The six-mile drive took three hours. Reverend F.A. Schreiber
welcomed them; and the house-keeper, Mrs. Eikel, gave them a
delicious meal. After supper they were shown to their small but
spotlessly clean, well-equipped house which they called Bethlehem.

The school was a two-room frame building. Each room was
heated by a coal stove. Sister Bernadette had the duty, early
each morning, of starting the fire. The school of eighty-five
pupils opened October 2, 1890. An exigency of the time, young
people moving to the cities, caused the school to close by 1915.

The next Ohio mission, St. Bernard's in Akron, is of long
duration and of great significance. On August 14, 1893, Sisters
Rose, Jordani, Yolanda, Hildegard, Gonzaga, Norberta, Thomasine, Beda, Hieronyma, Scholastica, Agnes, and Aloysius arrived in Akron. Throngs of people gathered to meet them. As
the devotion of Forty Hours was in progress, the Sisters accompanied Father Broun to the church.

The first convent of the Sisters was in the basement of the
church. A wide entrance opened on a spacious community room

and oratory; on the right were the kitchen, laundry, music room, and a sleeping room for three Sisters. A yard led to a red frame building which served as an additional dormitory. Though the railroad ran behind this house, the Sisters became accustomed to the noise and slept most comfortably.

When classes opened in September, there was an enrollment of five hundred pupils. Discipline proved difficult because many of the students were too old for the assigned grades since there were few educational opportunities before the Sisters arrived.

Several amusing experiences which dot this pioneer effort add color to the story. Sister Beda was quite ill. When the Sisters returned to the red frame house, they found a large sign tacked up by the health department: MEASLES. The Sisters wondered whether they should obey it. They decided instead to pray that no one would catch the disease, and no one did.

Another night while the Sisters slept in the upper room of the main house, they heard strange sounds like stealthy footsteps below them. They were frightened; they could not move. When the place returned to dead silence, they went down only to discover that all their canned goods had been stolen. The local community came to their aid and restocked their pantry.

One day when several Sisters were chatting with some students, one of them who was a non-Catholic said he was deeply grateful for everything the nuns were doing but that he had one question. "Sisters, why do you ladies insist on wearing your nightgowns to school?" The Sisters quickly explained the significance of the habit.

Father Broun had erected a new church and rectory by 1902. He encouraged the Sisters to purchase land and to build a convent and an academy since the potential enrollment of female students seemed to warrant it. The Community purchased two houses across from the church. The small one was used as the school, the larger as the convent. Mr. John Byrider, a generous benefactor and the brother of Sister Mary Charles, worked to obtain funds to furnish both buildings. By 1904 the

Academy of the Sacred Heart was built, and then an even larger structure was built in 1914.

Mother Mechtilde opened additional missions. In each place the pastor had provided a suitable convent, and grateful parishoners assisted the Sisters in getting everything in order.

The year 1923 is a pivotal year in understanding the final decision to separate the Ohio missions from Caldwell. The Community felt that the interest of the Akron people and the projected increase in enrollment warranted the construction of a larger facility than Sacred Heart Academy. They also pondered the need to open an Ohio Novitiate, since the number of candidates from the West was increasing steadily. When Bishop Schrembs, the Ordinary of the Diocese of Cleveland, learned that the A.H. Marks Estate on West Market Street in Akron was up for sale, he encouraged the Sisters to purchase it for $325,000. This spacious house with its surrounding grounds seemed to be the perfect setting for an academy, the proposed Cleveland Novitiate, and a Western provincial house.[33]

Though no definite action was taken, at this time, to apply to Rome for the right to erect a province or an alternate Novitiate, the Sisters, urged on by Bishop Schrembs, made the initial real estate contract. Since the property was landscaped with a preponderance of majestic elms, the convent was called Our Lady of the Elms. Mother Mechtilde was appointed the Prioress; Sisters Aloysius and Beda, the principals of the high school and grade school, respectively. Sister Agnes became the music director and Sister Matilda, the art instructor.

The convent was blessed by Bishop Schrembs and Right Reverend Monsignor T. O'Reilly. The five Sisters moved into the convent on the eighteenth of September. That night they were awakened by a strange sound coming from the terrace. Since Sister Matilda was the youngest, she was sent to investigate. She discovered the noise was simply the rain hitting one of the plants on the terrace. The Sisters all went back to bed.[34]

The dedication of the Convent and Academy was set for October 11. It was a gala event for the town; and representatives from the municipal government, the business community, and Catholic societies attended. A special bus was put on so that 3,000 townspeople were able to get to the ceremonies. Mother Avelline, representing the Administration, Sisters from the sur- rounding Ohio missions, and members of other religious com- munities gathered among the excited throng. While they waited for the ceremonies to begin, not even a heavy Ohio downpour could dampen their spirits. Bishop Schrembs began the pro- cession at three o'clock and Benediction was held in the convent chapel, followed by several addresses.

Mayor Rybolt in a short address remarked: "Akron is a community of many groups, but there is one thing in which we are all united and that is our effort to put into the minds of our youth a higher degree of intelligence. This is an industrial center in which men make their living by engaging in various indus- tries. But the world has learned that man cannot live on bread alone, for the religious and spiritual things have a great value in life."[35]

P.R. Kolbe, the president of Akron University, accented the role of the school in relation to the growth of the city. "All educational systems are working together for a common cause. The development of the mind is the purpose of all. . . . Ours is a world where thoughts are too much of dollars and cents. The spiritual side of our lives must be emphasized and the material side stressed less."[36]

The Right Reverend Patrick O'Leary, the chaplain, intro- duced Bishop Schrembs and applauded his efforts on behalf of this community and religious education in the diocese. His Excellency challenged those assembled to remember their role as pilgrims on earth who journey to God more easily when they recognize the primacy of spiritual values. He spoke passionately and at great length about the continual labors of the good Sisters of Saint Dominic. "They live a life of service for man for the love of God. They assemble several times a day to pray to God to have pity and mercy on human weakness. They become intercessors between God and the world. They instill in the youth entrusted to them an everlasting lesson of purity, holiness, honesty, respect for law and authority. Apart from their spiritual purpose, they are educators of the highest calibre."[37]

The ceremonies encouraged everyone. On October 13, thirteen students enrolled in the new school.

On December 10 the deed was signed by A.H. Marks and his wife, Lydia Locke Marks. Accompanying the deed was a quit claim deed for the same property signed February 9, 1921, by Florence W. Marks, the former wife. A mortgage of $320,000 was forwarded to the bankers of Guarantee Title and Trust Company, Cleveland, Ohio.[38]

Now that the property had been secured the Community applied to Rome to erect a Western Provincial House and a Novitiate. On August 16,1924 Bishop O'Connor informed Mother of Rome's response.

> Dear Mother Avelline,
>   Enclosed please find a translation of a document received from Rome, regarding the proposed separation of your houses.

> Rt. Rev. Sir:
>   Mature considering the prayers of the Moderatrix of the Sisters of the Third Order of St. Dominic, in your Diocese, in which the faculty was asked to institute one Province of the Institution with a Provincial house in Akron, Diocese of Cleveland, and of their erecting a Novitiate this S. Congregation of Religious answers, it is not expedient as asked. But thinks it opportune, that the Institution be divided into three or four Provinces, if that can be done. Otherwise, permission may not be sought from the Holy See of Canonically erecting a Novitiate in the City of Cleveland.[39]

In light of this letter it is difficult to understand that on the twenty-seventh of September the same Congregation approved the establishment of the Akron Novitiate.

> N 3903/24   F. 48a
> In virtue of the faculties granted by our Most Holy Father, the Sacred Congregation placed in charge of the affairs of Religious

grants to the Most Reverend Ordinary of Cleveland the faculty of proceeding to the canonical erection of a Novitiate in the aforesaid city, provided all things are observed which are required by law according to the norm of the Most Holy Canons 554 and 564 of the Code of Canon Law.

All things to the contrary notwithstanding.

Given at Rome on the 27th day of September, 1924.[40]

Bishop Schrembs went to the convent attached to Sacred Heart Academy to tell the new postulants (Geraldine Pangburn and Dorothy Riffel) and the four young women who had been accepted for Reception that the Ohio Novitiate had been approved. The candidates for Reception began a ten-day retreat on October 11, and the ceremony was held at St. Bernard's Church on October 22.

Preceded by the plumed Knights of St. John, the color guard carrying the American flag, thirty-four white-clad girls carrying chrysanthemums, thirty-four boys clad in red cassocks, the four postulants in bridal attire accompanied by bridesmaids entered the church. Slowly the bridesmaids removed the bridal wreath from the veils of the brides and placed them on their outstretched hands. Facing the Congregation the postulants said: "With this wreath, I renounce the world with all its vanities and pleasures." They prayed, "Accept, O Lord, this crown and bestow upon me an eternal one." The postulants then received the holy habit, the rosary, and their names in religion.[41]

Saint Catherine's, the house which had served as the elementary school,[42] was converted into the Novitiate. That building and the adjoining hay loft were divided into two floors. The dormitory was upstairs while the community room and classroom were placed on the lower floor.

The next series of events led directly to the separation. In November, 1924, an application for a decree of recognition or praise (*Decretum Laudis*) was signed by Mother Avelline and the Council. It was to be taken to Cardinal Laurenti by Bishop Schrembs on December 3, 1924.

Though no discussion is recorded, it appears that the Community leadership desired to have the Secretariat update the Constitutions and to approve the change from episcopal (diocesan) jurisdiction to pontifical status.

The letter from August Fiducchi explains the fate of this proposal.

Rome, 28th, June, 1925

Very Reverend Mother Superior,

...His Lordship, the Bishop of Cleveland, a few days before leaving Rome, called to the Secretary of the Sacred Congregation of Religious and had an interview both with him and me about establishing the Province of your Institute in his diocese. The Secretary explained to him the impossibility of granting such a thing and repeated the same reasons already said by me. Then I proposed again to him to appoint a Representative of the Mother General, who shall have the charge of governing all the houses existing in the diocese of Cleveland. This representative shall be appointed under your direction and responsibility, but she shall enjoy larger responsibilities than any common local Superior. The Bishop seemed to agree with this proposal.

The Bishop declared also to withdraw in your name the application made for getting the *Decretum Laudis* for your Institute. Thus, my long work of translation and confirmation of your Constitutions to the Code of Canon Law has been useless.[43]

The Annals of the Community state that Mother Avelline did not ask Bishop Schrembs to withdraw this application and that Bishop O'Connor was not informed of the withdrawal of the application for Apostolic approval.[44]

The next mention of the situation took place in August, 1925. At a special meeting of the Council, the Akron situation was discussed at length. Though there is no record of the exact nature of the discussion, it was decided to make no change in the status of the houses and/or the superiors in Ohio.[45] Life went on as usual, and relationships seemed satisfactory and even amicable.

On May 20, 1927, Bishop John Joseph O'Connor died. He was replaced by the Bishop of Trenton, Thomas J. Walsh, who was consecrated March 2, 1928. Since the new Ordinary was most anxious to ascertain the spiritual and temporal welfare of all communities and institutions in the diocese, meetings were arranged with administrators.

Mother Joseph, who had been elected at the Third General Chapter, July, 1927, met with the Bishop in early June. In her report to the Council she spoke about the Bishop's concern over the distance of the Akron missions and their indebtedness. She said plainly, "The status of the Novitiate in Our Lady of the Elms must be clearly defined."[46]

It is obvious that Mother Joseph had discussed her future plans for the new Mount Saint Dominic Academy and the projected debt to be incurred. While the Bishop agreed with the construction, he looked with serious alarm on the financial position of the Community.

The question of finances as regards Our Lady of the Elms and new policies issued by the Cleveland diocesan School Office created a dilemma both for the Community and the Diocese of Newark.

Early in April, Doctor J. Hagan, superintendent of schools in the Cleveland Diocese, had issued a letter establishing a diocesan normal school and outlining requirements for teachers in that diocese:

(a) In the future no Sister will teach in any school in the Cleveland Diocese until she has completed the state requirements for teachers and has received the teaching certificate issued by the Department of Education.

(b) Sisters already involved in teaching may continue, but they must take classes on Saturdays and at summer school toward the desired certification.

(c) No one can replace a Sister in the diocese unless (she is) already certified.[47]

Though Mother Joseph was able to make practical arrangements with Doctor Hagan concerning the acceptance of New Jersey certification for those Sisters already teaching in the Cleveland Diocese, the situation concerning future assignments seemed questionable. The economic factor and the question of diocesan jurisdiction augured the eventual move to separate. A special meeting of the Council was called for August 13, 1928. "The purpose of the meeting was the discussion of the status of the Akron Novitiate and the voting upon the propositions of obtaining consent of the Council for establishing the autonomy of the Cleveland Community should such be the pleasure of the Bishops of both dioceses."[48]

The result of the balloting was unanimous for separation. Mother Joseph visited Bishop Schrembs in September, and he gave "hearty approval of the pending establishment of Our Lady of the Elms as the Motherhouse for the future independent community."[49]

The welfare of both dioceses and the future of the two communities were considered in all negotiations. Differences of vision and the hopes and fears of each person and group involved formed a complex web of circumstances between 1928 and 1930.

Mother discussed the canonical procedures with Reverend Meagher, the Dominican provincial. He recommended Reverend Edward Celestine Daley, O.P., who was the secretary at the Apostolic delegation in Washington. Father Daly suggested that the separation should be conducted with the bishops and that, when the terms had been determined, Bishop Schrembs would simply seek Roman approbation.

The Sisters of the Community were informed of the pending separation by circular letters. On November 26, Sister Aloysius wrote to the Sisters: "Reverend Mother earnestly advises that the Sisters consider this matter (of separation) carefully and that furthermore she suggests that a Novena be made in every house before the feast of the Immaculate Conception, in order to obtain God's light and direction in this important affair."[50] Each Sister was advised to report her intention of remaining with Caldwell or affiliating with Akron by January 1, 1929.

It is difficult to capture the mood of the times since the response was personal. The pain of decision was severe. Several letters are extant. "It is a real sacrifice to leave the East, so I hope our dear Lord accepts it as such and that it will be a benefit to my spiritual life. It just about tears the heart out of me, yet it must be." A Sister professed forty years wrote: "This is to inform you, dear Mother, that finally after many interior battles and fervent prayers to God for guidance, I know what to do. I believe I should use my remaining strength to aid, in whatever way I am able, the new foundation." Another simply said, "I hope the affair can be settled speedily for it is a great worry to the Sisters and you."

By January of 1929, all the Sisters had declared their intentions in writing. Mother Joseph visited all the convents to verify each choice. She and the Council continued more specific plans. "It was decided at the suggestion made by Rt. Rev. Bishop Walsh that all the money paid by the Caldwell Community on the Mark's Estate will have to be refunded with the interest on the same, furthermore that the new community pledge itself to refund all the assessments paid by the Ohio missions to Our Lady of the Elms."[51]

On March 5, the canonical forms were forwarded to Mother Mechtilde with these instructions: "Please notify the Sisters to come to the Elms to sign, and make it clearly understood that once signed, if the project goes through, there is no chance of ever returning to the Caldwell Community."[52]

Three days later, Mother Joseph and the Council signed the formal approval of the separation.

We, the undersigned Mother General and the Members of the Council of the Sisters of the Third Order of St. Dominic of the American Congregation of the Sacred Heart of Jesus of Caldwell, New Jersey, in the diocese of Newark, after having taken a vote of the members of our Congregation, knowingly and freely give consent to the projected establishment of an independent Congregation of Dominican Sisters which is intended to be established in the Diocese of Cleveland by the separation from the Congregation of those houses and convents which we now hold in the Diocese of Cleveland, as well as of the members of our Congregation, who are now actually resident in the same diocese and who expressed in writing their will to be separated from the Congregation of Caldwell and affiliated to the proposed Congregation in the Diocese of Cleveland.

The very next day the sixty professed Sisters and seven novices affiliated themselves to the Akron community.[53]

On April 19, Bishop Schrembs wrote to Caldwell: "Mother realizes, I am sure, that when the separation is to be consummated, I am not expecting to receive a corpse ready for burial. Whatever conditions are proposed must be of such a nature as to give the Community a fighting chance at least, otherwise there will be no separation."[54]

The very next day Bishop Walsh met with Mother Joseph. He examined the canonical forms and found them satisfactory. "His Lordship suggested that an agreement with Rt. Rev. Bishop Schrembs, D.D., Bishop of Cleveland, should be entered into at the earliest date, and that the papers containing the signatures with the projected community should be sent to him with the declaration of the Council of the conditions under which the Community will surrender the titles to Sacred Heart Academy and Our Lady of the Elms. Those conditions being drawn up and duly signed were sent to the chancery office, Cleveland, Ohio."[55]

The terms of the contract were drawn up from the bursar's report of the monies expended for the initial payment, insurance, and taxes plus interest, as well as the total amount of assessments to Our Lady of the Elms since 1923.[56]

On April 26, Mother Joseph accompanied by the Secretary General, Sister Aloysius, had an interview in New York with the

Rt. Rev. Joseph Schrembs and his secretary, the Rev. George Habig. At this meeting Rt. Rev. Joseph Schrembs drew up a document agreeing to the stipulation set down.

CHANCERY OFFICE
DIOCESE OF CLEVELAND

Cleveland, Ohio
April 26, 1929

Sister Mary Joseph Dunn
Mother General
Sisters of Saint Dominic
Caldwell, New Jersey

My dear Mother General:

I hereby acknowledge the receipt of your several letters of March 8, 1929, and April 22, 1929. According to the tenor of these documents, the General Council of the American Congregation of Sisters of the Third Order of Saint Dominic, of the Sacred Heart of Jesus, of Caldwell, New Jersey, in the Diocese of Newark, after having taken a vote of the members of said Congregation, knowingly and freely give their consent to the establishment of a separate and independent Congregation of the Dominican Sisters in the Diocese of Cleveland, to be established by the separation from the Congregation of Caldwell of all the houses and convents now existing in the Diocese of Cleveland, as well as of those members of the Congregation now actually resident in the Diocese of Cleveland and who have expressed in writing their will and consent to be separated from the Congregation of Caldwell and affiliated to the proposed Congregation in the Diocese of Cleveland as per schedule signed by them and attached to this document.

It is mutually understood and agreed that the Congregation of the Sisters of Saint Dominic of Caldwell, New Jersey, shall transfer all claims and titles to Sacred Heart Academy, 274 South Broadway, Akron, and to the convent of Our Lady of the Elms,

West Market Street, Akron, to the new Community of the
Cleveland Diocese, upon the receipt of seventy-five thousand
dollars cash or a note for the same amount. This sum of seventy-
five thousand dollars shall constitute the whole and only financial
obligation of the Cleveland Community to the Community of
Caldwell, covering in round figures the interest and insurance
paid on the Convent of Our Lady of the Elms by the Caldwell
Community from September 23, 1923, to June, 1929. It is
mutually understood that the Community assessments in the sum
of twenty-seven thousand dollars transferred from the Caldwell
Motherhouse to the Convent of Our Lady of the Elms for the
past five years are hereby cancelled.

It is furthermore agreed mutually that the Caldwell Community
shall continue to assist the new Community of Cleveland by
supplying seven Sisters for St. Joseph's School, Alliance, and
three Sisters for SS. Peter & Paul School, Doylestown, at least
until June, 1932. It shall be understood, however, that the new
Cleveland Community may assume control of these schools at an
earlier date if they find themselves in a position to do so.

In view of the authentic documents of the Caldwell Community
of the Sisters of Saint Dominic signed by Sister Mary Joseph
Dunn, Mother General of the community, and Sister Mary
Avelline Quinn, Sister Mary Veronica Murrer, Sister Mary
Aloysius Amann, Sister Mary Clarissa Attenberger, and the
authentic roster of the Sisters who have of their own volition
elected to become members of the new and independent Community of Cleveland, and who have signed their names to the said
roster, I, Joseph Schrembs, Bishop of Cleveland, hereby confirm
aforementioned agreements, and in accordance with a resolution
of the Diocesan Consultors, I accept the newly organized Community of Dominican Sisters abovementioned as a recognized
Diocesan Community of the Diocese of Cleveland.

Given at the Chancery Office, Cleveland, Ohio, this 26th day of
April in the year of Our Lord, 1929.

(signed) + Joseph Schrembs
       Bishop of Cleveland
(s)   Sister M. Joseph Dunn
       Mother General
(s)   + Thomas J. Walsh
       Bishop of Newark

Witnesses:
(s)   G.N. Habig, Secretary
(s)   Sr. M. Aloysius Amann
           Secretary General
Given at the Bishop's Office
31 Mulberry St., Newark, N.J.
May 10, 1929 A.M.
P.S. In view of the fact that there are only three small Communities of the Sisters of Saint Dominic of Caldwell west of the
Diocesan line of Cleveland within the territory of the Diocese of
Toledo, namely: five Sisters at Bucyrus, four Sisters at Upper
Sandusky, and three Sisters at Norwalk, I would suggest that it
be understood and agreed upon that said Communities shall
belong to the jurisdiction of the newly established Community in
the Diocese of Cleveland and that the official line of separation
between the Cleveland Community and the Caldwell Community
shall be the eastern state line of Ohio.
I would furthermore suggest that in view of the present agreement you would be kind enough to appoint a vicaress from
among the Sisters who have opted for the Cleveland Community,
who will serve until such time as I return from Rome to preside at
the first election for a Superior of the new Community.[57]

Sister Beda served in this capacity until the Bishop returned
from Europe.
Bishop Walsh signed the document on May 10, 1929. Upon
his return to Akron from Europe Bishop Schrembs assisted at
the First General Chapter of the Akron Community. The newly
elected administrators of the Akron Community and the Chapter delegates contested the terms.
Surely the new Community was confronted with a great
economic difficulty. Sixty-seven Sisters earning $30.00 per
month had to absorb an exhorbitant debt. At this time $245,000
was still due on the A.H. Marks estate; $85,000 was due to the
diocese of Cleveland; $25,000 to Bishop Schrembs; $50,000 to
the Akron Bank; and $7,000 to individual benefactors.[58]
Strained relationships and continuous letters marked the
period June, 1929, through November, 1930. Mother Joseph,

Sister Aloysius, and Sister Rose felt that the terms, especially after the deletion of the assessments, were not only just but generous. Bishop Schrembs and his chancellor, Monsignor McFadden, demanded that the interest payments be lessened to simple rather than compound rates. Though Sister Rose felt she had computed the sum according to proper business practice, the Caldwell Community deducted $424.59 as suggested. On the following November 10, 1930, the Community of Akron presented the Caldwell Community with a check for $75,000 which represented funds for all interest, tax, and insurance payments made by Caldwell prior to 1928. The titles of the promised properties were transferred and relationship between the mother-daughter communities stabilized.[59]

The formal document of separation was issued in 1930, and in the same year the community was affiliated with the Dominican Order as the American Congregation of the Immaculate Heart of Mary.

The path toward separation was marked by hard decisions on every side. In the midst of that story the Third General Chapter was held on July 12, 1927. Reverend J.A. Hinch presided over the election in the name of Rt. Rev. J.A. Duffy, who was acting as administrator since the death of Bishop O'Connor. After three ballots Sister Joseph Dunn was elected Mother General. Mother Mechtilde, Sister Veronica Murrer, Sister Clarissa Attenberger, and Sister Aloysius Amann were her councillors. The Chapter legislated directives concerning suffrages for the dead; a change to the soft collar on the habit; and a cloak with a high standing collar, so that it could be worn over the soft collar; and the regulation of home visits.[60]

When Mother Avelline looked back on her fifteen years as Prioress and Mother General, she could be justifiably proud of her leadership. Her gifts of boundless energy, foresight and determination had borne rich fruits.

Marie Quinn was born in New York City on October 7, 1864. Her parents, Peter and Ellen Grinnon Quinn, natives of Ireland, sent her to Holy Cross Academy, Brooklyn. At age eleven, she transferred to St. Dominic Academy, Jersey City. Her residence among the Sisters nurtured her vocation. She entered the Congregation of the Holy Rosary in 1880 and received the habit November 26, 1881. Less than a month later she affiliated herself with the Jersey City Community in which she made profession on August 4, 1883.

Mother Avelline taught music in Jersey City prior to her assignment as Superior of Mount Saint Dominic, 1892–1912.

Bishop James McNulty reminded those gathered for her funeral liturgy that "as a young girl Mother Avelline made a contract with God."[61] That contract meant a struggle to be a faithful steward in leadership roles as a local superior, Prioress, Mother General, and Council member from 1892–1945. "She had brought to the Community fine intellectual equipment, deep spirituality, and a capacity for guiding others. She had an innate ability as a teacher and molder of souls."[62]

As Mother Prioress and later Mother General, she showed great affection for the postulants and novices. Her understanding of human nature and her ability to show firmness with a gentle touch can be illustrated in this anecdote.

Homesickness and a feeling of loneliness are common occurrences among those in formation. It was especially true of the young women who entered from Ohio. One postulant recalled, "Almost every Saturday night after profound silence I would go to the Chapel. I knelt in front of the Blessed Mother's statue, but my presence was hidden by the confessional. I would cry a bit, tell Jesus how much I wanted to be a Dominican but that I really missed my family, and then remain there for quite a while. When it came time to be interviewed before Reception, Mother Avelline told me that she had been praying in the Chapel many a time and she knew how homesick I was. Mother said, 'You can feel homesick but stop crying, or go home.' I determined to stop crying.

"After the Reception ceremony Mother told me to walk my parents to the train. This seemed like an extraordinary permission but I responded. I walked proudly down the hill, kissed my parents good-bye, and felt like I flew back to the Mother-house. As I walked into the Refectory (dining room) Mother Avelline said, 'Sisters, look. Sister isn't crying anymore.'"[63]

This combination of sternness tempered by a genuine concern characterized Mother's relationships. Father Paul C. Perrota, a young Dominican who had come to Caldwell College in 1942, felt moved to write a personal tribute to Mother on the occasion of her death.

> Our recently departed Mother Avelline has given the most vivid impression of a genuine Dominican life beautifully and saintly lived.
> ...Deeply Dominican she was most loyally attached to all the traditions of the Order. Particularly characteristic besides her amazing energy and vitality in advanced age was her expansive Christ-like charity. Only one who loves God much could love her fellows as warmly and generously as she did. She blessed every thing she touched and everyone she met. She exemplified well the Dominican ideal of storing up inward grace by prayer and contemplation and then giving others the fruits of it through the action of charitable services.[64]

Mother Avelline possessed an apostolic heart. During her administration, Lacordaire in Upper Montclair, eleven parish schools in New Jersey, and several in Ohio, were opened.[65] Her zeal for professional excellence and ongoing evaluation of the schools are her legacy to the Caldwell Community sense of mission. She remained very supportive of Caldwell College and attended every affair in order to encourage the faculty and students.

In her last years Mother is remembered by the young Sisters as the kindly old Sister who would come up behind you, poke you with a rather boney finger, and then ask why she hadn't seen you lately.

April of 1952 found her in a small Infirmary room just waiting for her Lord to call her home. As she had knelt so many times before the Blessed Sacrament, she now bowed low and "like her Lord in the dark afternoon of Good Friday, April 11,

1952, simply said, 'Father, into thy hands I commend my spirit.'"[66]

The death of this woman of indomitable spirit and intense commitment to Catholic education provides a fitting transition to the next period, 1929–1945, which emphasizes the Dominican sense of mission and the growth and development of Community-owned schools.

NEW CREATION
AMIDST DEPRESSION

1.

5

> "We should each feel that in some small way we can make our community of today, worthy of its glorious past."
>
> Mother Joseph Dunn

2.

CALDWELL'S
FIRST DAUGHTERS
CLASS OF 43

3.

5

*1-Mt. St. Dominic Administration Building,
Caldwell, New Jersey
2-Mother Joseph Dunn
3-Marker for Traditional Caldwell College Dogwood
Tree*

The election of Mother Joseph in 1927 and her long administration of eighteen years illustrate how the vision and charism of one person can empower an entire Community to become most worthy of its glorious past.

Sister Mary Joseph Dunn, Mother General from 1927 through 1945, possessed the gifts of assertive leadership and definite purpose which were necessary to guide the Caldwell Community through the pain-filled separation toward a hopeful future. By nature she was reflective; by education she was a scholar. A close-knit family experience had molded her capacity for accepting responsibility and her Community appointments prepared her to chart a responsible course of action.

Her love for history and her deep belief that the Catholic Church had played a distinctive role in the western world's glorious past, and would hold a significant place in the American future, compelled her to place her talents at the service of Catholic education. The prefaces of the books she co-authored[1] called generations of teachers and students to find out what was achieved by those who helped build our country and what must be our part to keep our country great. Though her life was marked by frequent illness, it appears that she never let an opportunity go by without making the most of it.

Even a cursory glimpse at the key events of her administrations makes it clear that she possessed a passion for truth and a conviction that the Catholic schools had a vital role to play in the development of intelligent, articulate, spiritual, and moral American citizens and leaders. In the preface of her last book, Mother wrote, "All that our schools do should be Catholic in tone and character." She and her Councils[2] made daring decisions in order to create new institutions and improve existing ones so that knowledge and faith, patriotism and Catholic action would be the fruits of Catholic education in the midst of depression and war, as well as, prosperity and peace. Her concern that the middle class and poor not be deprived of excellent education and a Catholic cultural atmosphere was a compulsion.

From the beginning part of the "Ratisbon Legacy" was dedication to Catholic education. To lead students to a greater consciousness of their dignity as children of God and their responsibility to take an active role in the transformation of the world into a peaceful, just society by the power of personal example and service is the foundation stone upon which the Community sense of mission rests.

In every decade the Dominican sisters were in the vanguard for developing proper techniques and methods appropriate to the readiness of the student. Long before the Second Vatican Council document was issued, Dominicans understood and proved that the Catholic school was unique and had distinctive purposes. It was to mold a Community atmosphere enlivened by the gospel. The course of study intended to develop the whole person: spirit, mind, and body. "It encouraged faith to illumine knowledge, knowledge to produce constructive criticism of society and courage to speak about necessary change." Effective Catholic education fostered self-discipline and motivation while inculcating a sense of values, a capacity for right judgment, and a readiness to accept the challenges of adult moral and professional life. (Declaration on Christian Education, 8,5).

The Dominican school and convent were to be beacons of light for all to see. The Dominican Sisters and all who were touched by their quest for truth and their determination to be witnesses of the Gospel and leaven for society were to be lights for the world.

To the Dominican, study is essential to human development. It is a multi-leveled reflective process. It implies the acquisition of skills necessary to gather data and collate it in a logical, cohesive manner. Its second stage is to reflect on the data, to see connections, and to apply the insights to life experience. Such meditative reflection is enhanced by frequent dialogue with others in order to clarify and synthesize. The last stage of study is to contemplate. In the stillness the Spirit prevails over the intellect, brings the abstract to concrete, the speculative to the practical plain, and enables the student to make an appropriate response. To be open to learn basic skills, to become involved in study as a reflective process, to contemplate and to share the fruits of contemplation—this is the Dominican direction.

"Though Institutions are never the whole story...they are accidental tablets on which the heart of a true history may be read."[3] To look with reverence at the history of the Community-owned schools (Mount Saint Dominic Academy, Lacordaire Academy, St. Dominic Academy, and Caldwell College) in order to capture in this microcosm the spirit of the Caldwell Dominican sense of educational mission is the central purpose of this chapter. It is hoped that the fragmentation of continuous chronological progression will not detract but rather add to the grasp of the depth of commitment and the continuing sense of urgency.

Since one of the first recommendations made by Reverend Mother Joseph was the erection of a new building to house Mount Saint Dominic Academy, the narrative begins with that community school rather than with Saint Dominic Academy, the oldest one. On September 23, 1927, Mother presented a rough draft of an outline drawing for the proposed building. A month later the plans of Mr. J.G. Shaw of Fanning and Shaw, architects from Paterson, New Jersey, were sent to Rt. Reverend Msgr. J.A. Duffy. There was a delay in response since no action could then be taken on the diocesan level until the new bishop was consecrated.

December 18 brought the approval of the Diocesan Building and Sites Committee which suggested a number of minor changes. Once all the possible securities were investigated and the plans proved financially viable, though risky, September 18, 1929, the occasion of Reception and Profession, was chosen for the ground-breaking. Mercedes Hall was demolished during the interim since it stood on the proposed construction site.

Though the ground had been broken and all plans had been approved, Black Tuesday, October 29, 1929, placed the construction on indefinite hold. Mother Joseph never gave up hope. She waited patiently until the business community had stabilized. By March 20, 1930, new contracts were signed. Since the estimated cost was $1,000,000, Mount property was once again mortgaged. Construction progressed rapidly and the laying of the cornerstone and dedication ceremonies were scheduled for September 23, 1931, in conjunction with ceremonies observing the Golden Jubilee of the Community in the Newark Diocese.

MOUNT SAINT DOMINIC ACADEMY

This dedication ceremony of the new Administration building, so reminiscent of the earlier dedication of the Motherhouse on May 22, 1893, seems a fitting place to look back in order to trace the story of Mount Saint Dominic, 1893–1981.

The actual history of the school stretches back to the earlier decade. The first Caldwell school was opened for boarders and commuting students September, 1884, on the grounds of the Harrison Estate, Roseland Avenue. The young girls lived in the convent with the Sisters and were placed under the care of Sister Beda and later Sister Emmanuel. The students loved the orchards of peach and cherry trees and enjoyed playing with the cow, Bella Cush, and the pigs and goats.

The number of students constantly increased; and their needs for education, recreation, and proper nutrition were well

satisfied as the school moved from Roseland Avenue, to Bloomfield Avenue, to the Motherhouse on the knoll of Mount Saint
Dominic.[4]

Though there are few records, the testimony of Sister Inez,
who came to the school in 1911, offers a glimpse into its spirit.
Sister Inez and her sister Marian entered grades five and three,
respectively. They made a relaxed, easy transition from the
Brooklyn Public Schools to the academic regimen of the Sisters'
school. A true family spirit existed between the students and
teachers as they went about many occupations, academic and
recreational, dramatic productions, concerts, trips, snow rides,
and hay rides. As they worked, played, and prayed together
under the guidance of assigned Sisters, each student developed
personal discipline and a proper sense of the careful use of time
and talents.

Classes were held on the first and second floors of the
present Convent building. By this time high school and grade
school girls boarded in dormitories and several private rooms
on the fourth floor of the Motherhouse (the present Formation
floor); while the boys, who could attend the Grade School only,
were housed in St. Catherine's Hall, the upper level of the
laundry building. Meals were served in the present assembly
room on the first floor of the Motherhouse, next to the Sisters'
refectory.[5]

When the Motherhouse was moved from Jersey City to
Caldwell in 1912 Mother Avelline began to consider alternative
places for the Grade and High School activities. By July of 1914
she obtained permission from Bishop O'Connor to build a hall
and dormitory if the sum did not exceed $7,000.[6]

Sister Inez again provides background information. In
1915 Mercedes Hall, a three story building, was constructed on
a site directly across from the porch of the Motherhouse. The
first floor contained a theater and auditorium. The second floor,
used for High School boarders, included a large central dormitory area with alcoves along the side which contained curtained
single rooms. The third floor was an open dormitory for grade
school girls. There was a beautiful grape arbor in the front; the

building was surrounded by beautiful rambling roses; and in the rear there was a tennis court.[7]

The boys[8] lived in Aquinas Hall, an extension of St. Catherine's, built in the fall of 1915 at the cost of $4,250. Msgr. Jarvis recalls that Sisters Isabel and Victoria were the first prefects there. He speaks of a genuine companionship between the boys and the Sisters. One interesting anecdote captures both the enthusiasm of the youths and the maternal attitude of the Sisters. On many occasions, the Sisters related stories of the Saints. The boys were impressed by the saintly spirit of sacrifice and decided to imitate their austerity. Who suggested the idea remains a mystery but each boy attempted to place his wash basin under the mattress and sleep on it. One by one in the stillness of the night the prefect heard the basins fall noisily to the floor. They all laughed, and Sister suggested more fitting ways to imitate the saints.

The Grade School Scrapbook recalls the efforts of Sisters Isabel, Victoria, Amabilis, and Laura to provide excellent academic programs in the three R's, Religion, elocution (taught by Miss Parmerly), and music and art. The tradition of the Spring Pageant and Fall Bazaar as major fund raisers began as early as 1916.

It would be impossible to trace a complete history in a book of this nature, but the Caldwell *Progress* article, "Everyone is Somebody at the Mount" (May 13, 1971), summarizes not only the dream of Sister Josephine Clare, the principal, but of all the Dominicans through the years. It was always the dream "to be able to create a learning situation that would give each child the self-confidence she needed to achieve to the fullest extent of her ability."

Even after a highly individualized program had been developed, enrollment continued to decline. The Community contemplated closing the school in 1977, but many Sisters felt very strongly about its continuing. Though the administration and faculty worked very hard to attract new students, enrollment did not improve. Due to financial reasons, the school was forced to close in June of 1980. The Junior High was incorporated with the Mount High School and opened with fourteen students, September 1980. The Grade School's achievements can best be known by its students who hold its past, present, and future in their lives which continue to reflect the values learned, the self-sufficiency and mutual respect acquired, and the Christian service orientation experienced during those eighty-seven years.

A closing Mass was celebrated by Monsignor Jarvis who had graduated from the school in 1918. The tree planted in the front yard of the school grounds opposite St. Dominic's circle commemorates the glories of this school, 1893–1980.

The narrative picks up the history of Mount Saint Dominic Academy High School with the dedication ceremony, September 23, 1931. The Sisters were proud of their new structure.

The main building in the $1,250,000 group follows the late Gothic architecture throughout and is in keeping with ecclesiastical precedent. A seventy-five foot tower is the predominating feature in the design and is flanked on both sides by the four story and basement main house. A two-story auditorium and chaplain's quarters are at either end of the building. The building is 315 feet long and runs 290 feet deep. To the rear is the wing housing school and dormitory partitions and is connected to the main house by a two-story covered way.

The entire structure is finished in a brown brick facing, trimmed with buff Indiana limestone. Topping the tower on either side of a heroic statue of St. Dominic are two large stone panels, one carved with the papal arms of the bishop of the diocese. At various points along the parapet surrounding the entire building are panels carved with symbolic insignias of the Dominican Order. The basement contains in addition to the various service rooms such as the boiler, refrigeration, and pump rooms, a large and well-equipped domestic science room and cafeteria. With its arched plaster openings, oak ceiling, leaded glass windows and carved entrance vestibule, the feature of the main floor is the entrance lobby. On either side of it are large reception rooms with oak wainscotting, ornamental plaster ceilings, and carved chimney pieces. An elevator, main corridor and the covered passage-

way are located near the lobby. The east end of the corridor leads
to the auditorium and the west corridor runs over 500 feet to the
chaplain's residence.
Between these points is a series of small reception rooms, library
and stacks and dining rooms.[9]

The second floor housed music rooms, offices, vaults, and
student rooms; and the third and fourth floors contained large
bedrooms and baths.

Bishop Walsh, who officiated, was met at Ryerson and
Bloomfield Avenues by seventy-five men of the Newark diocese.
Michael J. Ripple, O.P., delivered the sermon at the 11:00 a.m.
Jubilee Mass. Samuel Simms, the town Mayor, introduced the
3:00 p.m. dedication services, and the sermon at that time was
preached by Rt. Rev. Msgr. John C. McClary, the Chancellor
of the diocese.

This is a day of joy and gladness not alone for those who bear the
Dominican name but also for that vast number of nearly a
million Catholics in this single diocese of Newark. For no one
better than they knows the great value to the Church, humanly
speaking, of the great Catholic system of schools. This is to them,
therefore, a symbol of the forward movement of the Church and
in it they rejoice and are glad.[10]

Reverend Michael J. Ripple, O.P., President General of the
Holy Name Society, spoke at the outdoor *Coram Pontifice* field
Mass which commemorated the Golden Jubilee of the Com-
munity. His words echoed the spirit of the hearts of many
Dominican women, deceased and living.

These decades of years seem to tell the Joyful Mysteries as we
think of their beginnings, in humility and sublimity, just as at
Bethlehem. Or again they breathe of the Sorrowful Mysteries as
they trudge along the rugged way of struggle and of pain, of
suffering and of sacrifice. But oh, today they seem fairly to sing
the Glorious decades of victory and triumph as we witness, on
this hill of sanctity and scholarship, the Crowning of fifty
masterful years, dedicated to the sacred ideals of Catholic

Education, with this magnificent gem of architecture, newly dedicated to that same holy purpose. This is indeed a beautiful building; beautiful in the symmetry of its lines that gladden the eye; remarkable in its well chosen site on the crest of the hill; wonderful in its appointments, its utility and convenience; and yet the greatest of all its charms is hidden from the eye.
It is the spirit of Christ our Lord that transforms this building of brick and wood and metal into a Sacred Edifice fixed to the Cornerstone of Christianity by the Divine Architect Himself.

Father Ripple outlined the history of the Church's interest in and influence upon education.

No institution or principle endures except for the truth that is in it. Time is the real test of both individual and organization. The Education of the Catholic Church has endured and will endure because of the ideals towards which she works; viz., the well rounded development of every child in its physical, mental and moral powers. As Ex-President Coolidge in one of his addresses said, "The mere sharpening of the wits, the bare training of the intellect, the naked acquisition of science, while they increase the power for good, likewise increase the power for evil. An intellectual growth will only add to our confusion, unless it is accompanied by a moral growth. I do not know of any source of moral power other than that which comes from religion."

Father then quoted from the June 1, 1925, Oregon School Law decision.

"The child is not a creature of the state.... The fundamental theory of liberty which all governments in this union repose excludes any general power of the State to standardize its children by forcing them to receive instructions from public teachers only."
Religion should permeate and revivify the education of childhood and youth.
We are pleased beyond words, that such a school is in the capable hands of the Dominican Sisters who today complete a half century of noble unstinting glory to themselves, of untold

blessings for those who have come within the circle of their influence.

May I conclude with this humble tribute to our revered Dominican Sisters who have labored with such conspicuous success among us; with the fervent prayer that God may bless with the same full measure of grace their every effort, that they may continue down the cloistered walk of the years, the same steady strides, accustomed to success, because they walk with Christ; and when this era closes may another voice tell the story of success that we know today, but may the story be replete with newer and greater accomplishments than we could dream of.[11]

Eleven days later on October 4, 1931, the opening of the Auditorium of the Mount was celebrated by the presence of Monsignor Fulton Sheen, already a renowned speaker. The text of his address affords a glimpse at the milieu into which Catholic education was immersed at that time.

Fulton Sheen entitled his address "Catholic Opportunities." He concluded that in these days "there are some conditions which are favorable and there are others which are not quite so favorable." The Monsignor decried the gradual de-Christianization of society and a laxity on the part of believers to understand and defend Christian dogma and morals. As a professor he had investigated contemporary thinking and he opined, "People are not thinking."

He sensed a decline of bigotry and a genuine search for the divine in a time of spiritual uneasiness. He insisted that Catholic youth and adults must learn to be gentle with those on the "outside" and to accept the challenge to go into the world and feed the hungry who are looking for something stable.

Catholics must be convinced and be able to convince others "that the things that make a millionaire do not necessarily make a man. Our first duty, then, is to go into the world and make our country conscious of our principles; and our second duty is to rely primarily on the spiritual." He deplored reforms "because reformers usually talk about reforming somebody else, and they generally reform the wrong thing." Reform is usually a matter of discipline but true conversion is a matter of turning to Christ through prayer, sacrifice and action.

In his conclusion he spoke prophetically of the on-going conflict between "the world of Peter (founded on the deposit of faith and morals interpreted by the successor of St. Peter, the Pope) and the world of Pan (those who want new ethics to suit the new unethical ways of living; new moral codes to suit an immoral age)."[12]

The audience applauded continuously to show appreciation and agreement. Father Rooney, the Mount Chaplain, responded, "The opportunities he spoke about, do not wait til they come to you, seek them."

The words of the impressive address and the festivities of both days still echoed in the hearts of those who were present when Mother Joseph and her Council were forced to realize that the depression and the commensurate loss of revenue, since many families had defaulted on tuition, caused them to be seriously in arrears of their promised payments to Fanning & Shaw.[13]

Mother and the Council knew the history of the Mendicant Order of St. Dominic well. They clearly understood how often in the past the Sisters of Saint Dominic of Caldwell had placed themselves in grave indebtedness to insure a continuance of their good works. Again on January 27, 1932, the Secretary General penned a "begging letter" to Mr. John Milton (attorney-at-law).

January 27, 1932

Mr. John Milton
1 Exchange Place
Jersey City, N.J.

Dear Mr. Milton,

Would it be possible for you to suggest or recommend a financial institution in Jersey City that would be willing to furnish a sum of money, approximately $150,000 to $200,000 on the Note of this Community with the endorsement of the Most Reverend Bishop of the Diocese?
As you probably know, we have recently completed our new

Academy Building at a cost of about $1,200,000. The Academy
Building together with a two-story Science Hall adjoins our
original Convent and is surrounded by approximately sixty acres
of land. We secured a first mortgage from the Mutual Benefit
Life Insurance Company of Newark, in amount of $500,000,
about two years ago, applying this sum as part of the cost of the
new Academy, using accumulated surplus funds belonging to the
Community and $200,000 borrowed from Montclair Institutions
on our Note. We have over $400,000 of our own funds invested in
the Building. The tract on which the buildings stand is estimated
to be worth about $250,000, while the original Convent would be
valued at about $200,000.

In addition to our new Academy property we have the tract on
Bloomfield and Ryerson Avenues, consisting of a frontage of
nearly 2500 feet. The Villa of the Sacred Heart, a Guest House, is
located on this tract. This later property is free and clear of
encumbrance.

We also own and maintain "Lacordaire," a private school for
girls, located in Montclair. The value of this property is estimated
at $125,000 and is likewise free and clear of encumbrance.

In Jersey City, we have the properties on Bergen and Fairview
Avenues, besides the new property on Bentley Avenue.

We should greatly appreciate if you would be willing to advise us
of any Institution that would be willing to advance the sum re-
ferred to in the earlier paragraph. Such money as we shall borrow
will be used to redeem the Notes held by the Montclair banks.
We realize the importance of your time and the numerous calls of
your profession, but we assure you that any advice or suggestion
that you care to give will be deeply appreciated.

Thanking you, we remain, etc.[14]

Once again Divine Providence rewarded the prayer and responsible action of the Community and the necessary funds
were made available.

Throughout the 30s financial strain plagued the Sisters.
Many companies including Langton Coal Company were forced
to stop deliveries. One collector's note is extant: "I failed to see
Sister M. Mannis (the bursar) but was given a check amounting

to $184.50 with the information that when further monies were received another payment would be made."[15]

While depression's children, poverty, unemployment, dehumanization and austerity of life, hovered closely, the spirit of the High School continued to be evidenced in its many activities.

1933: First liturgical demonstration Mass.

1934: Five-act historical production of *Mary, Queen of Scots.*

1935: Junior Varsity Basketball team started. Catholic University exams mandatory. Iota Delta Alpha Sorority initiates members without hazing.

1936: "An active discussion was held on preparation for exams... A pledge of loyalty and honor was taken by all students as a result of the discussion. A war on slang was declared by the Junior class, who will publish a daily bulletin with captions 'from the front.'"

1937: The federal theater project, sponsored by the Works Progress Administration of New Jersey and Mount Saint Dominic, presented the Marionette Theater.
Aquinas Debating Society hosts Symposium on Catholic Education for Catholic Schools' Week, November 14.

1942: Undefeated basketball season.[16]

Reverend Paul C. Perrotta spoke at the commencement exercises, June 17, 1942. Amid the news of the ravages of war in the Pacific and in Europe, the speaker acclaimed for this and all later generations to hear:

The human heart seeks what is beautiful, noble, true, and good. Man will ever resurrect himself, for undying in him is his call to civility and culture.

Here is beauty: these graduates are fresh, vital, attractive, noble, with high ideals and motivated by the self-effacing desire to contribute to the progress and joy of the world. They were taught to try to live in the spirit of Him who is the Way, the Truth, and the Life. War is youth's worst enemy, a loathsome thing that rapes and desecrates virginal temples, that starves the intellect, that

encloses the will, and that kills the soul's finer impulses. Its
graduates are not sweet, pure girls like these, but the maimed, the
diseased, the outraged and the prostituted girlhood of conquered
countries...
You will discover many seamy sides of life that will do violence to
the ideals you have fashioned for yourselves. Be practical and
adjust yourselves but do not scuttle your ideals.
Yes, love will find the way. If you have really the love of God in
your hearts, all the problems of your life will vanish. There are no
problems. His light will reveal the path to follow and His grace
will give you the strength to pursue it.
Retain in your hearts the principles these nuns have taught you;
that you continue in virtue and chastity; that you improve your
science and your service; that you grow up to be splendid
Catholic ladies, a joy to your families, an honor to your Church,
a pride to your country.[17]

While the commencement address highlighted the goals of
education, moral development, and Christian service, the Academy brochure in the early 40s accented academic credentials,
the natural beauty of the campus, a select curriculum, and a
Catholic cultural experience in aesthetics and the social graces.

Throughout this decade enrollment increased steadily and
by 1948 the Senior class peaked at fifty.[18]

Though the Middle States Association had evaluated the
Academy as superior in both 1943 and 1953, applications began
to far exceed available facilities. Expansion seemed imperative.

In 1954 Sister Germaine, the principal, turned to the
parents for assistance. The greater Mount Saint Dominic Fund
was formed under the chairmanship of Edward F. Hackett. The
Parents Association defined itself simply:

1. We are a modest group. We are willing and able to make a
   modest contribution to a most worthy cause.
2. We recognize that the Sisters of Mount Saint Dominic
   Academy have given our daughters the education and guidance to bring them through the most critical years of their
   lives.[19]

The desired improvements were begun in 1959. When the school discontinued taking Grade School boarders,[20] their dormitory space was converted into additional classrooms. Donations obtained from fund-raisers along with Community loans led to the renovations in 1960 which provided needed classroom and office space on the second floor and improved Library and storage room facilities on the fourth. At the same time high school students shared the college science laboratories in order to provide maximum use of the facilities and a quality educational experience in these technical fields.

A final extension of the physical plant was made in 1962 when the Postulate (fourth floor) was changed into additional classrooms.

Necessary adaptation of space and facility to meet student needs was paralleled by changes in curriculum design, modular scheduling, expanded athletic opportunities, and the increased participation of students in the decision-making process concerning school policies and discipline.

Though administrators and faculty have changed frequently in the last decade and the Board of Trustees repeatedly has been tackling the momentous task of accelerating programs to meet contemporary needs while seeking to balance the budget amid spiraling cost escalations, the spirit of the school and its outstanding achievements have not waivered. The student publications, *Argosy* (newspaper) and *Golden Fleece* (literary magazine), continued to be medalists; the forensic league fostered a host of articulate future Christian leaders; the Sodality and League of the Sacred Heart sponsored spiritual as well as outreach programs to alleviate the "hunger" of the human family; and the Essex County Search Program provided additional experiences in Christian Community and leadership.

The Student Handbook (1980–1981) makes a contemporary statement about the Institute's eighty-seven year old, three fold mission, "to proclaim the gospel as it applies to the world today, to proclaim it as a loving Community visible to all, and to serve with whatever gifts and in whatever capacity the Spirit wills."[21]

CALDWELL COLLEGE

Throughout its history the Caldwell Community has always maintained concern for the professional, academic preparation of the teaching Sisters. This attitude and the financial burden involved in educating the Sisters at many institutions prompted Mother Joseph to seek permission to erect a Junior College at Caldwell. The request was forwarded in 1927, plans were worked out by Monsignors McClary and Duffy, but by 1929 Bishop Walsh refused to grant permission for a state charter. He felt the diocesan need for a woman's college was being met adequately by the College of Saint Elizabeth at Convent Station.[22]

Mother Joseph accepted the refusal and proceeded to arrange Fordham extension courses to be offered at Caldwell and Jersey City. In September of 1932, when Fordham's new administration discontinued the service, courses were continued through the Manhattan College extension.

Mother had never abandoned her dream for a college. She continued to prepare a Sister faculty and made other remote preparations. The creation of the Newark Archdiocese and the formation of the independent diocese of Paterson in the spring of 1937 created an opportune moment for Mother to congratulate the Bishop on his promotion to the Archbishopric of Newark, April, 1938, and to remind him that "there was no college for women in the archdiocese."[23]

After assisting at the General Chapter, June 21, 1939, the Bishop announced that a college for women would be opened in Caldwell by September. He appointed a committee to investigate the proposed facilities.

On July 3 Msgr. J. McClary (chairman), Msgr. J.G. Delaney, Dr. James Kelley (President of Seton Hall), Very Rev. Thomas Boland (chancellor of the Diocese), Msgr. W. Lawlor (Superintendent of the Schools), and Father Furlong (chaplain of MSD) made their inspection and advised Mother Joseph to contact Dr. Roy De Ferrari of Catholic University, the only Catholic member of the Middle States Association of Colleges and Secondary Schools, to get his recommendations.

After his visit on July 8, Dr. De Ferrari recommended the formation of a Junior College affiliated with Catholic University since Middle States would not give formal recognition of an independent college for two years.

Mother persisted in her dream for a four-year college where the "Sisters, as well as women from middle-class family backgrounds, could procure a broad-based liberal arts education in a Catholic cultural environment." The Bishop agreed with that vision and sent his written confirmation on August 1. He suggested the name Caldwell College for Women and the Council approved it unanimously.[24]

Mother Joseph and the four Councillors became ex-officio members of the Board of Trustees; and they appointed eight additional members: Mother Mechtilde, Sisters Raymond, Aloysius, Perpetua, Mannis, Hilda, Thomas and Eileen. On August 7 Frederick J. Gassert (attorney) drew up the certificate of incorporation which was signed and filed in Trenton by August 18.

Under the terms of Incorporation, Caldwell College for Women was legally authorized:

1. To provide and furnish instruction in the arts, sciences, and professions and in all fields of learning;
2. To establish and maintain a college for the purpose of giving instruction and education in all fields of learning;
3. To give diplomas and to grant and confer any and all degrees in accordance with the laws of the State of New Jersey;
4. To do all things deemed advisable to advance the cause of education generally and particularly education of Catholic women;
5. To receive and acquire by gift or otherwise and to hold or dispose of real and personal property; to lease and sell these holdings; to make investments of its funds; to borrow moneys secured by mortgages on its property or otherwise to accept gifts and bequests, and to act as executor and trustee whenever necessary in connection therewith and in the case of bequests to apply the principal or interest as may be directed by the donor or as the Board of Trustees of this corporation may determine in the absence of such direction;

6. To have and to hold, to buy and sell such property, real and personal, as may be necessary to carry out the purposes for which this corporation is formed and to borrow money for its uses and purposes and to execute and deliver notes or other evidences of indebtedness for the same;

7. To do such things to carry out its general purposes as the Board of Trustees of this corporation shall deem requisite and as are permitted to corporations of similar class and to have all other powers with which such corporations are endowed by law;

8. To join or consolidate with and to enter into agreements and co-operative relations not in contravention of law, with any persons, firms, associations, or corporations, governmental, municipal or otherwise, in order to better achieve the purposes for which this corporation is formed.

According to Article II of the Statutes of the College:

The purpose for which the institution exists is the Catholic higher education of women and the conferring of degrees upon those who successfully complete the prescribed course of study. This purpose is attained by instruction in the principles of Catholic religion and philosophy, by instilling high ideals of character and conduct, and, in short, by developing the religious, social, and intellectual powers that should distinguish a cultured Catholic woman.[25]

Everything happened very quickly. The General Council of the Community approved Mother Joseph's list of faculty members.

Department of Religion is to be placed in charge of a priest who would be appointed by the Archbishop of Newark.
Department of Philosophy, Sister M. Aloysius
Department of English, Sister M. Hilda
Department of Mathematics, Sister M. Corita.
Department of Latin, Reverend Gabriel Lucarelli, C.P.M., Ph.D., was appointed by the Archbishop as head of that Department
Department of History, Sister M. Hubert

Department of Business, Sister M. Alma, Sister M. Clement
Department of Education, Sister M. Anthony, Sister M. Fortunata
Department of Science, Sister M. Joanna
Department of Art, Sister M. Victoria, Sister M. Ancille
The Head of the Department of Music to be selected from the
following names: Sister M. Laura, Sister M. Mercedes, Sister M.
Alicia, Sister M. Celine, Sister M. Annuciata, Sister M. Corine[26]

By September 19 Sister Raymond was appointed Dean; Sister
Marguerite, Registrar; and Sister Eileen, Librarian. The Arch-
bishop was named President of the College; the Mother General,
President of the Board of Trustees; and Monsignor Kelley,
Chief Diocesan Advisor for Caldwell College.[27]

The solemn opening of the College, September 22, 1939,
included a Mass of the Holy Ghost celebrated by Msgr.
McClary. Students of the Academy Grade and High Schools
formed an honor guard in the procession of faculty members,
administration, and thirty-four students of the new college.
Classes followed immediately after the reception.

In the fall of 1940 Sister Joanna (Science), Sister Francis
(Modern Languages), and Sister Alma (Business) joined the
college faculty. By 1941 Reverend Paul C. Perrotta, O.P., was
appointed to the Department of Religion and History, Sister
Clement to the Business Department, and Sister Inez to the
English Department.

Several drafts of the Constitution were written between
1939 and 1945 when Monsignor Kelley wrote the final draft
which was approved by the Board of Trustees in August, 1945.
This document outlined the views and aims of the Institution.

Caldwell College was founded in 1939 by the Sisters of Saint
Dominic. It is a standard four-year college, affiliated with the
Catholic University of America. Its general aims are to align itself
with the oft-repeated cry of Catholic Action and to offer to young
women desiring knowledge, a training that will make them
dynamic personalities; for knowledge, if it is truly such, should be
an instrument for the enrichment and control of action; and
"personality is that perfection by which a being has control—

control over self, and over others"... Its specific aims are: to
provide a college education for young women at a moderate cost
that will have both a cultural and practical background; to
educate such to use their leisure time to the best advantage and
their busy time profitably and intelligently; to train them to be
womanly and all that term connotes, whether they be found as
homemakers, professional or business women; to instill a right
attitude towards life and to evaluate properly human events in
the light of a life to come.[28]

Sister Raymond's report to the Commissioner of Higher
Education (1942) provides essential information about nascent
growth and development.

> Who is admitted? The third quarter of the class
> Actual admissions: 1939 (40); 1940 (13); 1941 (19)
> Faculty: 1 cleric, 13 religious, 2 lay women
> (teachers of speech and physical education)
> Class size: 2–27
> Degrees pursued: B.A (14); B.S. (26)
> Credits required: 130 (36 in major field; 60 liberal arts; remaining
> electives)[29]

By 1947 the enrollment had increased to 170 (only one was a
non-Catholic, who had to attend all religion classes).[30]

The faculty and student body were close-knit. This spirit of
family was nutured by many traditions designed by Father
Perrotta and fostered by the Administration and Sister faculty.[31]

The College staff continued the Dominican tradition of
doing great things on a shoestring budget. Revenue from the
$150 tuition and $400 room and board was scarcely enough to
make ends meet. Mother Joseph was often heard saying, "if
God wants the College, God will bless the College, all you have
to do is your work as best you can."[32]

Sister Raymond in a very special way offered an effective
role model for the students. She was extremely lady-like,
sensitive, and charitable. Her gentility and warm smile gave her
a winning way. More by who she was than by what her very

deep voice said, the students got the message. Catholic cultured women do not use slang and do not shout. They develop decorum and work for peace and harmony.

The first commencement was held June 8, 1943. The Archbishop presented the degrees and Monsignor Kelley gave the formal address. One invited guest, Philip H. Cummings of Verona, captures the spirit of this momentous occasion.

> Dear Sister Raymond:
> ...I am a Protestant, you may wonder what the First Commencement of Caldwell College meant to me. To begin with, I am an American and all Americans value education highly. When men make war it is up to women to uphold tradition and that of education fostered by these young women and under the leadership of the great Sisterhood of the Dominican Order will go on to make the future generations better and with the past protected and preserved and transmitted to them. Secondly, in those very words of Monsignor Kelley regarding the bigotry and racial prejudices of the materialistic world, there is a glimpse of the power for good both spiritual and civic in the greatest community of the Christian world, the Holy Roman Catholic Church. Against the "idolatry of the state" your Church stands as the one supreme bulwark.[33]

Spurred on by the evident witness value of their work, Sister Raymond and Mother Joseph strove to have a realistic and progressive attitude in regard to the development of the college. With the help of Reverend Chandler, O.P., President of Providence College, they fashioned a comprehensive curriculum which provided a framework in which practical problems could be controlled.[34]

In spite of intense effort the Community was disappointed when the College did not receive a favorable evaluation from the Middle States Association in 1949. The scholastic phase of the Institution had received a superior rating. Student services and general spirit were highly praised. But the evaluating committee questioned the financial administration of the college revenues and the Community's ability to make adequate provision for the continued education of future Sister faculty. The members felt that the system of recording college revenue and expenses in the general Motherhouse accounts made it impossible to judge the Institute's ability to sustain itself and foster its own development.

In 1950 Sister Servatia, the former Dean of Women (replaced by Sister Anthony in 1947), and the Community Secretary General recorded the situation succinctly. "Let us keep in mind that we have met all the requirements except two of the most important requirements, namely the education of the Sisters and a complete separation of College and Motherhouse with regard to maintenance."[35]

Mother Joseph, who had already submitted her letter of resignation as President of the College to be accepted upon receipt of accreditation, offered timely suggestions. With the assistance of Monsignor McNulty, Reverend Joseph C. Glose, S.J. (Chairman of the Evaluating Committee), Mr. Cook (the financial experts on the Inspection Committee), and Mr. Duplessis (a certified public accountant) a satisfactory plan was formulated.

1. The recommended library had been erected between 1949 and 1952, and an adequate staff was assigned.
2. The college became a separate corporation and the Community received rent for the land and facilities which were used.
3. A separate college treasurer, Sister Alma, was appointed, and Mr. Waldorf of Fordham University assisted her in drawing up a budget and making an annual report that could show the true financial picture of the Institute.
4. The Community determined to set aside a minimum of two Sisters each year to do advanced work in order to have sufficient numbers to meet the growing requirements of the college.[36]

Finally accreditation was received in May, 1952.

While the College was preparing for Middle States evaluation and reorganizing so that its standards could be met, Sister

Inez had been appointed Assistant Dean in 1947. It is difficult to explain why, but in 1951 when Sister Raymond resigned she was replaced not by Sister Inez but by Sister Norine (a member of the Community council).

Sister Norine became ill in 1952. Since Sister Inez had been very involved in all the Middle States communications, she worked closely with Father Glose during 1952 when the final recommendations and reports were accepted.

Sister Inez's name was presented to the Board of Trustees in June 1952; but she was not confirmed as Dean until May of 1953 since Archbishop Boland had only been installed as the new ordinary in January of that year, and the appointment needed his approval.

In September, 1953, Caldwell became the sixteenth college in the country to have a research unit affiliated with the *Institutum Divi Thomas* in Cincinnati. Sister Joanna and Sister Bernadette Agnes had spent three months during the preceding summer working at the Institute's headquarters. The research foundation was begun in 1935 by Archbishop John T. Mc-Nicholas, O.P., to foster research on cancer, the "black plague" of modern times. The Institute contracted to supply the cultures and the animals to insure uniformity of experiments from unit to unit while the college provided the physical space, Mendel Hall (a renovated milk shed), and absorbed additional costs related to the Junior-and Senior-year student research projects.

An article which appeared in *The Advocate* (the Diocesan newspaper) conveyed the spirit of Caldwell into the 50s. A faculty member remarked, "You see we try to stress happiness here." The text went on to highlight the college's cooperative spirit which made it possible for all to work together "quietly and efficiently, without publicity, doing a wonderful job."[37]

Tension between schools that share facilities is bound to happen, but in a time of need the "family spirit" emerges triumphant. The completion of the College Library was one such occasion. "The time was short and thousands of books had to be moved from the old library (in the Mount Saint Dominic Administration Building) to the new one. And so, as in the old 'bucket brigade' style of fighting fires, students from Caldwell College and Mount Saint Dominic Academy formed a human transmission line from the old library to the new one—and handed the thousands of books from one to another until the huge job was done."[38]

The graduates of the college in the 50s recall its distinctly Catholic, religious atmosphere. Resident students who desired to attend daily Mass simply put a sign on their doors and the President of the Student Council awakened them. Attendance at retreat and the more solemn college liturgies was mandatory. The social graces were experienced in the dining hall and residents were expected to dress appropriately for meals and to assist with table service. Holiday banquets were gala affairs waited for expectantly and attended with enthusiasm.

Between 1958 and 1961 the college enrollment had doubled; the faculty had expanded;[39] and Sister Marguerite, the college president (1952–1968), pleaded for the construction of a sorely needed residence hall and an extension to the Science Building which would provide additional classrooms and more modernized labs. The proposed buildings were incorporated into the Dominican Sisters Development Fund Campaign (1960). With the money gained from the drive and the assistance of government loans, the Mother Joseph Residence Hall, which cost $1,687,448, and the extension of the Science Building, Raymond Hall, which cost $316,174.93, were erected and dedicated on October 1, 1961.

After the blessing of the cornerstone for Raymond Hall the long procession of ecclesiastical and civil dignitaries, religious, students, and dedicated benefactors made its way to the field opposite the Residence Hall. The Honorable Alexander P. Waugh, Superior Court Judge of New Jersey, life-time resident of Caldwell, and friend of the Sisters of St. Dominic, addressed the joyous crowd.

His honor told of his visits to the Mount as a delivery boy for the Post Office. He sensed the serenity of the surroundings and he experienced the generosity of the nuns in the Villa kitchen, who always had cake, pie, and milk for a hungry boy.

As he reflected on the progress of his own life from student, to lawyer, to judge, Judge Waugh exclaimed that in all those years the "Dominicans were not standing still. Great things were happening... Mother Joseph's name was legendary in the Caldwell Community. She knew what Almighty God wanted her to achieve—and she knew how to obtain material to achieve those objectives. That quiet, able nun on the hill was a mental match for anyone in this Community."

It was clear to the Judge and to all present that the words of Psalm 126, "Unless the Lord build the house, they labor in vain who build it. Unless the Lord guard the City, in vain does the guard keep vigil," applied aptly to this dedication ceremony. "The Lord, acting through the instrumentality of Mother Joseph did build this house (the Mount and College), and Mother labored not in vain. The Lord will guard this city. This house dedicated to Mother Joseph will endure. God's work will continue here."

The address extolled Sister Raymond for whom the Science Wing was named as a "valiant Sister." It explained that just as "the Beatitudes were first delivered on a Mount, so they are proclaimed and lived out on this hallowed Mount. Dominicans from the beginning were called to be defenders of the faith and lights for the world. This city set on a mountain top cannot be hidden because many saintly women have worked here and continue to work here for the everlasting honor and glory of our Father."[40]

The prose and poetry of the yearbooks (*The Carillon*) of the 60s frequently extolled the virtues of the firm liberal arts background, the integration of knowledge and life, the guidance of faculty and administration who helped the students realize that "the college is exalted as the student soars, for the fulfillment of the teacher lies in her student's love for truth."[41]

The 60s were characterized not only by an increase in students, faculty, and buildings; but also by an intense effort to improve academic excellence through the incorporation of an honors program, and to provide for better academic advisement. Sister Inez contacted the deans of other institutions in

order to share their insights. She then asked willing, qualified
faculty members to create policies and programs which answered
Caldwell's needs.

The example of the Dean seemed to be catching. No matter
how good the program was, everyone expected and wanted it to
be better. Her ability to identify and direct another's talent
brought with it a personal sense of accomplishment and generally a better atmosphere and spirit among the faculty and
students.

On August 22, 1963, *The Advocate* published the article,
"Caldwell: First Quarter Century," in which Sister Marguerite
noted that the college had gone through these phases: 1) the
internal recognition of its excellent academic and extra-cur-
ricular schedule; 2) the inter-collegiate recognition; and 3) the
present phase of encouraging personal enrichment through the
best possible use of all the college facilities.

The students were learning to develop personal initiative
and to direct their energy toward meaningful action. One
concrete realization was the formation of a student fund to
beautify the campus. Their money went first not to aesthetics
but to a very utilitarian end, the modernization of parking
facilities in 1963.

On September 19, 1964, the College celebrated its Silver
Jubilee with great pomp and circumstance. *Honoris causa*
degrees were awarded to the Honorable Governor Richard
Hughes, Mother Dolorita, and Doctor Roy De Ferrari, Secretary
General of Catholic Univesity. Her favorite Dominican son,
Paul C. Perrotta, whose heart was in the college and whose
spirit had become so much a part of the past twenty-four years,
gave the formal address. His opening remarks, echoed the
inaugural of John F. Kennedy.

> Tell not what I have done for Caldwell: ask rather what Caldwell
> has done for me and for the thousands whom she has taken under
> her roof.... In its warm aura of home rather than the cold aura
> of school, Caldwell seeks to develop Christian women who aspire
> to merriment in play, seriousness in study, devotion in prayer and

union in vision... Others may seek to follow the will-o-the-wisp of untrammeled freedoms and the lure of ultra-liberalism; others may concentrate exclusively on technology and the sciences or seek the sophisticated and the socially elite: Caldwell College would rather adhere to the maxims of the Sermon on the Mount: seek ye first the Kingdm of God and his justice; she remembers the saying of the Great Teacher: you are the light of the world; she keeps in mind her motto: Sapientia et Scientiae; and in compliance, she cultivates the wisdom that rests in God's ways; she disciplines the will into virtue; and she imparts a knowledge of worldly things calculated to ensure a better society.[42]

The next fifteen years will be telescoped since the nature of this work requires it. Caldwell College in its fortieth anniversary year (1979–1980) looked back to 1968 when the Student Center was built to provide adequate athletic and cafeteria facilities, additional classrooms, office facilities for faculty and staff, and a fine arts wing.

In order to extend Caldwell's educational opportunities to women who could not avail themselves of its full-time program, the office of Concurrent Curriculum (now Continuing Education) was started in 1969. In the past decade seminars and workshops have been offered to assist the returning women.[43]

During the ten year term of Sister Anne John (1968–1978) the college looked critically at its past and future. Under her direction and in conjunction with the Middle States Association and the National Association of State Directors of Teacher Education, the college entered an intense four year self-study program (1971–1975). The efforts of students, faculty, staff, and administration enabled the college to look more realistically at its past experience and to make viable plans for the future.

This summary of the final report provides significant insights.

Although the future facing any independent institution and particularly a small women's college has aspects of precariousness, Caldwell College has a number of factors operating in its favor: a well-thought-out educational program; an excellent plant; a uniquely widespread awareness and understanding on everyone's part of the college problems and possibilities; a population characterized by dedication, common sense, humor, and tolerance.... There is an *esprit* at Caldwell which we feel ultimately is its greatest and most sustaining asset.[44]

Though changes were made in compliance with the recommendations, and subsequent Analytical Study Groups forwarded additional constructive criticisms, by 1978 it became more evident that the college needed professional assistance if it were going to remain competitive and recruit some of the dwindling market for eligible students. With the assistance of the Community and the support of the Board of Trustees the services of the Stewart Weiner Marketing firm (now Weiner Ingersoll and Associates Inc.) were placed at the service of the college. The raw data obtained from broad-based questionnaires became the material from which new programs like the Total Student Development Program, the External Degree Program, and more sophisticated recruitment and retention programs were fashioned.

"As the college responds to the needs of the contemporary woman and to the changing educational patterns, I am inspired by recalling the vision and courage of Mother Joseph, the foundress, and the faith and dedication of all who have brought Caldwell College to its first forty years."[45] These words of Sister Rita Margaret, the present Academic Dean, serve to have us look back to the dream that became a reality amidst depression. The same dreaming and responsible planning is still happening on the hill. In her Annual Report 1979–1980 Sister Edith Magdalen offers the hope of meeting present and future challenges.

The problems facing Caldwell College are not unique to Caldwell alone. The shrinking pool of students, governmental attempts at control, a decrease in funds available from public and private sources, new demands being made on education, escalating costs and inflation, adversely affect every institution of higher education today. The challenges that lie ahead for Caldwell must be faced and met with confidence and unity. Plans are being formulated which would revitalize the college's financial condition, address the recommendations made by the Middle States Association, enable the college to undertake a systematic evaluation of all college personnel, and foster a better understanding of and commitment to the External Degree Program. Our confidence in God and in the characteristic dedication and goodwill of every member of the college community enables us to join in unity as we enter another decade with a sense of pride in and recommitment to the mission of Caldwell College.[46]

LACORDAIRE

One year after the Sisters of Saint Dominic opened the grade school at Mount Saint Dominic, Caldwell, Doctor Morgan W. Ayres moved into his new home on the corner of Lorraine Avenue and Park Street in Upper Montclair. No one could have realized then that twenty-five years later, in 1920, the famous handsome Ayres homestead would be purchased under the direction of Mother Avelline to be the site of Lacordaire.

> The Community of the Sisters of Saint Dominic, one of the oldest and best known of the religious communities of Europe, has acquired through purchase the brownstone residence and grounds situated on the northwest corner of Lorraine Avenue and Park Street, formerly the property of Dexter N. Force. The building will be used as a school for girls, with a kindergarten and grammar grades, and special departments of art, music and modern language.[47]

According to the earliest annals, "the aim of the school was to introduce the young child into a homelike atmosphere where it will become familiar with the common every day expressions of French life simultaneously with the formal study of the English langugage."[48]

By a constant systematic stress on the cultural aspects of education and its concrete expression through dramatic recitals, education week programs, plays, debates, pageants, and contests in French, Lacordaire evolved from a small experimental educational center to a well-established institution, unique in its type and effective in its training.

On September 15, 1920, Sister Concepta (principal), Sister Aloysius (high school teacher) and Sister Andrea (grade school teacher) welcomed two students. It is hard to imagine either the feelings of these Sisters or the two young girls. These humble beginnings bore fruit because by 1923 the faculty had increased to five and the enrollment to twenty-three.

Sister Raymond became the principal in that year. She and Mother Alacoque, the superior, organized special activities intended to publicize the experimental nature of the school and to attract new students. Evidently, newspaper coverage of Education Week, November 1923, and poster exhibitions at the Mt. Hebron Public School and the Bellevue Branch of the Public Library, as well as fine coverage by the *Montclair Times*, bore rich fruits. The enrollment for 1924 was forty-three students.

In May of that same year the school hosted its first annual Lawn Party in the enclosure of the main building. The *Annals* record the gala event and capture the spirit. "Old Chinese and Japanese lanterns found in the barn had suggested the idea. Mothers, nurses and babies received small hand-painted imitations. As a result, so many chubby youngsters, hardly beyond the creeping stage, dotted the lawn as the party opened with a special program of dances, songs and recitations, that our school yard looked like a Day Nursery." Primary grade enrollment was increased effectively because of this annual recruitment effort.

By the fall of 1924, enrollment justified a concentration on day pupils only so boarding was discontinued.

The year was so filled with blessings that Sister Raymond and Mother Alacoque decided that a grotto should be built as an act of thanksgiving to the Blessed Virgin for her continuing intercession on behalf of the school. Sister Raymond had charge of the First Communion class and she decided that during their three day retreat, she and the children could collect enough stones on the grounds to start the foundation for the coveted shrine. As they worked Sister told them stories of Ireland's heroes and saints who had built churches in much the same way. When the grotto was completed, since the Sisters were too poor to purchase a statue for it, Sister Raymond borrowed a small white one from Sister Aquinas who was Novice Mistress in Caldwell.

On the day of the dedication, the priest who blessed the shrine asked "if the Sisters, always hopeful for better things expected it to grow into a big Blessed Mother," and the answer was "Yes." In fact, it was replaced by the statue of Mary which had been in the original Motherhouse of the Community.

This statue which had been in the Novices' Dormitory at Saint Dominic Convent, Jersey City, was brought to Caldwell where it rested until Mrs. Arthur, a benefactor of Lacordaire, offered her big Pierce Arrow with her uniformed chauffeur to transport the iron statue to Lacordaire. She accompanied Mother Alacoque and Sister Raymond to Caldwell. On the way to the Mount they stopped to see the new Saint Aloysius Church. The pastor, Reverend Father McEnery, happened to be in the church at the time. On hearing of their errand he offered them the newly decorated statue of the Blessed Virgin which had been in the old church at the foot of the hill in Caldwell. It had often been the object of devotion to the Community, so it was received with joy and placed in the Pierce Arrow. Then they went to the Mount and claimed the original statue. After it had been put in the car beside the other, Mrs. Arthur laughingly remarked that "her car looked like a Barclay Street[49] store moving along Bloomfield Avenue."

The Mother's Club was begun in 1925, and it began its annual tradition of card parties to acquire funds to equip the school.

The year 1926 marked the Golden Jubilee of Mother Alacoque and a year of new growth for Lacordaire. Its enrollment reached sixty-seven and it was formally approved by the State of New Jersey. This approval along with its earlier affiliation to the Catholic University in Washington (1923) completed its professional organization. To commemorate both occasions, Mrs. Arthur donated the beautiful marble St. Dominic and granite pedestal which still grace the front lawn.

Gradually improvements had been made in the Gymnasium Building, and the renovated barn rooms were decorated by the students for various activities. The ladies of the Tabernacle Society of Saint Cassian's Church in Upper Montclair, many of whom had daughters in the school, used the Assembly room to do their sewing and other charitable works. They outfitted the entire kitchen facility and in gratitude supplied the Convent chapel with exquisite linens.

In 1927 lightning struck the tower of the main building which then had to be reshingled and painted. This costly, hazardous job, as well as the providing of a new fence to separate the property from the Gould's at the end of the lot on Park Street, the widening of the road into the property, and the painting of the exterior of the two buildings was accomplished by Mother Alacoque by dint of sacrifice and the help of the Mother's Club.

Patricia O'Callaghan, class of 1931, expressed well the outreach of Lacordaire's spirit in a clever paper presented in the *Montclair Times*, "Lacordaire, An Active Unit in Montclair Civic Life."

> Some people often think perhaps that because Lacordaire is a private school, conducted by ladies who have voluntarily given up the social and domestic joys of life, it can be only a passing unit in our civic life, a place where youthful minds are trained and developed, it is true, but where no current from the great outside can enter.
>
> This is decidedly false. From the first year of its inception, Lacordaire interested itself in local activities, such as the Junior Red Cross... we are constantly reminded that we should be leaders in correct English, lady-like deportment, and above all in moral conduct. This, it seems to me, is one of the best things Lacordaire or any school can do for a community. If we succeed in this, we shall not have lived, nor shall Lacordaire as a school

have been established in vain, for good example is the brightest star in the world's firmament.

The onslaught of the Depression in 1929 did not seem to have a deleterious effect on the school. In fact, in 1931, the high water mark in attendance was reached, eighty-one pupils, all paying full tuition. In the latter thirties, the number fluctuated between sixty and seventy and most paid full tuition. Sister Veronica, as superior, tried to grant rebates according to individual circumstances. "This led however to an abuse, for people began asking for a lower rate where there was no apparent need."[50] Reverend Mother Joseph put a stop to any reductions or free scholarships in September, 1934.[51]

The Golden Jubilee year of the Community, 1931, was also a year of great rejoicing for Lacordaire. Sister M. Veronica, as Superior, paid off the remaining debt. As the venerable annalist humbly records, "We felt that our trial and sacrifice were now amply rewarded when every nook and corner of the stately Tudor-Gothic building with its spacious grounds belonged to us. It will always remain a creditable monument to Reverend Mother Avelline who, as head of the Community, negotiated for its purchase and to Sister M. Concepta who was its first superior and principal."

This decade saw the beginnings of the school newspaper, *The Tower Journal*, which later became *Les Nouvelle*. Its first edition was printed in longhand by four ambitious students. In 1935 it was a printed tabloid and in 1965 its name was changed to *The Checkerboard*.

The years 1931–1934 were undefeated seasons for the school basketball team. They had to play their games in the public school gymnasium since the school gym did not have a regulation size court. The annalist notes casually, "Lacordaire needs badly a new building which will contain a chapel, gymnasium and science rooms."

Alice McWilliams, a star athlete who had transferred with her sisters, Helen and Bertha, from Mount Saint Dominic to

Lacordaire in 1924 spoke more dramatically of the drastic need
in the following lines adapted from Shakespeare:

> Nature that framed us of four elements
> Warring with our breast for regiment
> Doth teach us all to have aspiring minds.
> Our souls whose faculties can comprehend
> The wondrous architecture of the world
> Now dare to do what clever Shakespeare did—
> Present a play, sans stage, sans scenes, sans anything
> Except ourselves most dear to you all.
> And never shall we rest until we see
> Gymnasium, swimming pool, and all the rest,
> That go with schools like Lacordaire
> To make life still more bright and fair.

This play written by Sister Raymond, *Faith and Loyalty*, and
many other benefit performances would be held before the
cherished building was erected in 1962.

Uniforms were also mandated during this economically
depressed décade: blue and white (grades 1–4) and black and
white for all other grades.

An amusing but embarrassing incident for the Community
occurred during this time. The Ayres estate had been sold to
D.N. Force in 1906. Madame Force, according to the agreement
of sale made for us through Reverend J.M. McGeary, left the
parlor and library furniture for our use. In the fall of 1932,
during the annual bazaar, Sister Raymond learned from Miss
Eleanor Peregrine that the furniture was simply loaned to
Lacordaire and that actually she owned it. She even had a letter
to that effect signed by Sister Concepta who had received the
furniture when the house was bought and was grateful not to
have to purchase items to fill the library and foyer. For some
reason the succeeding principals and superiors were not cognizant of the agreement.

Sister Raymond learned that Miss Peregrine had been
travelling in the West and Europe for twelve years. She was
indignant that she had been ignored by the good Sisters since no

one ever had sent her any manner of greetings or invitations to school affairs. She explained that she wanted all her furniture so that she could use it toward payment of board in the European convent where she hoped to live.

Since some of the furnishings had been given to Mother Joseph to decorate the parlors in the New Mount Saint Dominic the matter was complicated indeed. Both Sisters Veronica and Raymond went to Caldwell to check the story with Mother Joseph and Sister Concepta. The Sisters decided to avoid further embarrassment by offering to purchase the furniture. Their prayers were answered. Since Eleanor was ill she had to defer her European vacation trip; Sister Raymond persuaded her to transfer all her furniture to Lacordaire except for some rare andirons, a painting, and an English chair.

In July of 1933 Lacordaire Convent was raised to the dignity of a Priory with Sister M. Alphonsa as its first prioress. Each year of her term brought new improvements to the school and convent. A vestibule was added to the back porch of the convent to provide better insulation; the children's dining room was redecorated with a lovely landscape done by Sister Veronica; and the Chapel was moved to the first floor of the Convent.

In 1936 Raymond Hall, the renovated barn, became a school of music and science. The upstairs was outfitted with gas and water attachments to provide for the laboratories. Again the venerable annalist remarks, "It is a bad combination, however, for both music and science teachers are annoyed by the work of the other... The girls must use our small gymnasium for practice... We really need a new building; but God alone knows when we can plan for it."

Mrs. Edson Heigel and Mrs. Harold Cummigliani arranged to hold a card party at the Coca-Cola plant near Newark on April 28, 1937. The net proceeds of $2,000, as well as a donation of $1,000 from Mrs. E. Tietji, were donated to the gymnasium fund.

By January of 1939 Reverend Mother Joseph had instructed Sister M. Raymond to consult Fanning and Shaw architects, who drew up plans for a small, semi-circular colonial building that would house about one hundred children and contain a large airy kindergarten, a teachers' room, and three other classrooms. A building campaign was launched which grossed $4,780, by June.

In early spring plans for the new building were put on hold because the large house opposite the school on Park Street was placed on sale. "With wistful eyes and yearning hearts the Sisters, especially Sister Raymond, took their evening walk in the school grounds, casting looks of holy envy over at the vacant thirteen room house." A novena was made to Kateri Tekawitha in hopes that the owner would sell the house without the land. The prayers were answered but when plans to transfer the house to the Lacordaire property required that some valuable old trees be chopped down, the owner, Mr. Scot, renegged. In July the house was demolished and Sister Raymond again turned her attention to the plans of Fanning and Shaw. The new wing, added to the carriage house, became the grade school.

The next twelve years saw a continuing rise in enrollment so that by 1958 the student body had definitely outgrown the Tudor mansion.

Sister Virginia who had been teaching at Lacordaire since 1936 became its principal (1956 to 1962). In February of 1958 she wrote Mother and the Council to assure them that a fund drive was absolutely necessary since the enrollment of 140 utilized every possible space. She explained that "the fathers of the students have formed a board. Donations have been made and pledges listed. The plan involves a mortgage to be amortized in twenty years. Lacordaire needs to be a separate corporation."[52]

The Council responded immediately. The attorney drew up the papers of incorporation. Mother Dolorita was named president; Sister Alouise, vice-president; and Sister Virginia, secretary-treasurer. By April Sisters Mary Dorothy, Marie, Mercedes, and Mary Edna were added to its Board of Trustees. The deed for the land was transferred May 18, 1958.

The Community, the staff, and the interested students and

parents never anticipated a long, drawn-out zoning variance clearance battle when they began plans for the new building. On September 28, 1958, "the town of Montclair gave permission to build but enumerated restrictions which seemed over-exacting (viz., limiting student registration to 290, stipulating that the present structure could be used only for housing faculty and administrative offices, and that the auditorium could be used only for educational purposes).[53] Several court appearances ensued.

Finally in June, 1959, the "State Court's Apellate Division by 6–0 vote upheld the action of the Montclair Board of Commissioners in granting a zoning variance to build a two-story brick L-shaped building to house 200 students."[54]

Plans drawn up by Fanning and Shaw were approved by the Chancery; the town authorities consented to excavating in order to obtain a more functional basement; and ground was broken on July 23, 1961. On September 5, 1962, the cornerstone was laid and the building was solemnly dedicated by Archbishop Thomas Boland.

The program *Joy in the Arts,* which was hosted in 1965, illustrates the educational thrust and cooperative spirit for which Lacordaire is well known. The administration, faculty, and student body throughout the years have ascribed to the belief that "it has never been enough to parrot the teachings of truth. Each generation must review knowledge, assimilate it, restate it—hopefully with beauty and emotion, selectivity and discipline. This is the role of the Arts in education."[55]

New recruitment programs and continued attempts to balance the budget have met with recent success. Five years ago the Grade School opened its classes, pre-school to sixth grade, to boys as well as girls. To accommodate the new students and provide for their needs the Community sponsored the renovation of the auditorium. From that one long room, three classrooms were made. Today the grade school with a full-time faculty of ten has an increasing enrollment. To meet the needs of working parents the school offers full day pre-kindergarten and kindergarten programs. The teaching of French continues from grades one through eight, and capable students may apply for advanced placement in the high school programs.

The High School is looking forward to Middle States Evaluation in 1982 and has already begun its self-study. The school continues to offer a well-ordered curriculum, small class sizes, and individual instruction and counseling opportunities. The present trend of increased enrollment and projections for gradual improvements in the physical plant, expansion of curriculum offerings, and the implementation of a debt reduction program while achieving a balanced budget seem to indicate a hopeful future.

SAINT DOMINIC ACADEMY

On May 24, 1978, Saint Dominic Academy celebrated its centenary as a Grade and High School.[56] The Vicar of Hudson County, Most Rev. Jerome Pechillo, members of the Community, parishoners, and benefactors of long standing, alumnae and their families assembled in St. Boniface Church to pay tribute to a hundred years of Dominican presence. Since it was the month of May the traditional Marian hymns, *Salve Regina* and *Inviolata* were chanted. A multi-media presentation highlighted the many ways that the Caldwell Dominican women have witnessed to the charism of proclaiming the Good News by word and example.

The collective memory of all those who have molded and remolded the spirit of the Academy was described simply by Jane Pichot (class of 1890) on the occasion of its 75th Anniversary: "there is no place like St. Dominic."[57]

The self-sacrificing Community spirit which resulted in the erection of the Motherhouse and Academy in 1878 has been described in an earlier chapter. From that date until 1915, commuting boys as well as girl boarders and commuters attended grades kindergarten through high school and commercial within the monastic-like structure.

The classrooms, dormitories, and dining facilities were located in the west wing. The kindergarten was in the basement, the commercial on the top floor, and music rooms were spread throughout until 1908 when a Music House was placed in the building adjoining the Academy.

During regular hours the students had a full academic schedule which included the study of German. Many students remained after 3:15 to take lessons in art, music, and stitchery. The school was well known for its yearly orchestral recitals and craft bazaars.

One tradition that deserves special mention is the *Dia Polla* Society. It was founded to encourage scholarship and improved articulation in history, art, and literature. The honor students learned much even as they socialized.[58]

The school regulations indicate the desired tenor of the building.

> ...A high standard of deportment must be maintained therefore prompt obedience and a respectful attitude are required of every pupil.
>
> ...Silence, the golden monitor, that points to success, is strictly required of the pupils, after the first sound of the bell, in the classrooms and halls, and while filing up and down the stairs during the hours of dismissal.[59]

Signs were posted in almost every room: Strict Silence To Be Observed Here. Pupils learned quickly that slang wasn't proper decorum and that cooperation was next to Godliness. Playful attitudes and sliding down the bannisters were tolerated in moderation and after school hours only.

Since increased enrollment warranted the expansion of facilities, two additional houses were purchased on Second Street in 1911.[60] Overcrowding and maximum use of facilities (persistent threads in the SDA tapestry) prompted another expansion in 1915.

Mother Avelline and her Council longed to move the Academy to "The Hill."[61] Finally it was decided "that a high school was to be opened in St. Aedan's Parish, 669 Bergen Avenue, to be known as St. Dominic Annex, since the High

School, commercial class, and Art Studio of St. Dominic's
Jersey City are to be removed to the above place."[62]

The Yearbook of 1916 reveals the mixed feelings surrounding the move. Since most students and Sisters loved the old
building it was hard to leave the dear *Alma Mater* even though
the new home in the transformed Johnson Estate was elegant by
comparison.

> S.D.A. Annex has not the severely plain exterior that one usually
> connects with a school building. Its wide porch, stately pillars
> and broad sweep of windows, curtained with dainty material,
> suggest the comforts and luxuries of home. This is just what it
> seems to us. Surely lessons were never studied under more ideal
> surroundings.
>
> On mounting the veranda steps and crossing through the vesti-
> bule, one enters the Reception Hall. To the left is a large sunny
> parlor over the door of which a beautiful porcelain tile, the gift of
> Mrs. Owen J. McWilliams, tells us it is Aquinas Room. The
> brown rug on the floor, the draperies, palms and ferns, comfort-
> able rockers and lovely statuary all form a harmonious whole.
> Only the cases of mineral specimens give an indication of the
> purpose of the building. To the right of the main entrance is Our
> Lady's Room. This is a music room and office. It also has the
> advantage of affording a comfortable retreat for a tired visitor.
> Over the lovely onyx fireplace hangs an excellent copy of
> Murillo's Assumption.
>
> On the same floor is St. Dominic's Room as the title tells us. This
> is used for Assembly purposes. There are also accommodations
> for recitation and study periods. After morning prayer and hymn
> the girls file to their respective classes. Many of the zoological
> specimens are kept in this room. Three large windows make it
> pleasantly bright and the sunny little First Year Girls delight to
> gather here. Broad winding stairs lead to the second floor where
> most of the class rooms are found. Directly to the left is the
> Studio from which a door leads to another veranda with a
> pleasant outlook on Bergen Avenue. Next comes St. Vincent
> Ferrer's Room with its daintily panelled walls, bordered with
> wild roses. Here most of the commercial work is done. Going
> along the corridor we come to St. Hyacinth's Room. This is a

perfect little gem with its Bird's-eye maple mantle, and soft brown paper bordered with large bunches of rich purple grapes. Recitation chairs, a teacher's desk, book-cases and a filing cabinet, with a few choice pictures, complete the attractiveness of this retreat. The Junior girls can usually be found assembled here.

St. Rose of Lima's Room is well named, for its walls are covered with a pretty paper in a rose pattern. The white wood work, large windows and dainty water-color sketches, all enhance the delicate beauty of this particular class room, the favorite retreat of the Second Year girls.

The Library is a small cozy room, whose brown covered walls are lined with well filled book shelves. The round table, chairs and davenport and mantlepiece are all of a golden oak, making the room a perfect study in brown. Here the Seniors may generally be found. The prettiest and sweetest room of all, however, is the Chapel. The beautiful altar, the gift of a friend, seems to be of the purest marble, and it is quite a surprise to learn that it is only a very fine imitation. A white marble pedestal supports the cut glass Sanctuary Lamp. On the walls are tiny Stations in old ivory finish. Small prie-dieux and chairs complete the furniture. St. Rita's Room, which is used for type-writing, is on this floor. A little hall leads to the rear stairway. On descending this, one enters the Laboratory in which the Sciences are taught. The large case in this room contains all the paraphernalia for experiment. Adjoining this is the Gymnasium. Indian clubs, hanging along the walls, denote the use of this room. Dainty curtains and the various class pictures with the well-used piano give, however, a homelike touch to this favorite resort, where we like to gather to eat our luncheon and indulge in schoolgirl gossip.[63]

On April 26, 1916, a Recital was held in Saint Aedan's Hall in order to raise money and to help make the school better known. It was well attended and this yearly performance by the Glee Club and orchestra was a very effective recruitment technique. Thanks to the generosity of Reverend Roger McGinley (pastor), graduation was held June 14 at St. Aedan's Church.[64]

The Grade School continued to be held in First Street until 1921 when it was closed. In that year Sister Andrea taught all grades, twenty-five students in one room.

Since living conditions for the Sisters at Bergen Avenue were very congested and to allow for more classroom space, a house was purchased on Fairview Avenue in 1925 and was used as a convent.

The General School Report for 1926–27 describes the Academy as a private Roman Catholic Secondary School for Girls established and accredited by the State of New Jersey in 1913. The curriculum included a four year academic program which prepared the student to pass Normal or Training School examinations, as well as a two year Commercial program. The enrollment included 145 girls and there was a full-time faculty of five Sisters and a part-time faculty of three women and one man. The school encouraged a balance between inductive and deductive methodologies, lecture and class recitation, and note-book work.

The continued growth of the Academy made it imperative to find additional space to expand facilities. The property of Mr. Gorman, adjoining the annex, was put up for sale in 1929 but $80,000 was prohibitive. Property adjacent to the Fairview Avenue house was considered; but building inspectors advised that the present Convent be demolished, so that option was scrapped.

Finally three lots, each containing a well-built frame building, became available on Bentley Avenue. When several mortgages valued at $125,000 were procured and underwritten by a bank note for $175,000 at 5% interest, the property was bought and necessary renovations were made.[65]

In August 1930 the Academy was moved to its new locations on Bentley Avenue. Two houses were used for the school and one for the Convent. During this decade a basketball team was formed, the yearbook was reinstated, and the news-paper *Diletante* was begun.

In 1938 it was decided to expand the physical plant by adding a portable unit of four classrooms if the funds could be raised by the Academy. There is no further discussion of expansion until July of 1941 when Monsignor McClary informed Mother Joseph that the elite men's club, the Carteret Club, was up for sale. Since he believed it was an ideal location and an appropriate building, the Council discussed the purchase provided the price did not exceed $50,000.[66]

By August a down payment of $5,000 had been made and Mr. J.G. Shaw had already suggested needed improvements. Monsignor McClary as Vicar General of the Diocese had negotiated for a diocesan loan of $110,000 at 3% interest. The additional $60,000 was for renovations. He wrote on September 1:

> I am awfully glad that this purchase now looks like an accomplished fact. Its location and the size of the property, plus the well constructed building, could not be duplicated, I feel, for less than $250,000 or $300,000, so I consider it a real bargain and another asset to the Community.[67]

Letters were written to Mayor Hague and the City Council for an abatement of the interest on the taxes which had accrued on the Carteret Club; for a similar consideration concerning past water charges; and for a tax exempt status. Each was readily granted.[68]

Work on the renovations was delayed because of the declaration of war, December 7, 1941.

The move was made on March 7, 1942. The residence at 2572 Boulevard provided nine classrooms, a science laboratory, a small library which was enlarged by 1944, an auditorium, gym, principal's office, and a reading room. The Convent living quarters included nineteen bedrooms, a kitchen, refectory, community room, music room, guest dining room, and laundry.

The actual move to the Carteret Club could be numbered among the "managerial wonders of the world." Since automobiles and trucks were rare commodities to begin with and since gas was rationed to assist the war effort, students were drafted to carry books and small pieces of furniture. The caravan began at Bentley Avenue where assigned Sisters organized "what to take and in what order." The long line of uniformed girls (approximately 100) made a steady parade (for at least 100 trips) with cartons, cases, and furniture. The bearers walked down Bentley Avenue, along Hudson Boulevard (approximately 10 blocks) to Duncan Avenue. The exhausted carriers were met by Sisters who again provided precise directions as to "where things were to be placed."

The move was made in three days (Thursday to Saturday). The following week classes began in the new school. Teachers and students enjoyed the larger classrooms and the better equipped laboratories, but most people missed the "coziness and closeness" of Bentley Avenue, for at least a short time. The Sisters were very excited with their more spacious living quarters.

The Carteret Club's physical transformation is hard to capture in words.

The former large club-meeting rooms on the first floor became classrooms, each named for a Dominican saint or Our Lady and the Sacred Heart. The large central crystal dining rooms became Madonna Hall, a parlor for visitors. (Students were never allowed to walk across it.)[69] The former bar with its beautiful stained glass windows and dark wood paneling was the perfect spot for the cozy chapel, which formed the far side of the center first floor corridor. A small library was made in the rear.

The ground floor became a very low-ceilinged gymnasium, locker room, storage space, and art room, while the beautiful swimming pool was converted into biology and chemistry laboratories.

The large ballroom with its stage (on the second floor) became the auditorium, and the anteroom was made into a classroom. The remaining rooms on the second, third, and fourth floors became the Convent.[70]

The decade of the 40s was marked by a very homelike atmosphere. Monsignor McClary, who had been appointed chaplain in 1942, treated "his girls" to movies every Thursday. The girls were helped to see this Convent School as a holy place because it was a place of unselfish regard for others, of dedication, and of high courage. Above all they reverenced it as holy because the Blessed Sacrament was reserved in the chapel. The sign, "Silence to be observed here," helped to remind everyone of His presence among them. The students imbibed the joyful cooperative spirit of the Sisters and were anxious to acquire habits of virtue, both intellectual and moral.[71]

Sister Madonna inaugurated the present school newspaper, *The Trumpet*, in 1943.[72] Three years later Sister Julia Maria reactivated the yearbook, *Dominica*.

Monsignor McClary died in 1952, and his presence was sorely missed. Into the 50s enrollment continued to increase, and the curriculum was changed to meet new needs. Freshman initiation took on a new sophisticated look: the rings received by Juniors were redesigned; the basketball team practiced in Mount Carmel gym and played its official games in P.S.8 on Franklin Street; the Forensic League attracted new members and won its share of trophies; the Sodality sponsored spiritual and social concerns activities; and the Glee Club and Dramatic Club sponsored Spring entertainment. Uniforms changed from blue serge jerkins (overvests) and pleated skirts to blue skirts and blazers; oxfords gave way to saddle shoes; and long hair to short.

In the early 60s the Science Labs were remodeled and throughout the next fifteen years Sister Eucharista nutured young scientists who became finalists and winners in the National Science fair competitions.

By 1964 enrollment warranted additional expansion. The large auditorium was divided so that another classroom could be added. Sister Julia Marie obtained permission to investigate the cost of an extension. In 1968 the Council denied the request because the time seemed inopportune since the Administration was near its end and the Community already had a high debt, but the Sisters were permitted to investigate financial alternatives. Though enrollment peaked at 518 in 1969–70, permission for the expansion was not given.[73] By 1976 the need to expand was so imperative that dialogue concerning a pre-fab building to be built on the front "tennis court" lawn was seriously considered. The plans were never approved so other alternatives were explored. Classroom space was rented in Carr Hall which

158   WOMEN AFTER HIS OWN HEART

was part of the near-by St. Paul's Episcopal Church. Doctor Coughlin, a member of the Board of Trustees, indicated that St. Peter's College was anxious to rent its Yanitelli Recreation and Life Center in order to obtain additional revenues. By 1978 the St. Peter's facilities were rented;[74] and athletic offerings were expanded to include swimming, tennis, karate, gymnastics, track and field, and weight lifting.

The year 1978–79 was labeled the "year of experiment" because of the many changes in the curriculum. In September SDA's facilities were supplemented by the use of St. Peter's College and the Hudson County Area Vocational Technical School.

Project Advance made it possible for Seniors with an average of 90% or higher to receive college credits for taking any of nine electives offered at St. Peter's College. Career-related electives were offered on the same principles at the Vocational School.

A new dress code was adopted which included the option of wearing brown flared pants and a short light-blue corded vest. The pants were permitted as winter wear and the vest in place of a summer blazer.[75]

If the year 78–79 was a year of experimentation, the next year was the "year of invading the Cloister." Since 1942 the entire front wing of the second floor had been "The Cloister." It contained several bedrooms. The need for additional classroom space as well as the expressed desire of some Sister-faculty for an alternative parish-based residence combined to promote the "invasion."

Sisters Joan Spingler, Jeanne Adrienne, Terry Puccio, Arlene Antczak, Debbie Lynch, and Eileen Ivory moved to Dominican Convent, a house on the property belonging to the Dominican Parish, Sacred Heart. The former second floor music room became a faculty lunchroom, and the bedrooms became classrooms and a conference room.

The year 1980–81 began on a very harsh note. On October 3, 1980, three Sister faculty members, Sister Eileen Imelda, Sister Grace Cassidy, and Sister Terry Puccio, were killed in a tragic accident with a jack-knifed truck. The faculty, students, all of Jersey City, the Dominican Community, and the entire Church of Newark mourned the loss of three vital, creative, faith-filled women. Their deaths focused attention on the mystery of death and the need to celebrate and share life fully.

The present Board of Trustees and faculty continue to make revisions in course offerings and grading evaluations to meet both the needs of the gifted and the remedial student. They continue to remain not only financially solvent but able to help other Community schools in their moment of financial need. Their recent brochure announces that the school desires

> to follow in the footsteps of Saint Dominic in the heart of Jersey City, where it has entwined itself in its very growth and has been a torch of learning to generations of young women who have come for the light of Faith, Knowledge and Love... We exist to develop Catholics, who can ask questions and who can give answers, who are understanding and understood. We instill the knowledge of how to serve and the love to want to serve. We train leaders whose faith will dispel apathy, whose spirit of hope will uplift a weary humanity, whose charity will light new paths.

Thus far this chapter has introduced the reader to the dramatic events which fostered the creation, growth, and development of the Community-owned schools during the three administrations of Mother Joseph and beyond them. It is now time to return to the chronology of significant activities which affected the regular life of the Congregation from 1929 to 1945.

Religious formation and continuing adaptation of the Constitutions according to the vision and needs of the contemporary Church remained a constant concern. In September, 1928, at the suggestion of the Diocese, the Community opened a Juniorate program. The Juniorate was a four-year program of educational and spiritual guidance for young women who wanted to live a modified religious life while completing the usual four-year high school academic requirements.[76]

Sister Clarissa was appointed the first Juniorate Mistress and her four young charges, Sister Mary George, Sister Mary

Elizabeth, Sister Dorothy Marie, and Sister Margaret Imelda, remember her motherly solicitude. When Sister Clarissa opted to join the Akron Community, Sister Amabilis was appointed to replace her.[77]

The mistresses strove to develop a homelike environment and to provide a gradual introduction to religious lifestyle and discipline. Prayers were said in common several times daily, attendance at regular high school courses occupied the bulk of time, and this heavy academic schedule was followed by the accomplishment of domestic charges in the school and Motherhouse.

Though each Junior's story remains a personal experience with individual sacred memories, it is possible to define a collective vision. The courses offered at Mount Saint Dominic Academy were academically excellent, but many Juniors felt somewhat bewildered—feeling neither a part of the regular school life nor a bona fide member of the Community. But their community life, under the direction of spirit-filled women and highlighted by the enthusiasm of dedicated youth, bore rich fruits in deepening their personal desire to embrace the spirit of Dominic: his quest for truth, his zeal for the work of the Church, and the prayerful joyous common life of the Dominican Sisters.

Sister Amabilis echoed the feelings of each mistress. "I am so happy about my girls who persevered and are now doing wonderful works for God and Community."

Just as the Diocese was anxious to encourage new vocations, the Order was concerned about directing its religious women toward a more simple ceremonial, a continuous religious formation program, and a better understanding of the meaning of temporary profession, both on the part of the candidate and the Community, and in relation to the final commitment.

In 1930, like most American Dominican Communities, the elaborate Reception ceremony, so reminiscent of marriage by virtue of its external signs (bridal gown and bridesmaids, etc.), was simplified. The candidate entered the chapel in her postulant dress and veil, the Bishop cut a small piece of her hair, and presented her with the habit. After dressing in the habit and white veil, the Novice returned to the chapel where she chose to wear a crown of thorns (symbolizing her renouncement of worldly ways) rather than to accept a crown of roses. She received the name and title by which she would be known in the Order, and she was presented the Rosary (a symbol of her dedication to contemplative life and a promise of Mary's protection).

The ceremony of Profession was also simplified. In 1930 it was decided that vows would be taken annually and renewed five times before final profession. The form of profession accented self-dedication and participation under obedience in the life of God, the Church (and in particular the diocese of Newark symbolized by including the name of the Archbishop), the Order, and this Congregation.

> To the honor of Almighty God, Father, Son, and Holy Ghost, I, Sister N., make Profession and promise obedience to God, to the Blessed Virgin Mary, to our holy father St. Dominic, to the Most Reverend Archbishop, N.N., and to Mother Mary N., Mother General of the American Congregation of the Sacred Heart of Jesus of the Third Order of St. Dominic, and to their lawful successors, according to the Rule of St. Augustine and the Constitutions of our Congregation (for one year or until death).

In 1931, Martin Gillet, the Master General, sent a circular letter to all Third Order Congregations encouraging the formation of a Scholasticate. This program meant that the newly professed Sister would stay at the Motherhouse for a year or two to complete her spiritual formation and to receive her Teacher Certification.[78]

The year 1935 witnessed the first convocation of the Dominican Mothers' General Conference which was held in Cincinnati, Ohio. The meeting suggested ongoing dialogue to achieve greater unity and uniformity in Dominican life. Several significant questions were raised: 1) Should there be greater uniformity in Constitutions, Ceremonials, habit material and

type of veil? 2) Even though most Congregations had decided
not to adopt the Divine Office in place of the Office of the
Blessed Mother, should the Divine Office be said at least in the
Novitiate House? 3) How can we assist one another to establish
Sister Formation programs for the religious and educational
development of new members according to the mind of the
Church? 4) Can we mutually support the foundation of a
Sister's hostel for education in Rome?[79]

There was no intention to amalgamate or federate. Each
Congregation simply responded to the questions after due deliberation. For the most part, the Constitutions and Ceremonials
were adopted according to required norms. The habit material,
a cream-colored mohair, was used by many; and veils became a
way to differentiate one Congregation from another.[80] Caldwell
never adopted the Divine Office in the Novitiate and attempted
to create a viable ongoing formation program. The institute
Regina Mundi for the study of spiritual life, Scripture, and
theology was founded in Rome.

The period 1929 to 1945 brought daily requests to supply
Sisters for newly erected parish schools. The Community responded unselfishly. Eight new schools were staffed.[81]

Many requests came from Missionary posts especially in
Latin America. Though the Community felt it was not opportune to educate Sisters for foreign missionary work, it decided
to establish a mission in the South or Southwest especially for
Sisters with lung trouble who could be stationed in a more suitable climate and yet engage in catechetical work at the same
time.[82]

The Chapter of 1939 mandated that the Community establish such a mission as soon as possible. As Providence would
have it, a medical doctor and acquaintance of the Sisters of
Saint Dominic of Perpetual Adoration in Newark, who was a
friend of Bishop Toolen, the Ordinary of the diocese of Mobile-
Birmingham, had heard about the Caldwell search. He informed Bishop Toolen who immediately contacted Mother
Joseph. Mother sought volunteers and when it was apparent

that Sisterpersonnel were available, the agreement to staff Saint Margaret's School, Bayou La Batre, Alabama, was confirmed.[83]

Saint Margaret's had been staffed by the Mercy Sisters of the Union in Baltimore. Bishop Toolen had heard through the proverbial "grapevine" that the Sisters were intending to withdraw from one of their Southern missions (probably St. Mary's, Cottage Hill). The Bishop informed the Congregation that he agreed to a withdrawal from one mission and had offered the Caldwell Dominicans Saint Margaret's.

The surprised Sisters of Mercy returned in haste from their summer assignments and prepared the house for the new Community. The pastor, Father Alexander O'Neill, was not at all happy about the episcopal decision. The pioneer missioners, Sister Ruth Durr (Grade 7–8, principal), Sister Benigna (1–2), Sister Leo (3–4), Sister Consuela (5–6), and Sister Anne Catherine (who replaced Sister Bernarda for one year since Sister Bernarda, who had volunteered, needed surgery) arrived with no knowledge of this intriguing background. Any feeling of displeasure on the part of the pastor or people was completely disarmed by the charm of Sister Ruth and the dedication of the Caldwell Sisters.

The annals of the early years provide comic relief, hindsight, but to the pioneers it was raw reality. They had anticipated "outdoor plumbing" but were overjoyed that they had one indoor facility. The night lights they had brought were needed during the many electrical storms which left them without heat, light, or refrigeration. Thanks to the needlework of Sister Consuela the house and sacristy needs for linens were satisfied. Though no money was allotted for the Mission, Sister Marie (the general bursar) managed to send $60.00 a month. This amount, as well as the $80.00 received from the pastor in return for the domestic work of the Sisters who cooked and cleaned for the Rectory, and revenues received from the Dominican Schools and Sister Bernarda's school lunch program, provided for the ordinary needs of the convent and school.[84]

In 1942 the Community also opened a convent to serve as a

catechetical center for the Black parish, Saint Peter Claver, Asbury Park.

The Community's concern for the poor and the needy is further demonstrated by its work at summer camps: Butler and Imelda.

Butler Camp was sponsored by the Saint Vincent de Paul Society for children from Jersey City who otherwise would not have time away from the hot, congested, urban environment. Sisters Camilla, Andrea, and Wilhemina formed the heart of this summer project while the Franciscan Seminarians and professed members of the Caldwell Community developed and executed the summer recreational arts and crafts and religious programs.[85]

The second summer camp, Camp Imelda, which was held at the Mount, began as a way of ministering to grade and high school boarders who had no permanent stable home life. It was opened in the summer of 1932 and provided a family and a religious environment accented by physical exercise and classes in French, dancing, music, swimming,[86] and arts and crafts.[87]

The year 1941 occasioned the Community's request to open a private elementary school in the vacant house on Bentley Avenue.

August 21, 1941

Most Reverend Monsignor McClary,
Reverend Mother said that we always had a call for a grade school in Jersey City, but since we closed the grades at First Street (1921), we have never had space for the elementary classes in the Academy until now. This is the first time we have had the rooms and the ideal situation of having the grades separated from the high school, together with an opportunity to help the Sisters at Saint Dominic Academy to take care of their debt.
Mother feels sure that the Most Reverend Archbishop will have no objections in granting permission for another Catholic private school in Jersey City which will take care of pupils who attend Protestant and non-sectarian private schools in that neighborhood.[88]

The request seemed very reasonable in terms of the educational needs of the area and especially since the Community had so recently spent money to repair the buildings that were vacated when Saint Dominic Academy moved to the Carteret Club.

Monsignor McClary recommended that a kindergarten be opened on a temporary basis mainly because then the Bentley Avenue house could retain its tax-exempt status and not become a financial drain for the Community.

Sisters Marie, Alphonsa, Gabriella, and Margaret opened the school in September, 1941. It was closed in 1947.

This overview of Community movements began as a tribute to the charism of Mother Joseph and to the dynamic faith and trust of Community leadership symbolized by their willingness to broaden Community ministry and deepen the bonds of common life. It concludes with a brief necrology of those facets of Mother Joseph's life and mission that have not been noted previously.

Mary E. Dunn, the daughter of John and Margaret Donovan Dunn, was born December 29, 1885. Her mother died; and she and the children were placed in the care of an aunt. Mary attended the public schools in Boonton until she entered the Community in 1902. Two of her sisters also became members of the Community: Sister Dolores and Sister Loretta Claire.

As a young Sister she taught at Mount Saint Dominic Academy; Saint Mary's (Leipsic, Ohio); Assumption School (Lawrence, Massachusetts); and Saint Aedan's (Jersey City). From 1915 to 1918 she was the assistant novice mistress and served as the Directress of Studies (1918–1927). During that period she received her M.A. from Fordham (1921) and her Ph.D. (1923). While she was a member of the Council (1921–1927) she served as the superior of Saint John's on Ryerson Avenue, the Community Infirmary, and began her career as an author of history books.

Her election in 1927 and re-election in 1933 were considered within the norm. Since she was involved so completely in the projected college and other grave financial considerations, when her term expired Archbishop Walsh suggested that she be permitted to run for re-election by postulation.[89] After much prayer and deliberation on the part of elected delegates, she was re-elected for a third consecutive term on the first ballot.

Mother Joseph had a "genuine enthusiasm for all things Dominican" and was a dedicated daughter of the Church. When our Holy Father Pope Pius XI issued his *Motu Proprio* on Sacred Music which abolished all figured music in Church service, the archdiocese enforced it strictly. The Caldwell Dominicans became the leaders in training the Sisters and their students in plain and Gregorian Chant. Small groups of Sisters made Saturday excursions on buses and the subway to attend classes at Manhattanville's Pius X School of Liturgical Music. In 1935 the diocese began the custom of celebrating a Demonstration Mass of Sacred Music sponsored by the St. Cecilia Guild and performed by select choirs from diocesan elementary and secondary schools.

During her second term the Community negotiated the sale of the original Motherhouse property in Jersey City; but a year later in 1934 when Mr. Levine defaulted on the payments, the Community reclaimed the property. Plans were made to renovate the building to make it servicable for some worthy project of Catholic action.[90] Bishop Walsh gave his permission on June 30, 1934.

The necessary renovations were completed in a year's time. On September 10, 1935, Siena Hall was opened as a residence for professional women.[91] A small group of Sisters coordinated the meals and maintenance until 1960 when the Community sold the property to St. Boniface Parish.[92]

Mother Joseph and her Council had done the impossible. They had created the Mount and the College amidst depression and war. Sister Aloysius remarked in the Annals of 1933 that "the depression did not pass us lightly by, but we felt ourselves singularly blessed in the knowledge that in spite of all our financial difficulties we were always able to meet our obligations. This was due in great measure to the heroic efforts of the

Sisters of the Missions and the earnest prayers of the devoted members of the Community."[93]

The fifty-four years of carrying and passing on the torch of truth and the zeal for the Church which marked the Dominican life of Mother Joseph Dunn ended on Good Friday, March 30, 1956. This determined devoted religious, brilliant scholar, great educator, and efficient administrator, who had struggled her entire life against the physical disabilities accompanying chronic ill health, has not been forgotten. Monsignor Furlong spoke for countless persons, "We do not grieve now the loss of this great woman. Rather do we give thanks to God for having had her. Nay, rather for having her still, for all things live unto God and whosoever goes to God is to be reckoned among the family of God. She is lost to earth through death, it is true, but only so that she may live forever in heaven."[94]

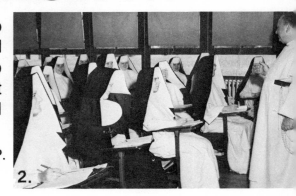

EXPANSION AND CONTINUOUS GROWTH

"Alone you can do nothing, but God and you will be able to do all that God wants. If it is God's work, he will bring it to fulfillment."

Sister Aquinata Fiegler, O.P.

2.

1.

6

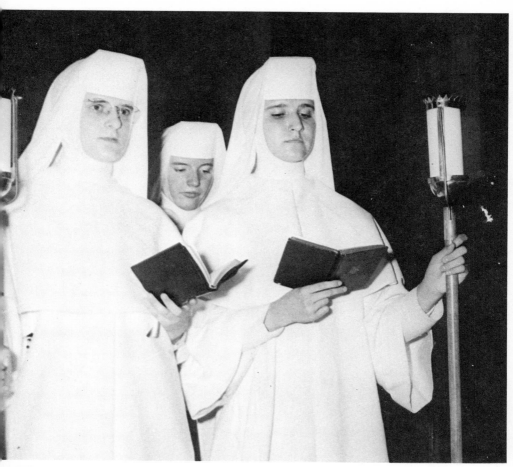

6

4.

1–Novices leading Salve Procession
2–Caldwell College Summer School Class with Father Perotta
3–Mother Aquinas Cooney
4–Archbishop Boland and Mother Dolorita Ansbro at Groundbreaking for St. Catherine of Siena Infirmary, Caldwell, N.J.

After sketching the overpowering events of the preceding eighteen years, the next twelve (1945–1957) take on a much more ordinary aura; but the last twelve (1957–1969) in this chapter are again somewhat overwhelming in scope and change. The two administrations of Mother Aquinas were filled with the pain and agony of constantly repairing the old properties and watchfully waiting to see the new ones develop. As Catholics who were born and raised in the urban ghettos of Hudson and Essex Counties recovered from wartime restrictions and moved to the suburbs, the Church of Newark witnessed a tremendous growth in new parishes. Since most pastors and parishoners considered the parochial school the hub of the parish and the pledge of future Catholicity, most parishes placed themselves in grave indebtedness to build a school. All communities of religious women responded to the call of the Church and tried to staff the new schools.

The baby boom associated with the 40s and 50s had a dual effect on the history of most religious congregations. While their schools were crowded with the younger offspring, the numbers of young women entering religious life also increased proportionately. During the entire period the Community opened many new missions since the numbers entering the Community seemed to indicate future personnel to staff them adequately. In 1957 no one could have projected zero growth (in the Community) by 1969 and the sweeping changes in Church and religious life fostered by the decrees of the Second Vatican Council (1963–1965).

The acts of the Community during this period which directly affected the Community-owned schools have already been described. In this chapter emphasis will be placed on the suitability of the personality of leaders to the specific needs of each phase, growth and expansion, and the initial steps toward renewal in formation, education, and general community life.

While the leaders of Russia, the United States, and England were meeting in Potsdam to discuss ways of rehabilitating war-torn Europe and of expediting the surrender of Japan in the Pacific, the Sixth General Chapter was opened in Caldwell on June 26, 1945. Two Masses of the Holy Ghost were celebrated, one by Reverend James Halliwell (Chaplain) for Sisters present in the Convent Chapel; and the second by Reverend Joseph H. Brady in the auditorium.

After the usual proceedings the twenty superiors, twenty elected delegates, and four ex-officio members elected Mother Aquinas on the second ballot. Her councillors included Sister Concepta (Vicaress), Sister Felix, Sister Servatia (Secretary General)[1] and Sister Victoria. Sister Marie was elected Bursar General.

The Chapter addressed itself to the formation program and the overcrowding of the Mount schools. St. John's was renovated according to the specifications of the Diocesan Building and Sites Committee and was used as a residence for senior high school boarders. Sister Flavia, the newly appointed Novice Mistress, discussed proposed Saturday classes for the postulants with Sister Concepta, the former Mistress of Novices and present vice-president of the College.[2]

Though the Annals of the local convents and parochial

schools would reveal much activity, the Community history (1945–1951) is easily summarized. Constant repairs on Mother-house properties and financial demands on the part of creditors forced the Community leaders to ask the Academies in Jersey City and Upper Montclair to assume increased responsibility for notes. In addition, each Sister was asked to raise $10.00 to help defray the cost of Motherhouse expenses.[3]

In 1946 Rosary Chapel on the second floor arcade of the Administration Building was furnished, then dedicated and blessed on September 14. By 1947 the Villa and St. Agnes' were renovated and equipped with fire escapes to insure the safety of the high school and college boarders, respectively.

The same year the Sisters' salary was increased in the Dioceses of Newark and Trenton.[4] The letter received from Bishop Griffin of the Trenton Diocese serves to help the reader understand the question of religious salaries. After the Bishop informed Mother Aquinas of his intention he added:

> ...The reasons for the increase are: first, the notably increased cost of living which has for so long universally affected house maintenance among the families of the diocese, as well as rectories and convents; and secondly, the impossibility facing parish convents of contributing a fair share of their income to the support of the Motherhouse[5] of the Religious Communities which have been so generous with us in supplying Sisters for the needs of the Diocese. This increase brings the Sisters' support to the normal economic level for this area...[6]

In spite of this increase, Community finances continued to be burdensome. The diocese was extremely helpful and covered most notes at a very low interest. Between 1946 and 1948 the properties on Bergen, Bentley, and Fairview Avenues were sold.

The Community was singularly honored on March 16, 1948, by the visitation of the Dominican Master General, the most Reverend Emmanuel Suarez, and his brother priests, Paul A. Shehan (Procurator General) and T.M. Sparks (Socius).

On October 22, 1949, "it was decided that only in business

transactions would the baptismal and family names be used. Hereafter the original plan of using only one name would take place in naming the Sisters at Reception."[7]

The Seventh General Chapter convened June 24, 1951, with a High Mass celebrated in the Convent Chapel by Reverend John J. Ansbro (Chaplain). Forty-eight elected delegates (an increase of eight in the light of new missions opened in the interim) re-elected Mother Aquinas on the second ballot. The new Council included: Sister M. Dolorita (Vicaress), Sister M. Germaine, Sister Norine (who died December 7, 1954, and was replaced by the conciliar appointment of Sister Anita), and Sister Servatia (Secretary General). Sister Adele was elected Bursar General.

Sister M. Adele, Chairperson of the Committee of Financial Affairs, reported that "the financial reports of all houses show an increase which is practically double the receipts of the previous six years. Of course, the expenditures were correspondingly high due to the increased cost of living."[8] Through the united efforts of all the Sisters the Motherhouse debt has been markedly decreased,[9] and the Diocese absorbed all remaining notes with a 3% interest which represented a decrease of 1%.

On September 26, 1951, Mother Aquinas promulgated the acts and regulations of the Chapter. She called the Community to renewed devotion to the Rosary and recommended the daily recitation of the fifteen decades. Mother advised, "if we are anxious to be successful teachers, we must first of all be good religious, and it is for this I am including some of the good resolutions adopted during the General Chapter."[10]

The regulations exhorted the local house to make proper use of the time of silence, the weekly Holy Hour, and common recreation. Particular attention was drawn to the significance of the habit and the proper practice of the vow of poverty. The Community was informed that there would be only one entrance date: August 30.[11]

By 1952 the Community suffered a severe cash flow problem and once again the Diocese met its need with a loan so that the normal bills for meat, food, milk, and coal could be paid.

During the following year the city of Caldwell had been contacted to investigate the possibility of constructing a heliport to act as a mail-drop center for the United States Postal Service. Such a site would have expedited mail delivery. Since the proposed site included 100 feet of Community property, negotiations began in the spring of 1953. The Diocesan Building and Sites Commission responded that "such a heliport would be dangerous to our property...and that the noise level would prove detrimental to our school..."[12] The project was shelved.

1953 was also the Centenary year of the archdiocese. On January 12 the bishop-designate, Thomas Aloysius Boland, took "canonical possession" of the diocese, when the Board of Consultors presented him with the appropriate papal bulls proclamating his appointment.

Two days later members of the hierarchy, clergy, religious communities, and laity assembled at Sacred Heart Cathedral for the solemn enthronement and pontifical Mass. Television cameras and radio transmitters captured the sights and sounds of the ancient ceremony. After the formal bulls of appointment had been proclaimed, the entire diocese was called to "receive Thomas Aloysius as your Metropolitan Archbishop-elect, filially as the father of your souls."[13] Immediately representatives of the clergy, religious, and laity filed out to offer homage.

In his usual simple but inspiring style, the new bishop explained, "The Church's material wealth is perceived easily and could be dispensed with; but above all, her wealth is found in the fidelity of her children to her precept and their devotion to the interests of God and humanity... I come to you today to be one of you and not apart from you, to be in your midst, to share your honors, your troubles, your joys, your sorrows."[14]

The Caldwell Community experienced the solicitude of the second Archbishop of Newark many times in the first three years of his episcopacy.

When Archbishop Boland made his canonical visitation in

January of 1956 he expressed particular concern about the
formation of postulants and the community life of the College
faculty. He recommended that the postulants not be sent out to
teach, that the office of President of the College be separated
from that of the Superior of the College faculty, that the Sisters
slow down the hectic pace of life, and that the local missions and
Community provide for enriching recreational activities and
summer vacations of reasonable length.[15]

In 1957 the high school boarders were moved to St. John's,
and their two dormitories were renovated as the Postulate. The
third floor convent building dormitory was redesigned as a
recreation room for the Postulants. Sister Maura was appointed
the Mistress of Postulants, and the class of 1957 was to be
assigned regular college schedules.

The implementation of the Bishop's recommendations concerning the best government and housing policy for College
Sisters could not be settled immediately since the Chapter of
1951 had placed the Sister faculty of the College under the
Superiorship of the president. But "after an investigation, it was
decided to place the members of the College faculty under the
authority of the Sister Prioress (at the Mount) in all affairs not
interfering with the work of the College which rested with the
President and the Dean."[16]

The final decisions concerning the lifestyle and residence of
the College faculty, and appropriate home visitation, vacation,
and recreational opportunities were to be left to the 1957
Chapter.

While the election of delegates for the up-coming Chapter
was being coordinated and the Council was preparing to render
an account of its stewardship, the Lord called Reverend Mother
Aquinas home to Himself. Though Mother had been ill, and
Sister Dolorita had assumed many of her duties, her death was a
shock. Sister Dolorita assumed the role of Mother General, and
preparations for the Chapter were set in motion.

On May 10, 1957, Mother Aquinas died peacefully. She is
remembered as a sustaining presence—a woman of prayer
whose gentle persuasion could convince anyone that they not

only could do whatever she asked of them, but that they also wanted to do it. Her benign personality was exactly what her time in Community leadership demanded. This virtue was further highlighted in the Most Reverend Bishop McNulty's (Ordinary of the Paterson Diocese) eulogy which insisted that, "Motherliness was an essential quality of Mother Aquinas, so approachable, of such sympathetic understanding, of marvelous patience, of genuine interest, of wise counsels based upon her long experience and motivated by her own love and her pride in her Dominican family."[17]

Christina Cooney was born on September 12, 1878, the third child of Patrick and Ann Collins Cooney. Another daughter, Sister Genevieve Cooney also entered, and died January 6, 1894. Even as a young girl in Our Lady of Mount Carmel Parish (Boonton) Christina's gentleness, kindness, vital faith, and devotion to our Lady were already evident. She entered in 1899 and was professed on December 28, 1901. During her teaching years at St. Mary's (Dover), St. Mary's (Rutherford), St. Dominic Academy, and St. Aedan's (Jersey City), she worked zealously because she understood that "while educating the young, she was also helping to fashion the character of a nation on solid principles and lofty ideals and worthy habits of life."[18]

Her leadership in Community included six years as Novice Mistress (1921–1927) and twelve years as Mother General. Like her holy father, Mother Aquinas chose to combat the evils of her day by achieving a personal holiness that made her a more efficient instrument for the will of God. Her devotion to Mary and the Rosary was particularly evident.

During her administration twelve new missions[19] were established. She encouraged principals and administrators to expand facilities and to constantly improve the educational opportunities. In her visitations she counseled each Sister to make time to be with the Lord, to confide in Mary, to be mindful of poverty, and to be ready to do His will immediately. Many Sisters recall being sent for by Mother. When you entered her office she was usually seated in her rocking chair, her Bible was opened on her lap. She would call you over and say, "Now Sister..." It usually meant pack your toothbrush and be at your new mission by tonight.

Her life was one marked by simplicity and quiet. And as the saying goes, "She died the way she had lived." In the silence of Friday, May 10, "we feel like her namesake Thomas, the Lord came to her and said, 'Mother, well have you witnessed to me, what reward would you like.' Our simple Reverend mother probably responded, 'Nothing but yourself, O Lord.'"[20]

The Eighth Ordinary General Chapter was formerly opened July 6, 1957, at 7:30 p.m. Sister M. Dolorita, Vicaress, presided. The six ex-officio members, twenty-seven elected superiors, and twenty-seven delegates assembled in the Chapel the next morning. They assisted at a low Mass of the Holy Ghost celebrated by His Excellency, the Most Reverend Archbishop, and after the singing of the *Veni Creator* and exhortations by the Archbishop, proceeded to elect Mother Dolorita on the first ballot. Her Councillors were Sister Alouise, Mary Dorothy, Marie (Secretary General), and Mercedes. Sister Borromeo was elected Bursar General.

Reverend Mother set the tone of her administration, announcing "that it was with sincere humility that she had accepted the trust placed in her, and that with God's grace and the cooperation of the Sisters, she would do her best to "uphold the Rule and Constitutions of the Community."[21]

These few words describe the primary spirit which empowered Mother to face the next twelve years.

Even at the beginning of the Chapter it was apparent that the tremendous growth of numbers in the Novitiate, in the College, and in the enrollment of our Academies would require changes in the formation program and a vigorous building project. These pressing needs occupied the first administration.

The Community has continually provided an excellent program of spiritual, Dominican, professional formation for its new members with obvious shortcomings because of apostolic demand. Even Rome was aware of this universal tension.

The notion of *aggiornamento*[22] predates Vatican II. It goes back to Piux XI at the First International Congress of Mothers General in Rome held in 1950. All of the activities in the 50s and early 60s were the obedient responses of American superiors and educators to the promptings from Rome.

Again at the 1952 Congress, Cardinal Larrona explained the need, purpose, and proposed form of Juniorates (Scholasticate is another accepted term).[23]

> In the Novitiate, the formation of the religious is begun.... In the Juniorate it is continued though not with the detailed program of the novitiate year. ...The Juniorate is intended to forestall the catastrophes which have sometimes befallen your professed Sisters who were sent into active life without any transition period to prepare them for the special problems confronting them in that life.... In the Juniorate, they are provided with opportunities to integrate their professional training with the demands of the religious vocation.[24]

The First National Congress of American Major Superiors was convened in the city of Notre Dame, Indiana, from August 9 to 13, 1952. Reports by Sister Madaleva, C.S.C., and others noted the urgency for change. By 1954 this body (not officially constituted until 1956), in conjunction with the National Catholic Educational Association, founded the Sister Formation Movement whose main goal was to encourage and facilitate all communities in the establishment of post-Novitiate continuing formation.

In 1957 Sister Maura Campbell was appointed Postulant Mistress. This class of postulants attended regular college class appropriate to their present level of higher education, completed the usual year Novitiate program, and became the first class to enter the Caldwell Scholasticate.

Sister Maura, as a member of the board of the Sister Formation Movement, was knowledgeable and prepared to take the nineteen newly professed through the first-year program. She had a clear vision of how to adapt the words of Elio Gambari, S.M.M.:

> The purpose of the Juniorate is to continue, consolidate and perfect the general religious instruction and at the same time to provide the professional education necessary for proper apostolic activity. The whole is to be guided by a personal religious development which is the individual's response to the religious and professional training. The Juniorate should be so organized as to assure this triple formation.[25]

It was a new concept fraught with possibilities, but open to misunderstanding by the larger Community who had not experienced it.

On June 17, 1960, Sister Maura (directress) and nineteen newly professed Sisters moved to St. John's on Ryerson Avenue. With great effort all necessary renovations were made; a tastefully but simply decorated oratory was placed on the first floor; a study room (called the Angelicum) was designed in the basement; and the open house was held early in the fall. Besides a heavy academic schedule, the Scholastics studied the spiritual life using Garrigou-LaGrange, O.P., as a "guru," and the religious life as portrayed in *The City of God* by Carpenter as a basic working document. These studies were complemented by celebrating community prayers and meals at the Motherhouse, assisting with domestic chores in the Infirmary, and working in local parish religious education programs.

By the next summer the class of nineteen was joined by twenty-four new professed. Every inch of space at St. John's was utilized, and Sister Maura rejoiced that both the first and second year programs were to be given simultaneously.

Between 1958 and 1960 Mother and her Council had received repeated requests from pastors and even the Bishop to send more teaching Sisters to staff the burgeoning classrooms. By April 11, 1960, the Council decided that "in view of the great shortage of Sisters/teachers, the Scholastics would be sent on mission and return to Saturday classes."[26]

The tension to be faithful both to the ideal of continuous formation and the obligation to staff schools adequately found its resolution late in August. No one who lived in St. John's that summer will ever forget it. Sister Maura had not returned with the Sisters to St. John's after supper. She had a meeting with Mother Dolorita. As she entered the house a very solemn, sober mood settled upon the group. Sister gathered the forty-three professed in the "Angelicum" and explained the need for teaching Sisters and the very hard decision the Council had reached. After the list of mission assignments was read, only eight professed were assigned as resident Scholastics. In 1961, five scholastics were in residence while thirty-six received Saturday spiritual life classes after attending prescribed academic classes.

The Scholasticate moved from St. John's to Rosary Hall and each year the residents were few while the numbers attending Saturday classes increased.

After the 1969 Chapter Sister Mary McGuinnes was appointed directress and lived for one year at the Mount and the next year the Scholastics lived at St. Philip's in Clifton. Sister Emma Patricia was appointed directress and she, along with Sister Agnes Bernard and Formation Committee members designed a program of spiritual formation which was open to all Sisters.[27] Each new development built on the firm foundations laid by the pioneers of the Sister Formation Movement.

Throughout the narrative it has been evident that the buildings on the Mount were always utilized maximally and that most areas have many different inhabitants and served multi-purposes. One group of Sisters who deserve special affection, heart-felt accommodation, and enduring prayer and respect is the infirm and retired members. They were often on the move.

As early as 1893 Mother Catherine envisioned the Motherhouse at Caldwell as a perfect spot for adequate health care and contemplative retirement. For a while the third floor of the Motherhouse with its sun porch, on the second floor across from the Chapel, facing the orchards, provided the site of the Infirmary. Then it was decided to move the Infirmary to St.

John's in 1917.[28] By 1932 the infirm were once again asked to move in order to make room in that residence for school boarders. The move was made smoothly and the Third Floor of the Motherhouse became the new—yet really the original— Infirmary. Physical conditions were cramped, but compassion and the best of nursing care were available. Nearness to the Chapel where so many memorable events had taken place was a special grace for these sick or elderly members who had served so faithfully.

When Mother Dolorita was asked to try to describe her terms as Major Superior, one of the first things she mentioned was:

> Along with our duties, my Councillors and I began to talk of carrying out Mother Aquinas' greatest desire, that of planning a building—a home for our sick and retired Sisters. We discussed our thoughts with Archbishop Boland and Monsignor Hughes (the Vicar General). They agreed we needed more adequate living quarters. Their concern was how we would finance such a project.[29]

Mother and the Council placed the entire project under the patronage of Saint Joseph. Each Sister and every local mission were asked to pray a particular petition daily. Its words remain imprinted in the hearts of the Sisters and are still said nightly by the Sisters in the Infirmary.

> O glorious St. Joseph, thou who hast power to render possible things that are impossible, come to our aid in our trouble and distress. Let it not be said that we have invoked thee in vain. And since thou are so powerful with Jesus and Mary, show us thy goodness equals thy power. Amen.
> Divine Providence can provide; Divine Providence did provide; Divine Providence will provide.

Once again the unbeatable combination of "working as if it all depended on you and praying as if it all depended on God" bore rich fruit. Divine Providence did provide.

On July 17, 1958, "the Bishop directed the Community to raise at least one-half of the sum desired before doing any definite planning."[30]

The Council requested Sister Alouise to begin a Dominican Guild[31] whose primary purpose would be to encourage fundraising for the proposed buildings.

On July 15, 1959, Sister Marguerite, president of Caldwell College, suggested a combined development fund drive to provide for a new residence hall, science facility, and the Community Infirmary. The Bishop approved of a consultation with representatives from the Community Counselling Service, Incorporated, of New York.[32]

The month of August witnessed the presentation of the plans to the Building and Sites Committee who, in turn, forwarded a favorable report to the Bishop. Permission was granted to seek loans to obtain funds for the initial stage of work. Bids were opened for contractors and the firm of Robert P. Moran & Associates was chosen.[33]

Four days later Sister Marguerite and the Council met with Mr. Joseph L. Reilly and Mr. Matthew Mahon who explained all the details of the development campaign. Mr. Ludwig was named director; Sister Margaret Anne Fahy, the Sister coordinator; and Sister Regina, the historian. Five thousand dollars was paid as seed money (half by the College, half by the Community). The superiors were sent questionnaires to offer names of potential donors and solicitors.

A detailed account of the three-phased plan[34] is not necessary for this narrative. What is necessary to be said is that the one and only Dominican Sisters Development Fund became a family affair. Everyone became an active campaigner. The newest postulants (who had entered five days after the campaign strategy was decided) and the novices became proficient "envelope stuffers." The professed members donated hours of time to collating names, interviewing, and evaluating. And last and most important, the infirm were the powerhouse of prayer and a source of ongoing inspiration and momentum.

The three letters of Mother Dolorita, Archbishop Boland,

and Bishop McNulty are included because each accents in a particularly personal manner the spirit of the drive, the support of the clergy and laity, as well as the dire need and deep gratitude on the part of the Community.

The campaign was advertised in an attractive brochure, *A Special Message for You and Your Family*, from the Sisters of Saint Dominic, Caldwell, New Jersey.

Dear Friend,

If you are the head of a household, you know that there is a point in the growth of your family where you must provide larger quarters and more extensive medical care. The Sisters of Saint Dominic are, in a real sense, a family, and the time has come for us to expand our facilities in order to take better care of our members, and those under our care.

The present Sisters' infirmary area at the Motherhouse is pleasant and attractive, but inadequate for our needs. There are 552 Dominican Nuns serving in the New Jersey area. However, only 10 Sisters may be taken care of in this facility at any time. In the near future, the Order intends to construct an Infirmary Building, which will not only provide adequate room for Sisters now in service, but will also contain a Geriatrics Center for retired Sisters.

For the past few years, both Sisters and students at the Caldwell Community—the location of our Motherhouse and College— have been seriously overcrowded. Since the Sisters of Saint Dominic have always been reluctant to turn away any qualified postulant or student, every classroom, laboratory and living space is being used. Conditions are such that, unless a new residence hall and science addition are built this year, we may be forced to curtail our educational activities at Caldwell, with the consequent result of affecting our quality of future instruction in the parishes.

As a responsible Catholic we are sure you will help us meet these challenges and carry on Christ's work with children. This prospectus outlines some of the memorial opportunities available in the buildings to be constructed. We fervently pray you will find it

in your heart, and within your means, to serve God and perpetu-
ate the name of a loved one. You may be certain the Sisters of
Saint Dominic will remember you and your family in their
prayers, always.
Most cordially in Christ,
Mother M. Dolorita, O.P.

The Catholics of the dioceses surveyed responded with
generous hearts; the Bishops supported the endeavor wholeheartedly.

Dear Mother Dolorita,
Your request for permission to conduct a fund-raising campaign
in the parishes where your Sisters staff our schools and institutions has my cordial consent. The contribution of the Sisters of
St. Dominic to Catholic education in our Archdiocese is inesti-
mable and will only be adequately known when the Book of Life
is opened to us. At present it is obvious that you will not be able
to accommodate the ever-increasing enrollment unless you immediately initiate an expansion program. An appeal for funds in
order to meet at least partially the heavy capital cost of your
college expansion program and also the construction expense of
the other building so essential to the Motherhouse, will meet an
enthusiastic and generous response from our good people.
Blessing all who contribute to the success of this worthy and
salutary project, I remain
Yours very sincerely in Christ,
Thomas A. Boland, Archbishop of Newark

Reverend dear Mother Dolorita:
Your announced Campaign for Funds to build a new Infirmary
for the Dominican Sisters and to expand educational facilities at
Caldwell College merits the hearty cooperation of our priests and
people.
I confidently assure you that my brother priests and devoted
parishioners of the seven parishes of the Diocese of Paterson,
where the Dominican Sisters of Caldwell labor so successfully for

Our Lord, will give generous support to your plea.

We are mindful of the personal sacrifices made by our nuns in educating generations of children to be worthy Catholics and splendid Americans.

We are sensitive to the obligation to say Thank You and this Campaign for Funds provides that opportunity.

Praying that God may bless you and your revered Sisters and that He may prosper this venture, I am

Devotedly yours in Christ,

James E. McNulty, Bishop of Paterson

The brochure further explained that the expansion required that the Sisters of Saint Dominic establish a Development Fund in the amount of $2,500,000. Five hundred thousand of this total had already been acquired through savings and special gifts. A loan for $1,000,000 was to be negotiated so that, though the fund, the generosity of benefactors would provide the remaining $750,000.

While the fund's phases passed one to another, Mother and Robert Moran made final decisions concerning the site of the Infirmary and a redesign to make best possible use of the natural setting and source of sunlight.

By April bids were opened for the proposed $1,500,000 structure.[35] The Building and Sites Committee approved the plans on the 26th, and Monsignor Hughes suggested that consultations with the Diocesan Liturgical Committee should be done in connection with the construction of the Chapel.[36]

The ground-breaking ceremony occurred on December 28, 1960, in the presence of Reverend John J. Ansbro, Lewis A. Springman, O.P., Reverend Arthur Little, members of the Generalate, Donald Lockward (Mayor), Robert Moran, Mr. and Mrs. Robert Brady, and about 250 Sisters. Not even the bitter cold day could mar the warmth and celebration of this momentous initial action.[37]

Mother and the Council watched the construction closely. A Sisters' Concert, dinner dances, Christmas sales, private bequests, small local fund-raisers, and personal donations from

Community members enhanced available funds. The name Saint Catherine of Siena Convent was chosen and the building which provides 100 private rooms for sick and retired Sisters, adequate examination and treatment rooms, nurses' quarters, solariums, a special diet kitchen, refectories, chaplain's quarters, general meeting rooms, and a large basement (home of the laundry, physical and occupational therapy rooms, storage areas) was blessed and dedicated by Bishop Thomas A. Boland on September 20, 1962.

Mother Dolorita recalled that when the building was nearly completed, we planned to have the Sisters who were patients in the Infirmary at the time visit their new home, select their own room, and choose its colors. Such visits and personal involvement made it easier to move them from the Motherhouse which they loved dearly.

"Moving Day" was one to be remembered. On December 12, 1968, the local Rescue Squad assisted in caring for the Sisters who were not capable of walking. The spaciousness and beauty (though the rooms were functional and simple in decor) of their new home was overwhelming. Some were confused by the buttons and bells to be used to call the nurse.

At that time there were fourteen patients and five staff members. They each helped each other get acclimated; tears were shed because of "missing the Motherhouse" and adjusting to so many new gadgets and routines.

The postscript which brings the "dream-reality story" up-to-date is that today there are eighty-eight infirm or retired Sisters being cared for. The quiet, contemplative environment with its flexible schedule removes the obvious pressure of a more structured program. Community Mass, evening praise, weekly holy hour, and a yearly retreat are highlights of the Infirmary liturgical life.

If it seems miraculous that the building was built, it is even more miraculous that the debt on the $1,600,000 building was completely liquidated by May 21, 1968, six years after its opening. "This blessing was the result of careful budgeting, and the cooperation of all the Sisters. Our Academies and Mission

Houses made definite monthly contributions. The College and Mission Sisters allocated the stipends they received for their speaking engagements. Royalties amounting to $6,800.75 from Sister Carmel's *Review Text in Health* and $1,500 from Sister Mercedes' Stamp Project were also contributed. A Dominican coloring book and albums of the Sisters' Concert were sold and the profit was applied to the fund. Finally the substantial donations of the Dominican Guild and the St. Dominic Guild must be acknowledged. The Development Fund Drive exercised an important role in helping us to cancel the mortgage."[38]

While the Community rejoiced in the completion of the Infirmary and prepared for the move into the new facility, a Church event that would affect every facet of Catholic life and every segment of its people was formally opened. Pope John XXIII had announced on January 25, 1959, that he planned to convoke the Twenty-first Ecumenical Council in Church history. The eighty-year-old Pontiff wanted "to open some windows" and to facilitate "a new Pentecost." The Council opened October 11, 1962. The first phase of consultations and deliberations ended December 8, 1962. Pope John, symbol of unity and beloved Father, died on June 3, 1963. The world mourned and then waited to see the fate of the Council. Pope Paul VI, elected June 21 and coronated on June 30, 1963, clearly expressed his intention to complete the Council and to implement its decrees.

At the end of the second session, December 4, 1963, the Constitution on the Sacred Liturgy was promulgated. Its implementation from 1964 through the 80s is so much a part of present Catholic life that the "old, familiar" ways are unknown to a whole generation. Greater participation of the laity in Mass, the use of the vernacular, altars facing the people, new lay ministries (lector, commentator, pastoral musicians, and extraordinary ministers of Eucharist) as well as Communion in the hand and Communion under both species are now all commonplace.

The fifth and final session began on September 14, 1965, and concluded December 8. The texts which most affect the theology of religious life and its appropriate place in the Church in the modern world as well as the call to *aggiornamento* were produced during this period.[39]

It would be impossible in this or any text to convey the complex web of personal and communal responses and the related tensions which, of necessity, emerged. Suffice it to say that change did not come easily but the Caldwell Dominicans gradually, thoughtfully, and for the most part with prudent discerning reserve tried "to undertake the quest for a deeper understanding of the spirit of the Council and the faithful application of the norms it has happily and prayerfully provided."[40]

In the midst of the Council session the Caldwell Community held its Ninth Ordinary Chapter, July 6, 1963. Mother Dolorita was re-elected along with her councillors Sisters Germaine, Miriam, Marie (Secretary General), Mercedes, and Borromeo (Bursar General).

Mother Dolorita again set the tone of her own sense of administrative mission in the age of change. "I pray that I may have the grace, wisdom and strength to lead the Community to a holier life for the honor and glory of God."[41]

Lucille Ansbro, whose parents came from County Mayo, Ireland, was one of twelve children. At great sacrifice her middle class parents managed to send their offspring to Catholic schools. One son, John Ansbro, a diocesan priest, former Motherhouse Chaplain and Vicar General of the diocese, and presently pastor of St. Aedan's Church, seems as much a part of the Caldwell Dominicans as the two daughters, Irene (Sister Roberta) and Lucille (Mother Dolorita).

Though no full account of her life is intended in this volume since she is still "making history" as Bursar of the Infirmary, it seems proper to salute her personal love and appreciation for the Dominicans who taught her at St. Dominic Academy and who nurtured her vocation.

She entered September 8, 1924, and the day after she entered she was assigned to teach first and second grades at the village school of St. Aloysius. Mother received the habit on April 14, 1925, and made profession the following year. After profession she spent twenty-six years as teacher and principal of St. Aloysius School until she was elected Vicaress and then Mother General.

In 1963 the *Advocate* named her one of the ten top women of the diocese and congratulated her on the calibre of her leadership and the charism to foster the expansion and development of Community properties and services.

To the diocese she was "about buildings," to the Community she was a woman of integrity and deep faith, schooled in the spirituality and sense of authority of the Pre-Vatican Church, who bore the heavy burden of leading the Community toward appropriate initial steps of renewal.

During the six years (1963–1969) classes entering became smaller, twenty-six sisters had died, thirty-four sisters requested and received dispensations from vows, four were on leaves of absence, and eighteen novices had decided to withdraw before Profession. The growth in membership that seemed so hopeful in 1957 had reached "zero" in 1969.[42]

Though new schools were opened, others were closed, or at least were no longer staffed by Caldwell Dominicans.[43] Caldwell Dominicans had been in the vanguard of adopting new methods of teaching religion, math, reading, language arts, and yes, even taking courses to introduce sex education in schools that piloted the program and only to students whose parents approved.

By March 25 of 1965 the Sisters were wearing a new veil which had been approved by the entire Community; and slight changes had been made in local horarium, the recitation of the Little Office, and other liturgical rubrics. Formal changes in the Constitution were held in abeyance since the decrees of Vatican II and a proposed new schema of Canon Law for Religious seemed to indicate "status quo" until a later time.

During her last six years, Mother was advised to sell Siena Hall to St. Boniface and to raze both the Villa and its annex, St. Agnes Hall, since proper renovations proved prohibitive.

After much consultation the Council decided that the first Special or Extraordinary Chapter of Affairs would be held in 1968. A program of self-study, a very Dominican approach which combined intellectual and spiritual formation, group reflection and dialogue, and the formation of structures to provide involvement from the "grass roots," was launched as a Pre-Chapter measure.

Our Program was divided into three phases—one from the fall of 1967 to March 2, 1968, another from March 2, 1968, to June 23, 1968, and then the Special Chapter itself.

The First Phase concerned itself with Self-Study for Renewal. A Chairman was appointed together with a Steering Committee selected from various categories—College, High School, Grade School and different age-groups. These Sisters made arrangements for the agenda of the General Monthly Meetings, procuring speakers as listed:

October—Sr. Mary Emil, I.H.M. "The Apostolic Outlook"
November—Rev. Thomas A. Collins, O.P. "The Scriptural Basis of Our Dominican Life"
December—Rev. Ambrose Clark, O.S.B. "Authority, Obedience, Freedom"
December—Very Rev. W. Bertrand Ryan, O.P. "Canon Law for Religious"
January—Rev. Giles Dimock, O.P. "Liturgy and Dominican Life"
February—Very Rev. William Ryan, O.P. "Poverty"
Rev. Andrew Newman, O.P. "Chastity" and Rev. Justin Hennessey, O.P. "Obedience"
March—Rev. James A. Egan "Unity and Community"

At all General Meetings there were group discussions followed by question and answer periods.

Phase I ended on March 2, and Phase II was initiated. The Steering Committee as such ceased; the members were designated as Consultors to the Task Force and the Constitution Committee; two were named Co-ordinators, and two were assigned to each Committee that would be operating, namely, Formation, Community Living, Apostolic, Government, and Personal Development. The Constitution Committee would handle the material sent to it by the various committees. . . . The Sisters were directed to list names of five finally professed Sisters whom they wished to nominate for the Task Force work; for the Constitution Committee they were asked to nominate three Sisters.

These Committees held weekly meetings, with the Chairman as the guide, and the Secretary making periodic written reports to each Convent. Much research was accomplished. Any Sister wishing to do so at this time was at liberty to write Position Papers; some were presented: "The Value and Need for Silence in Our Religious Lives," "Poverty and the Apostolate of Service," etc. Each Task Force Committee prepared Proposals for presentation to the Chapter. The Constitution Committee took these proposals and put them into a uniform style so that they could be voted upon by the Chapter Delegates. A complete set of Proposals was sent to every Convent two weeks before the Special Chapter.

When the delegates to the Special Chapter were elected, each one was assigned to a Special Chapter Committee named the same as the Task Force Group. On June 23, 1968, His Excellency, The Most Reverend Thomas A. Boland, S.T.D., L.L.D., Archbishop of Newark, offered the Mass of the Holy Spirit in the Convent Chapel, thereby invoking blessings on the Chapter.

The Opening Meeting was held in the Residence Hall with Rev. Mother Dolorita as Chairman. Each Chapter Committee elected its Chairman; the Chairman elected two Co-chairmen to assist Reverend Mother at the General Sessions.

The Committees conducted individual meetings and priorities were decided regarding Proposals to be made at the General Chapter Sessions. The Chairman of each Committee presented the Proposals for discussion and voting.

Daily reports of the General Sessions were sent to the Convents by the Chapter Secretaries who had been suggested by Reverend Mother and the Council with the approval of the Chapter.

Very Rev. Father William Ryan, O.P., Canonist, was present at all our sessions.

The First Session ended on June 29. Similar procedure prevailed at the Second Session of the Special Chapter of Affairs which lasted from August 29, 1968, to September 2, 1968, and also at the Third Session from December 21, 1968, to December 24, 1968.

Interim Acts of the Special Chapter of 1968 were sent to the Sisters for immediate implementation.[44]

The Interim Acts legislated new directives concerning vacations, home visits, suffrages for the dead, more responsibility on the local level for setting up the horarium and implementing personal and communal prayer options, the formation of a Committee to work at alternatives to dress experimentation, and a contemporary dress for postulants.

More significantly, the Standing Committee Structure was confirmed and the committees were empowered to make necessary studies, appropriate recommendations, and to collate and make ready for Chapter presentation proposals received from the Community. The Convents were divided into four regional groups which held regular meetings and forwarded group responses to the appropriate committee.

The Community voted in a new method of electing Chapter delegates which was approved by the Bishop. Throughout the voting period and during the entire proximate preparation time for the elective Chapter, the delegates and each Community member were encouraged to understand the reason and limited scope of appropriate experimentation, to be open to alternatives since "where there is unanimity in essentials, there may be diversity in means,"[45] and to be most willing to follow the spirit of Dominic.

A spirit of *faith* deepened by the assiduous study and contemplation of Sacred Scripture.

A spirit of *prayer* nourished by constant fidelity to religious observance and a deep appreciation of silence.

A spirit of *charity* which fostered a burning desire for personal perfection and forged a determined will to devote oneself entirely to the salvation of souls in imitation of the Saviour who offered Himself for our redemption.

A spirit of *involvement* which impelled him to be aware of the needs (of the) men of his age and produced a zeal to provide for them in a marvelously adequate way.[46]

As the General Chapter convened June 15, 1969, each Committee reported on the activities of the interim year. The approval of Project Link, an experimental junior high school in Newark,[47] and the establishment of a first foreign mission in Abaco were highlights of the apostolate reports.

It was clear to the assembled delegates and to the entire Community that the work had only just begun. Again Mother Dolorita's words in the Community report serve as an appropriate ending to this Chapter and a prayerful introduction to the next.

> God has visibly blessed the work of the Congregation. The accomplishments are indicative of the cooperation manifested by each and every member of our esteemed Community.
> ...We give you thanks, Almighty God, for these and all the benefits which we have received from your bountiful hands.[48]

2

3.

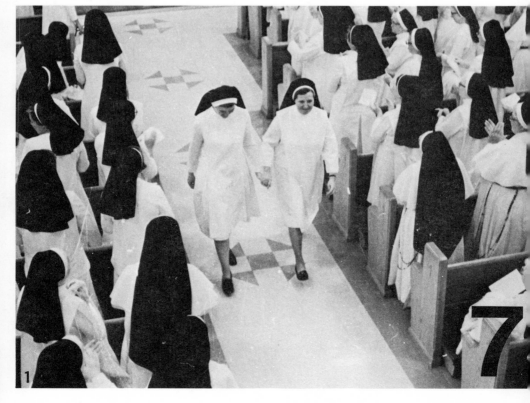

1

7

"To study the history
of any community
caught in the
throes of reform
is to look deeply
into the heartbreak
of many souls."

Sister Therese Catherine, O.P.

TOWARD RENEWAL

1–Liturgy of Installation for Sister Margaret Thomas McGovern
2–Dominican Institute, 1974
3–Sister Catherine Waters
4–General Chapter Session, Mother Joseph Residence Hall, Caldwell College, Caldwell, New Jersey

The years of experimentation encouraged by the Vatican Document *Perfectae caritatis* (1965) and implemented by Pope Paul VI's *Motu Proprio, Ecclesiae Sanctae* (1966) admonished all religious communities to be "on the way" toward renewal and adaptation. The Caldwell Dominicans, always prompt to obey even the suggestions of the Church, entered wholeheartedly into renewal, *aggiornamento*, —a deep questioning of who they had been, who they were now, who they wanted to be, and how they could integrate the best of the past into contemporary language, life experiences, and structures.

This ecclesial call to change made it quite clear that appropriate renewal of religious life involved two simultaneous processess: 1) a continuous return to the sources of all Christian life and the original inspiration behind a given Community, and 2) an adjustment of the Community to the changed condition of the times. (*P.C.*, 2)

This was a challenging call to reflect deeply on the spirit of the founder and foundresses in order to discover the essentials, the radical elements, and then to discern how to adapt these to the signs of the times. With hindsight it seems to this author that the call was a gift, especially to the Ratisbon-rooted American Dominican congregations. Rather than a Pandora's Box, the process by which individual women Dominicans and congregations began to study the past history,[1] to examine their European roots and the course of their American experience, provided an excellent opportunity to reclaim much of the Dominican tradition, to uproot or to adapt customs that were no longer producing the desired effects, and when necessary to create new ones. The process was and still is painful but perhaps there is a valuable lesson to be learned from the Old and New Testaments.

The scriptural and theological revolutions have enabled us to understand the ongoing nature of revelation and its "forever-newness" and to perceive the call to change as a new word from the Lord. Hopefully it is not far-fetched to see *aggiornamento* and corporate response to it as God's way of making contemporary the word of Isaias 43:18–19. "Remember not the events of the past, the things of long ago, consider not. See I am doing something new. Now it springs forth, do you not perceive it?"

In light of the belief that He desires and is, in fact, doing something new through history, a short reflection on one notion in the Gospel of Mark provides a key to adopting an attentive disciple's posture as the Community continues on-the-way toward renewal. Many times this evangelist uses the expression "on the way" and he usually follows it with "Jesus asked his disciples this question" or "Jesus explained the parable," the paradox. As women of the Word, modern disciples, and contemplative apostles, all attempts at renewal must flow out of a posture of listening to the Spirit of Jesus, a readiness to risk letting go of the known in order to discover His "new way," and the childlikeness to question Him and one another in order to clarify alternatives, live with paradoxes, and evaluate the results. Dominic would expect nothing less and demand nothing more.[2] The Lord will provide the strength and light which is needed to remain open-hearted and make every effort to achieve "truth in charity."

Though the concept of "future shock" and the aftermath of Vatican II may at first appear to many as having destroyed the unity, security, peace, and apostolic effectiveness of an earlier stable time, surely it is premature to make prophecies that the new Jerusalem is here or around the corner or that doomsday is already upon us.

This final chapter will attempt to sketch the spirits or be–attitudes which lie at the heart of those changes (both those evident to the broader church, as well as those sensed more by community members) which have shaped the agony of decisions and the struggle to celebrate oneness of mind and heart and sisterly charity amid a diversity of expressions which, if left misunderstood, sullenly tolerated, or totally rejected, could polarize and permanently destroy the very essence of the Caldwell heritage.

Each error must be judged in the light of its prevailing spirituality (vertical, God and me; or horizontal, God and me for others) and its theology. The 70s and 80s are attempting to integrate the two types of spirituality and to concretize the theology into life-giving symbols, structures, and lifestyles.

The statement issued by the 1972 Extraordinary Chapter of Affairs provides the rationale for all change.

> In the ongoing revision of our Constitutions we sincerely attempt to re-examine the fabric of our community living, reweave and replace the worn spots, and weave the fabric anew to create unity, community, and union with God—for ourselves and for those whose lives we touch. But it is as simple as this: General Chapters alone do not restore, rebuild, or revitalize Community; the sisters living with each other do. Therefore, acknowledge the need to translate the idealism of our commmon goals, *always open to critical evaluation* (italics mine), into daily realities. The reality is this: that we Caldwell Dominicans will survive on the local level or we will perish; that we will grow on the local level or be dwarfed; that we will pray on the local level or lose the presence of God; that we will be present to one another (*qualitatively*) on a local level or remain alone among the lonely, the alienated.[3]

The General Chapters of 1969, 1975, and 1979 and the Chapter of Affairs of 1972, as well as all pre-Chapter processes, attempted to involve the total Community in providing grass roots information and feelings which guided the elected representatives, the Chapter delegates, in forging Constitutions whose concepts and contents reflect an awareness of the religious life in mission to a Church in the modern world; a deliberate intention to foster personal holiness, the need for a supportive contemplative atmosphere for community living, and an untiring effort to fashion ministries to meet the contemporary needs of both the American and universal Church.

The earlier Chapters and the Constitutions of 1909, 1916, and 1945 were modeled on the legalistic and pastoral norms of their times. Changes were made to meet the new directives of Canon Law or the vision of the Ordinary. They rarely reflected the diverse opinions in Community (and there was always diversity), and they often ignored or sanctified some of the unnecessary struggles involved in faithfully responding to some ordinances. But it is not to be denied that those very documents and customs promoted personal holiness, Community visibility and credibility, and apostolic fruitfulness.[4]

In the past eleven years the Church has issued a call to understand that there is a common holiness that can be achieved in one's personal God-given, freely chosen lifestyle through which personal gifts and corporate resources are placed at the service of 1) liberating the captives, 2) preaching the Gospel, and 3) bringing about the renewed world described in Isaias 65: 17–25.

It is hoped that this telescopic view of a cataclysmic period will at least provide the reader with an initial impression of the tenor and intention of the times. There will be no attempt to cover the spirit, acts, and implementation of each chapter. General trends will be highlighted. The topics that will be covered are Leadership, Person and Community, Formation, Government, and Apostolate.

LEADERSHIP

The Chapter of 1969 elected Sister Vivien Jennings (Major Superior) and six councillors, each assigned to chair a particular

Standing Committee[5] and to assume responsibility for ongoing dialogue and development in the area of her concern.[6] Sister Vivien was re-elected in 1975.[7] Before the election of 1979, with the strong recommendation of the present Council, the vote of the entire Community, and the approval of Bishop Gerety, the Generalate was limited to the Major Superior and three councillors.[8]

Regardless of its size the Council attempted to exercise leadership which in Sister Vivien's words was *avant garde* and *radical*—"avant garde as the needs of the apostolate demand and as truly radical as the Gospel."[9] Though specifics will be covered in greater detail in later sections, the general concerns of the leaders will be cited here.

In order to face the vocation crisis (departures from Community and fewer candidates entering) attempts were made to update personal understanding of the vows and religious commitment; counselling and spiritual direction were encouraged; experimentation in local Community lifestyles was supported; and vocation personnel and updated materials were provided.

The Community's dedication to education was broadened as to ways of implementation (beyond the classroom) and to new channels of communication. Its corporate commitment to excellence of education in the inner city, urban, and suburban areas was constantly evaluated, and hard decisions about the feasibility of maintaining the Caldwell presence in particular schools were made sensitively and prudently after consultation with people involved on every level.

Tension became more evident and diversity of approval and disapproval accompanied the attempts to complement personal initiative, community discernment, and corporate responsibility in the areas of: *obedience* (as regards placement in ministry, election of Superiors and reintroduction of House Meetings); *poverty* (the introduction of personal minimal budgets and the need to hear the cries of the poor while providing effective witness), *chastity* (honoring individual differences in need for deeper personal faith and life-sharing and appropriate "intimacy," and fostering education and local community challenge to the responsible use of "new freedoms"), and *collegiality* (the call to engage everyone in the decision-making process).

For those who led and for those who followed, this brief summary is fraught with memories. All Chapter reports reveal a continuing thread and a very basic intention for all the Councils: to be thankful for the graces of Community and to accept the challenge of responsible stewardship. In 1976–77 the Council challenged the Community to "own the future together." The next two years the identification of personal giftedness and the need for openness and trust in dialogue were emphasized. The 80s opened with a call to remember "He is the Vine and we are the branches." And in 81, the Centenary Year, Sister Margaret Thomas recalled the Spirit of the first Sisters of St. Dominic who came from Germany to Brooklyn, New York, Jersey City, and Caldwell. Sister proclaimed that each of us carries within us the golden thread of that spirit so we can rejoice together in the faithfulness of the past 100 years while asking for the graces of fidelity to Christ's light—wherever we are—in Jersey City, Newark, Bridgeport, the Bayou, Abaco, Guatemala, or El Salvador. For we are one body in the Lord.[10]

The words of Sister Vivien in her report to the Chapter of 1979 highlight the incisiveness and charism of her leadership and accent the flow of activity.

> There is an appointed time for every thing
> And a time for every affair under the heavens:
> A time to be born and a time to die,
> A time to plant and a time to uproot the plant,
> A time to work and a time to laugh,
> A time to scatter stones and a time to gather them...
> A time to love... and a time of peace.
>
> In the life of the Caldwell Congregation, the 1970s seem to have been years that embraced the whole gamut of experiences described in these lines of *Ecclesiastes*.[11]
> ...And so the future dawns once more.
> ...Above all, as we move toward and beyond our hundredth anniversary in 1981, we pray that in the Lord's plan the immediate future will be for the Congregation and for each sister personally "a time of love... and a time of peace."

PERSON AND COMMUNITY

The Constitutions of 1969, 1975, and 1979 state emphatically that the unity of Community is based on the bond of charity which exists among the members. They describe the *ideal* in which "each Sister is respected as one who brings to community her unique contributions and rightly receives from the community loving encouragement and support."[12]

In the past eleven years Sister Rita Margaret, Sister Margaret Thomas, and Sister Patricia Mahoney, as well as their dedicated committee members, have worked to bridge the gap between the *ideal word* and the *real world* of convent living. They have facilitated the changes which continue to foster personal growth and development in a community context.

Each committee explored the meaning of personal chastity, a total self-giving which leads to intimacy with the Lord, charity toward "the Sisters," and appropriate relational and service response to all. Their reports encouraged a personal poverty which produces a reverence for all the gifts of life, a detachment from worldly comforts, a desire for simplicity of lifestyle, and a determination to use time and talents to bring about systemic changes so that the poor and the powerless can be served more equitably. The Community dynamics strengthened the concept that obedience involves a surrender of personal freedom in the light of Community discernment in order to make the best individual contribution to the life of the Community and the achievement of the comon goal—to make Christ present and to preach the Gospel by word, example, and meaningful service. The contemporary concepts of theology and psychology were applied both in the consideration and implementation of significant change.

Perhaps only the women who have struggled through the process can appreciate the paradoxes involved at the beginning and the need for evolutionary rather than immediate change in this religious congregation.[13]

The initial paradoxes cited are based on the Caldwell Community responses to the 1968 National Sisters Survey.[14] The five hundred-four Caldwell Dominicans overwhelmingly indicated a desire for more personal responsibility in daily living, less structured relationships between superior and subjects, and greater flexibility in frequency of contacts with family, friends, parishoners, and clergy. At the same time their responses to Community surveys demanded that the government structure and new Constitutions set up uniform parameters concerning night curfew, home visits, the presence of laity in the convents, and appropriate guidelines concerning the use of secular dress.

The majority of members wanted more individual choice in personal spirituality but again looked for congregational guidelines in regard to Community worship: office, Liturgy, availability of assigned confessors. While the Community apostolic demands created a large number of small convents and diversified ministries, and allowed individuals to work in one school and live in another convent, Sisters longed for larger communities to support a more regular common life. This sampling of diverse needs is sufficient to help the reader understand the complexity of feelings and directions which faced the leadership in this critical life area.

From 1969 to 80 changes were made with comparative ease in the areas of daily scheduling, adoption of the use of the Liturgy of the Hours (psalmody, readings, and prayers of the universal Church) instead of the Little Office;[15] encouragement of personal responsibility for the times and place for meditation, monthly recollection days, yearly retreats, spiritual direction, and summer spiritual renewal programs; the accomodation of Dominican devotions: the Rosary, *Salve* Procession and suffrages for the dead to local situations; and openness to longer vacations and diverse recreational, educational, professional, and civic involvements.

But the search to find the appropriate Dominican religious response to the deeper questions: finding time and space for silence and reflective study amid the bustle of demanding apostolates and diversified lifestyles;[16] facing the need for pre-retirement education and quality retirement experiences; and discerning community readiness and willingness to accept options in regard to wearing the religious habit, is still continuing.

The past decade has provided innumerable opportunities for enrichment in the studies of the vows, Scripture, and theology. Various models have been provided to facilitate local house and regional cluster discernment concerning methods of convent goal setting; appropriate flexibility and experimentation as regards silence, group study, and dialogue; and any other issue that is disturbing sisterly charity or convent tranquility.

Since 1977 several programs[17] have been offered to help Sisters approaching retirement to set future goals, define alternatives, and make a prudent personal choice after communal discernment. As of 1980 there are sixty-five Sisters living in St. Catherine's Infirmary and fourteen others who are retired but living in a local mission.

Though Sister Vivien was very right in her perception that in 1969 the Caldwell community "is united in the need for the habit as a visible witness to the fact that we are living a religious life," she was optimistic but not correct when she said, "so what could be a considerable distraction if the debate went on for 10 years is now a closed issue."[18]

The habit was a continuing distraction and the debate continued for ten years. Like most Communities each Chapter explored the appropriate response to the call of the popes who continually reiterated the importance of its sign value; Dominic's desire that the Dominican be a visible presence; the question of the luxury of anonymity when the world yearned for visible signs that commitment was possible; and the question of financing a secular wardrobe in the light of each Chapter's mandate to more radical simplicity and poverty.

The Pre-Chapter process provided open forums to expand information, assess the variant community stances and provide for adequate exchange of insights. The delegates to the Chapter of 1979 decided to use an adaptation of the Ignatian discernment process to confront this emotional, critical, and divisive issue. No one except the delegates can understand the depth of openness and trust, pain and joy, question and clarity that gave birth to the present Caldwell response to the wearing of the habit. "The Dominican attire consists of a simple white habit

worn with a scapular, jacket or vest, and a black veil. The habit
shall be worn for apostolic ministry."[19] Individual Sisters opt to
wear the traditional or modified habits and several veil styles;
while others seek individual dispensation from wearing the
habit and/or veil.

The debate has ended; the deeper questions continue. As
the Community learns to live with and appreciate this diversity
in external appearance, how can it remain visible and poor in
such a way that the world will see the good that it does and give
glory to God? Deeper immersion in the life of Jesus, heightened
awareness of the crying needs of a consumerism-driven society,
and significant presence "where the action-for-change" is happening will provide a continuous appropriate mode.

Eleven years later words written in the introduction of the
Master Plan for the Congregation of the Sisters of St. Dominic
still permeate all dialogue. "Common life is to be seen not as
conformity and regimentation, but an internal dynamism which
recognizes and respects individuality even as it creates a climate
to facilitate mutual support and growth."[20]

It is the season to claim roots and to dig them more deeply.
It is the hope of the future to acknowledge the hurts of the past,
to be a healing presence to each other, and to embrace the words
of Catherine of Siena who reminds the world that the Lord is
the true doctor who gives whatever is needed to bring about
perfect health and lasting unity.

FORMATION

One of the familiar verses that is repeated frequently to
demonstrate the personal character of God's love in the context
of a community covenant is "I have called you by name, you are
mine." (Isaias 43:6) The Spirit of God names, calls, lifes,
empowers, and frees the individual within and hopefully because
of the witness and support of the covenant community, but the
community response will only be as constant and faithful as that
of each member.

This spirit of providing an ongoing program which enables

each Dominican candidate and member to hear the call and to understand the connections between personal call and response and the corporate vision, lifestyle, and direction is at the heart of all formation endeavors from 1881 to 1981. The words change to express the contemporary but the ideals are "ever ancient yet ever new."

Sister Agnes Bernard and Sister Patricia Mahoney, along with the various directresses[21] and committee members, guided by the ecclesiastical norms; assisted by national and regional study/support groups; and challenged by Chapter mandates; fashioned a program step-by-step, that reaffirms the unity and balance of the contemplative attitude with apostolic service. Their documents and structures encourage personal response at the level of individual readiness and giftedness; and challenge those in initial formation,[22] scholasticate[23], and all final professed members to re-evaluate faith in the Dominican charism at both the individual and community level.

The six year term of Sister Agnes Bernard stabilized committee membership and scope; inaugurated an academic program for immersion into Scripture and Theology called IRFBTS (Institute for Religious Formation in Biblical and Theological Studies);[24] and began the work of formulating more specific programs for vocation awareness and recruitment, applicancy, postulancy, novitiate and scholasticate.

Sister Patricia Mahoney, who had been the postulant directress (1973–1975), was elected Councillor for Formation in 1975 and again in 1979.

Her report to the General Chapter emphasized the good-working order of the committee structure and directions of all programs. In 1975 the affiliate program[25] was adopted on a week-end basis under the direction of Sister Patricia Crowley, the postulant directress, and in 78–79 a live-in full-time affiliateship was opened. There were 2 live-in affiliates in 79 and one in 78.

In 1977 the postulants[26] began to live in a mission. St. John's on Ryerson Avenue was chosen for Jayne Sadowski who continued her college work; while Linda Dowling resided at St.

John's, Jersey City, where she taught, and returned to Caldwell on weekends. In 1978 there were no postulants. Since 1979 the postulants have lived in the Motherhouse Formation Community which is composed of affiliates, postulants, novices, and professed Sisters.

From 1976 through 1980, since their numbers were few,[27] the Novices have participated in a three month live-in Dominican inter-community Novitiate program sponsored by the Dominican Fathers at St. Stephen's Priory, Dover, Massachusetts. The program complemented rich liturgical, personal direction, and academic experiences with diverse apostolic exposure.

The Scholasticate program[28] from 1975–79 took on a different tone of accountability. The Junior professed Sister on-mission designed her own "home program" attended minimal peer group yearly enrichment programs, and took an active part in her evaluation by her local superior, principal, and formation councillor. Renewals and Final Professions were requested according to personal preference (yearly, three years), and the ceremony could take place either at the Motherhouse or Church of the Sister's choice.

In 1976 the Dominican Apostolic Volunteer Program[29] began which enabled women to choose to join a Community living situation and a particular ministry for a time of their personal designation with no commitment of actual application to the Community.

In 1977 Sister Frances Sullivan was appointed part-time vocation directress. She formed a Vocation Team and sponsored weekends and days of reflection. She and her successor, Sister Patricia Stringer (who will be full-time as of 1981–82), have attempted to involve the entire community in the recruitment process by sponsoring days of recollection and study at local missions, tapping artists and writers to produce brochures, ads and slideshows, and encouraging days and weeks of prayer for vocation awareness.

After two years of work a personal formation journal, *Formation Focus* was presented, first to the Chapter delegates

(1979) and then to each house. It reminds the members that "the Caldwell Dominican is by birth, baptism, and vow called to be a responsible, active member of the ongoing daily formation focus for self and others."[30]

Since 1975 there has also been an intense effort to encourage ongoing formation on a spiritual, academic, and personal level for all community members.

> Empowered and freed by the Spirit—gifted with the time to be a contemplative apostle—our Covenant life moves us gracefully toward the fulfillment of our vowed life-poor-chaste-obedient-until death-the final freeing of the Spirit—(a final call and a personal response just like all the ones through life)—Here am I Lord, take me![31]

GOVERNMENT

The Government committee was responsible for facilitating the creation of structures for the General Chapters and local house through which the spirit and fact of all implemented change was placed in operation. The present *Constitutions* states that

> the dynamism and solidarity of any society demand a governmental structure which will allow for both personal growth and perpetuation of the Institute in a contemporary setting. The government of this Congregation shall reflect and apply the principles of collegiality and subsidiarity[32] at every level of community life.[33]

As early as 1967, Sister Mary Luke Tobin challenged the members of the International Union of Superiors General to change from a pyramid (hierarchical) model of government to a collaborative one which fostered and developed the constructs and skills to use a consensual decision-making process whenever possible.[34] Throughout all the activities from the Self Study of

1968 until the present, Caldwell's leaders and members have been gradually (or not so gradually in some cases) introduced into group dynamic skills.

Synergy is defined by Webster as "combined action" and synergism as "cooperative action of descrete agencies such that the total effect is greater than the sum of the two effects taken independently." Countless synergy sessions with tons of news-brainstorming records long since discarded, and reams of facilitator's, recorder's, and secretary's reports on file, attest to the "Caldwell Olympian response" to collaboration and the struggle to reach concensus.

Sister Catherine Bernadette and Sister Alice Uhl and their committees defined their main focuses as the promotion of collegiality, the improvement of communication among superiors and between superiors, the committee and the Generalate, and the promotion of viable community government structures on the local level.

The period 1969 through 1975 was marked by a new, more truly representative system of electing delegates to the Chapter.[35] The traditional Dominican custom of a local house electing its superior rather than having one appointed was offered as an option.[36] The roles of superior, principal, and house bursar were separated in most cases and the latter was elected by the house. Local superiors were offered many opportunities for spiritual enrichment, community support, and education in values clarification, administrative skills, and relationship interaction a-wareness.

As the 1975 General Chapter was convoked, Sister Vivien and the Government Committee suggested the introduction of a new pre-Chapter process. In a document entitled *A Possible Approach*, issued January 1975, the process is simply defined.

> Affirmation is an approach to Chapter preparation and to the working of the Chapter itself. It involves the entire community, prayerfully reflecting together on the vital issues of religious life, then working toward and finally formulating consensus statements on these major issues. As such, the single statements (few

in number) will form a *credo*, a "this we believe," about our life together as religious women in the Church. The expression of these affirmations will help us to identify the areas on which we are united as a community.[37]

At the Chapter no proposal which contradicted the faith-statement could be accepted.

For a complex web of reasons the Community did not vote favorably to use the approach.

Sister Alice Uhl was elected the Councillor for Government in 1975. Throughout the next four years[38] the potential power of the house meeting was stressed. Models were suggested to make the house meeting a viable structure for handling ordinary house business; shared prayer and study; sensitive dialogue concerning personal or group fears, hopes, and dreams; and serious discernment to achieve grass roots response to critical church, world, and community issues.

More workshops were offered to Superiors and Community members to strengthen communication and confrontation skills. Regional clusters were organized to help local houses explore the use of the Goal Achievement Chain spectrum to develop shared goals and appropriate structures for their achievement and evaluation. It was suggested that each house make a personal covenant statement to convey its own spirit of sisterly love and concern.

On the parish level Sisters became very active members of parish councils, spiritual renewal teams, and adult study groups. While in the diocese members joined and even held key offices in the Newark Sisters' Assembly.[39]

The eighteen month pre-chapter process (1977–1979) was designed and coordinated by a steering committee composed of members of the Council, the Government Committee, facilitators and facilitator trainers as well as elected regional representatives. The process involved the total Community and incorporated the house meeting, regional meeting, and total Community meeting schemas in its reflective-dialogue stages.

Two summer Think Tanks (1977, 1978) involved sixty-five

Sisters in the study of critical Community issues and in the formulation of alternative responses.

Throughout 1979 the Community worked at every level to produce belief statements that identified areas of unity; critical issues which indicated diverse and in some cases divisive elements; and a range of possible solutions and proposals to promote a deep unity through that very diversity. The final tabulations were used by the Chapter delegates in order to assess the Community 'pulse' on any particular proposal addressed at the June Chapter.[40]

The Pre-chapter Counterpoint sessions provided input and promoted dialogue on community lifestyle models (based on an adaptation of Avery Dulles' *Models of the Church* emphases) and the issue of the habit. It became clear that the very sensitive issues required a different chapter approach if true resolution were to be achieved. The delegates were introduced to the Ignatian Method of discernment with the assistance of two members of the team from the Center for Spirituality at Wernersville, Pennsylvania.

By June the delegates decided to adopt the process to the discussion of the habit and corporate commitment. Concensus was reached and the agony and ecstasy of the process had to be conveyed to the Community so that a united response to and respect for the difficult decision could be achieved.

In the area of government the Community has come a long way. Continued attempts to broaden implementation of collegiality and to insure the application of subsidiarity on every level and the more extensive use of discernment and concensus are hopes for the immediate future.

Though the belief statements affirm Community unanimity on the need for a common life that balances prayer, study, and service, tensions still exist when a small group after prayerful discernment and articulation of specific goals seeks permission to establish a small community living situation that meets their needs and the Community guidelines.

Some forms of diversity still breed a threatening fear, but diversity is a part of the fabric of Community life. Sister Vivien's words in her letter of the convocation of the 1972 Chapter provide one perspective on relating to the issue. "By and large we are—and as Dominicans ought to be—independent thinkers, individuals who can probe objectively the merit of an idea (and its concrete expression), assess its values and limitations and then come to a genuine concensus in the best interest of the Community and of the Church."[41]

Structures will be continually evaluated. Greater accountability is already being demanded of individuals and groups within the Community. And each idea, local or larger Community experience, will be judged by its fruits. Chapters and processes do not make a Community. Personal responses to the group direction will either continue co-founding the whole or confounding it, because it takes a whole Community to sustain its charism. Government is no longer a matter of law but a recognition of the grace that Community dynamism rests on a personal and corporate call to be and to become all that the Church, the Order, and the world need in order to believe the *Good News* and to accept the challenge of continuous renewal and reform.[42]

APOSTOLATE

The first three topics focused attention on those aspects of renewal which attempted to strengthen the bond of love and establish a dynamic internal structure to promote stability and encourage new development.

All of these internal changes are important, first because they establish the environment in which holiness happens, and second because the more holy and contemplative the religious woman and Community become the more enlightened will be the sense of mission and the more fruitful the ministry.

That distinction between mission and ministry lies at the heart of all decisions made in regard to the Caldwell Dominican apostolate.

Just as the mission of the Church is to be the sign of Christ's continuing liberating, prophetic presence in every age, the Dominican religious Community is to be a microcosmic sign. The Caldwell Community is "in-mission"—sent by the Church for the glory of God to be "a blazing emblem of the heavenly kingdom." (P.C.1) Since from 1906 this Community has been incorporated into the Dominican Family as an active congregation rather than a contemplative one, it is also associated with a ministry—a specific service or services based on the founder's charism (preaching and evangelization); community history and professional training (education); and contemporary Church needs.

The mission of the Community was stated simply in the Apostolate Committee Chapter Report 1979: "To be and to become witnesses and disseminators of the Word, utilizing and developing each other's gifts and living a Dominican lifestyle for Caldwell Dominicans as ecclesial women are sent to proclaim the Word in truth."[43] Its application to service (Ministry) is defined in the Constitutions.

> Caldwell Dominicans, in witnessing and servicing, accept the specific ministry of communicating truth. In order to develop strong Christians at every level of society, efforts are directed especially to those who are in the greatest spiritual, economic, and cultural need.[44]

Each member is supported in her unique attempt to achieve contemplative apostolic integration. The hours needed for prayer, for study, and for common life cannot be habitually put aside for other activities.

Specific ministerial choices will be honored which contribute to the broad areas of communication of truth within the limits of personnel, the expressed desire to cooperate with ecclesiastical authority, and the spirit of the Constitutions.[45]

The Chapters of 1969 and 1972 mandated that the Community lifestyle and ministries should reflect concern for the Christian transformation of the social order, especially in the urgent areas of justice, peace, the dignity of human life, and commitment to the promotion of a proper understanding of the place of women in the modern world.

In 1969, nineteen sisters had volunteered for service in an English speaking[46] area outside the continental United States. Four Sisters, Marie Therese, Helena, Denis Marie, and Virginia Mary, were assigned to staff the school of St. Francis de Sales Mission, Marsh Harbour, Abaco, Bahamas, in September. The school is supported by Community donations, school contributions, and some funds from the Bahamian government.[47] The Sisters continue to offer excellent school and adult education, and the simplicity of their lives is a powerful witness among the poor.

In the same year preparations were made to begin a private non-denominational Junior High School in Newark to provide personalized Dominican education for those of God's poor who would not otherwise share its benefits. Sister Vivien and Sister Amelia were appointed coordinators. The plans were approved by William H. Warner, Director of Secondary Education in September 1970.

The school, called Project Link, and its convent for the five Sisters, Joan of Arc, Patricia Dominic, Melchior, Veritas, and Catherine Daly, began in two buildings on Hunterdon Street. Today (in its Irvine Turner Blvd. location) it continues to attract foundations and other funding groups because of its quality educational, social, and cultural experience for inner city students, grades 6–8. The religious and lay administration and faculty are assisted by Jesuit volunteers. Public school administrators, councillors, and teachers yearly make recommendations of students (the gifted, the potential leader who in the present setting is average, and the remedial) who would benefit most by the educational and social programs that provide maximum encouragement and personal attention during the crucial transitional years.

Throughout the 70s workshops were sponsored to help school personnel incorporate Christian principles of peace, justice, and human dignity into the curriculum and to encourage outreach assistant programs. Like most communities during this period, Sisters of the Community worked in Saturday and summer academic and recreational programs in the inner city. Others worked to lobby for specific concerns and to raise awareness about the inequities in housing, education, and health care.

For Sister Bertrand, who was the Councillor for the Apostolate from 1969–1979, that decade was one of continuing evaluation of educational commitments, adjustment of ever-decreasing personnel, and an ongoing attempt to meet personal needs for ministry counselling and preference through community structures; yearly preference sheets, interviews and recommendations from personnel directors.

The work of Sister and her committee members and various ad hoc groups, whose hours of reflection and decision cannot be recorded extensively in this work, will be evident to anyone who understands the "behind-the-scenes" deliberations implied in policy statement and action response.

According to the apostolate Committee Report 1979, "In the past decade, and more extensively during the last four years... Individually and corporately, this ongoing assessment of personnel and ministries has led us to acknowledge both the value and the difficulties of corporate commitments, Community-owned schools, and diversified apostolates."[48]

The Community situation was simply a microcosm of diocesan and national trends. Most parochial schools experienced a decline in student enrollment and religious staff which made it necessary to continually raise tuition and fees to meet current expenditures. As financial concerns and examination of the feasibility of religious communities maintaining commitment to all their parish schools (because of declining numbers and the rising median age of available personnel) intersected, action was indicated.

As early as 1972 the Chapter mandated planned withdrawal. Dedication to education demanded that some schools be retained while others be dropped. Careful criteria were drawn up, diocesan and parish administrators were kept informed, consolidations and regionalization were explored, but final decisions had to be made.

By December of 1978 the Apostolate Committee, after much consultation with personnel at every level of involvement, arrived at its recommendation to the Council, if feasible:

> retain 15 or 20 elementary schools
> retain all high schools unless critical conditions arise to indicate curtailment
> retain the two community elementary schools and continue to examine these to ascertain if significant information points to a different direction over a period of three years, remove presence from those schools not cited for retention.[49]

In April, 1977, a Community education day provided dialogue for further Community input. The refinement of the criteria for remaining in parish schools was accomplished, and volunteers for the formation of a School Study Retention Team were sought. Fifty sisters volunteered and, from April to June, designed and executed a process which produced reports and recommendations. Through a process of discernment, concensus for the retention of twelve schools was reached; then four additional schools received sufficient votes for retention. These sixteen were added to the list of four (Abaco, Bayou, St. Ann's, and Bridgeport) which the Council had already designated for retention. By January the time-line for withdrawal was formulated and notification sent out to the parishes scheduled for withdrawal.

As the Chapter of 79 approached, the Chapter delegates chose ministry, especially the tension-filled relationship between corporate commitment and personal preference for diversified ministries, as an issue for discernment/concensus rather than parliamentary procedure/voting.

The concensus statement reads:

> Within this Congregational Mission which is the communication of truth, the religious are committed to maintaining corporate commitment to the people of God. The Congregation hopes to

retain commitments to community-owned, parish, and diocesan institutions which remain viable in regard to personnel, finances, and apostolic effectiveness. There is support for those diverse ministries which emerge after personal and communal discernment.[50]

As the centenary continues and the next one hundred years begin the Community will experience a great deal of dying to self daily in the generous expenditure of apostolic energies and a need for continuous reflection in every area of mission and ministry.

In 1979 Sister Doris Ann Bowles became the first woman superintendant of schools for the Archdiocese of Newark.

In the same year the New Jersey Housing Finance Agency approved state funding for the building of Marian Manor, a 159 unit senior-citizen housing complex which now stands on the grounds of the former Villa. Occupancy began in August 1981. As Sister Vivien noted in her Chapter Report, "There has been a special public witness in our community's perseverance through the long delays and litigation which the project has involved (since 1973)."[51]

The fruits of the common and apostolic life of Caldwell also nourish national and regional leadership groups. Collaboration with other Dominican Congregations has enriched the past decade. The Community co-sponsors the Las Casas Fund which provides legal aid and other services for the Cheyenne-Arapaho Indians in Oklahoma. Active participation in the Inter-Dominican Community efforts to maintain the Mariandale Reflection Center in Ossining, New York, continued 1976 through 1978.

For the past two years Caldwell has not been involved in full sponsorship, but individual Sisters participate in its enrichment programs.

If the 70s demanded constant vigilance and critical decision-making, the 80s will require even more re-evaluation of individual and corporate effectiveness in providing a Gospel-centered creative response to evolving spiritual and social needs.[52]

FINANCE

One of the hardest realities for the Community to face throughout its history but, in a more dramatic sense, in the last decade is that the ability to continue good works requires a very heavy financial commitment. The Councillor for Finance, Sister Edith Magdalen (1969–1979), constantly reminded the total community that

> we, as Caldwell Dominicans, through our religious commitment, and through our poverty which we have voluntarily embraced, have established an interdependent relationship among the Sisters. We do not save for our personal needs but rather to help provide for the needs of others in the Community. And after we have provided for our own who have vowed to be poor, do we have additional resources which could be utilized in the service of the other poor.[53]

Community funds are used to provide for the physical needs of unsalaried Sisters (those in staff work, members in Formation, the sick and retired);[54] to maintain the Community land and Motherhouse and Infirmary buildings at Mount Saint Dominic; to support the education fund which supplies money for all continuing professional education and enrichment; and to increase the Community endowment fund which provides revenues for the future support of the ever-increasing number of retired members and, if necessary, may be used to defray current expenditures of the Infirmary.

For the past ten years, in addition to the aforementioned areas, the Community has subsidized those Community-owned institutions which were experiencing financial difficulties. Presently the Boards of Trustees have been informed that the schools must provide sufficient revenues to meet rising costs and to make every effort to include yearly Community-debt reduction payments.

Since the Community Bursar and her Finance Committee and advisors have kept a close watch on the flow of Community cash and have made every attempt "to tighten-up" expenditures, the financial structure is stable. But like every religious congregation, movement into the 80s raises the specter of a rising retiree population and continual departures from Community which will result in a decreased income, during a period of escalated costs.

Since this is the last chapter of a one hundred year history, it is obvious that the Community is still involved in repayment of the long-term debt on the Administration Building. So a careful plan of more rapid debt reduction seems necessary. The Community is deeply indebted to Sister Edith Magdalen and all who assisted her, and presently assist Sister Alice Matthew (Treasurer) and Sister Helen Marguerite (Councillor for Finance) in analyzing trends to make careful use of Community funds and provide for the future.

Since 1969 three significant aspects of Community finance need brief explanation. In order to assist with the increasing costs of care for the retired, this religious congregation (and most congregations) applied to enter the Social Security System. Great sacrifices were necessary in order to involve the Community retroactively to 1968 even though the decision was made in April of 1973. But after consultation on the national and diocesan ecclesiastical levels the move seemed propitious and necessary.

Each Chapter reminded the Community of its commitment to hear the cries of the poor and to provide a base of power for the powerless. As revenues decreased and Community costs escalated, smaller funds were available to actually assist "the poor." The Community decided to seek membership in the interdenominational organization called the Corporation for Responsible Investment. The group guides members to purchase small portfolios of stock in companies whose policies presently endanged the environment, exploit the workers, or support anti-racial and anti-human rights governments, so that pressure may be brought to bear upon the Boards of Directors by stockholders who are interested in people not merely profits.

As Community membership decreased and costs continued to escalate the congregational bursars encouraged continual dialogue to negotiate viable salary contracts for those who worked in parochial or diocesan institutions.[55]

As the Community looks forward to perhaps even harder times and more critical decisions concerning the financial feasibility of certain Community institutions, each member must deepen her understanding of the concept of interdependence and corporate responsibility. Involvement in discernment and critical personal and communal analysis of financial patterns will be a part of the immediate future. The sense of poverty which institutions face serves to call them to radical conversion and abandonment to His provident plan as it is revealed through Community decisions.

PUBLIC RELATIONS

Since this history was commissioned as a centenary task it is fitting to conclude the final chapter with the words of Sister Margaret Thomas and Sister Lenore De Coster, Councillors for Public Relations, as well as the Community Secretary Generals from 1969–1979. Accuracy of minutes and constant record keeping often go unnoticed until someone needs a particular piece of information, yet this type of work occupies much of the time of this councillor.

In 1975 the Chapter, cognizant of the up-coming centenary, called for the establishment of a permanent historical committee. The original committee members suffered from ill health; one died suddenly; and another left the Community, so its tasks were assumed by several Ad Hoc committees. Materials were gathered from all over the Mount and stored in the archives, then a small office adjoining the House of Prayer. Interviews with senior Sisters were begun, pictures and memorabilia were collected and placed in some kind of chronological order, and houses were asked to restore the practice of keeping annals.

Throughout 1978–1979 Sister Irene Marie and Sister Lois Curry began initial efforts at starting the official archives and history on a part-time basis. During 1980–1981 both were full-time, and their work progressed. By December 16, 1981, the actual date of the centenary, the history will be published and distributed and the archives, a heritage room (for memorabilia), and historical display reception parlors will be formed as a permanent historical center on the first floor of the Mother-house.

All the history: remote, proximate, and present, took on new meaning as the 369 Caldwell Dominicans gathered in the Convent Chapel for the first of many Centenary Liturgies of Thanksgiving. The honored guests were not civic dignitaries or ecclesiastical leaders but the infirm and retired who came walking, in wheel chairs, and one by ambulance. The prayer of Sister Caritas, a member of the Community for fifty-four years expressed the sentiments of all.

> O my God, I am deeply grateful to you for the many graces and blessings you have bestowed on our Community during the past Century.
> Much praise and glory to those who have preceded us, for the number of sacrifices they made and the spiritual benefits we are enjoying today because of them.
> Dear Jesus, we thank you for the success of our material progress, and for the educational and social projects that our Community has undertaken.
> Dear Lord, may we appreciate and never forget those Sisters whose prayers, works, and sacrifices enriched our Community. May we continue their efforts for God's praise, honor and glory.
> May our Blessed Mother and Saint Dominic bless us and enable us to continue to praise and give glory to Jesus Christ, Our Lord.
> May our Divine Redeemer reward and grant eternal rest to all our Sisters in our cemeteries.
> Amen.

This centenary year is another sign that the Caldwell Dominicans can make great things happen quickly. The committee, under the direction of Sister Maura and Sister Maureen James, has organized a series of events which will involve the Sisters, members of their families, benefactors, and friends—all who are so much a part of the fabric of the story. Sister Mary

Ann O'Connor and her fifty-voice Sisters' Choir have provided the musical leadership which has highlighted the Community and County Liturgies of Thanksgiving. Sister Gerarda and her staff of volunteers have published frequent Centenary News-letters which make is possible for even a broader range of people to join in the celebration.

The shield which appears on the back cover of this text was designed by Sister Gerarda and was presented to each Sister on December 16, 1980. It serves as a reminder of personal commit-ment to the Dominican charism and is also an identifying symbol for the Community.

The Caldwell shield is a more contemporary design of the modern black and white shield of the Dominican Order. The two larger segments of the Caldwell shield symbolize our affiliation with the Order, while the red denotes this Congrega-tion's dedication to the Sacred Heart.

The adaptation of the Order's shield to express the Com-munity identification is symbolic of the whole of this Commun-ity History. Throughout the decades the Community has at-tempted to serve the Church and the Order by adapting the traditions of each to contemporary settings. Words found in the position paper on the Dominican charism issued by the Domi-nican Leadership Conference in 1975 express well the dominant character of the Caldwell stance:

> The Dominican charism is contemporary and timeless, ever probing the signs of the times in order to discover with contem-plative sensitivity not just quick reforms but the deeper causes of current ills, taking the reflective position in order to get to the heart of the matter.[56]

EPILOGUE

In the beginning St. Dominic had a dream.
Today his dream has become a world-wide Order.

In 1853, Mother Benedicta Bauer had a dream.
Today there are twelve American Congregations which
trace their roots to Ratisbon.

In 1893, Mother Catherine had a dream.
Today the Mount with its one hundred-acre natural
setting houses many buildings in which her spirit
of prayer and service abides.

In 1931 and 1939, Mother Joseph had a dream.
Today the Administration Building and its
schools from Junior High through College continue
to reflect quality education in a
Catholic cultural environment.

In 1955, Mother Aquinas had a dream.
Today because of the vision of Mother Dolorita and the

227

*spirit and generosity of Sisters and benefactors, the sick
and retired can be cared for properly.*

*In 1969, Sister Vivien had a dream.
Today Dominicans are involved in education among the
poor and in using the media as a tool of proclamation.*

*In the 1970s, the Chapter delegates had a dream.
Today the Community is still attempting to meet
the "Timeless Challenge."*

In 1981 the Community members have many dreams.
These will shape the next hundred years—but only if each
dreamer dares to articulate her dream and create a vehicle for
making it a reality.

**To Dare
    To Dream
        To Envision
            To Plan
And To Have The Courage To Change
This Is The Caldwell Heritage.**

The Heritage is enfleshed in each age by women of the
Word, daughters of the Church, and contemplative apostles
who respond to new needs by the creation of structures which
free each member and the Community as a whole, to claim the
past, shape the present, and plan wisely for the future so that
God may be praised, our love may be a source of blessing for
many, and the Gospel may be preached.

NOTES

I. IN THE STILLNESS

1 Sister M. Augusta O'Hanlon, O.P., *Saint Dominic Servant and Friend* (St. Louis: B. Herder Co., 1954), p.51 which is taken from Bl. Humbert, *Life of Saint Dominic*.

2 In 1218 Reginald of Orleans had decided to enter the Order but became seriously ill. St. Dominic prayed for his recovery. Our Lady appeared to Reginald, anointed him with perfume and showed him a long white scapular which was to become part of the Dominican habit. Reginald recovered, received the habit and scapular from the hands of St. Dominic, and went to the Holy Land where he preached zealously until his death in 1220.

3 William Hinnebusch, O.P., *The History of the Dominican Order*, I (Staten Island: Alba House, 1965), p.98. A very complete, highly documented account of the foundation of Prouille can be found in Pere Mandonnet, O.P., *Saint Dominic and His Work*, pp. 365–379.

229

4 Sister Therese Catherine, O.P., *An Emerging Woman* (Staten Island: Alba House, 1970), p.5 explains the many names of Ratisbon and their meanings. In this narrative Ratisbon is preferred. "Regensburg, a city of seven names, dates back 3,000 years and rests at the northerly point of the largest river in Europe. It has been in turn, a Celtic settlement (hence the more ancient name, Ratisbon), the Roman stronghold of "Castra Regina", the capital of Bavaria, a ducal, regal and episcopal city at one and the same time, a world famous commercial city in the middle ages, a free Imperial City."

5 Sister Mary Hortense Kohler, O.P., *Life and Work of Mother Benedicta Bauer* (Milwaukee: Bruce Publishing Co., 1937), pp. 8–9 calls these women *Beguines*, "One who took vows, could return to the world if she would, and did not renounce her property." This critical edition provides the most authentic account of the early history of Dominican women who have roots in Ratisbon.

6 Extracts from the Holy Cross Chronicles translated in the Caldwell Motherhouse Archives.

7 Sister Mary Philip Ryan, O.P., *Amid the Alien Corn* (St. Charles, Illinois: Jones Wood Press, 1967), p.24.

8 Kohler, p. 26.

9 Ryan, *op. cit.*

10 Sr. Therese Catherine, p. 11.

11 Kohler, p.30.

12 Reverend Eugene J. Crawford, M.A., *The Daughters of Dominic on Long Island* (New York: Benziger Brothers, 1938), pp. 43–44.

13 *Ibid.*, p.45.

14 *Ibid.*, p.42.

15 *Ibid.*, pp.47–48.

II. AWAKENINGS

1 Ryan, pp.3–4.

2 Most sources state that when Nicholas Balleis, O.S.B. arrived at the Redemptorist rectory he arranged that the choir sisters would stay in New York with the Ziegler Family, relatives of Sister Rita Margaret Chambers of the Caldwell Community. He took the lay sisters to his parish in Newark where they were housed by the Blaggi Family.

The Blaggi family remained benefactors of the Jersey City Community and their generosity is memorialized in a stained glass window at the Caldwell Motherhouse.

3 Crawford, p.50.

4 *Ibid.*, pp.53–57 make a careful analysis of the letter.

5 *Ibid.*, pp.94–95.

6 *Ibid.*, p.100

7– *Ibid.*, p.76

8 *Ibid.*, p.81

9 MSM, unpublished thesis, Sr. Marie Thomasine Blum, O.P., *History of the Sisters of the Third Order of St. Dominic of the Congregation of the Most Holy Rosary* (Washington, D.C.:, Catholic University, 1938), pp.20–21.

10 *Ibid.*, p.22

11 *Ibid.*, p.23

The foundation of the independent Holy Rosary Convent was governed by the law regarding the foundation of Second Order monasteries formulated by the Council of Trent: Sess. XXV de Reg. Cap. 3:

1°, that the numbers in the community do not exceed that which could be conveniently supported; and 2°, permission of the Bishop of the place in which it was erected. It was not required that this permission be given in writing, nor was any formal decree of approbation required. (Blum, 26). Further Father Crawford states that the Bishop preferred verbal agreements and therefore documentary evidence for change of canonical status is often not available (p.117)

12 Sister Mary Philomena Kildee, O.P., *Memoirs of Mother Aquinata Fiegler, O.P.* (Grand Rapids: James Bayne Co., 1928), p.24

13 *Ibid.*, pp.24–25

14 MSD, Mother Mechtilde who was present at her death bed placed the copy in the archives.

15 MSM, unpublished materials of Sr. Eugenia Globb, p.6 Since the house was not canonically dedicated as a Convent, the Sisters could not have a Chapel where the Blessed Sacrament was reserved.

16 Kildee, p.7

17 *Ibid.*, p.8

18 MSD, unpublished materials *300R*, p.11

19 Kildee, pp.29–30

20 *Ibid.*, p.31

21 MSD, *300R*, pp.11–12

22 AA, 2:38 *M.A. Corrigan Papers*, "Clerical and general correspondence." In a later correspondence, January 10, 1878 Father Kraus sent an updated report. He stated building costs at $30,000 and expressed the hope that "his orphan children" could be placed in the Sisters'

boarding school instead of his paying higher board for them in other institutions. At this time the separation of the Jersey City Community from New York was also suggested.

23 MSM, Globb, p.16
24 AA, 2:38. Since the original letter was very long and emotional in tone, paraphrasing seemed most expedient.
25 MSM, Blum, p.41
26 AA, *Bishop's Registry*, November, 1878..., pp.79–80
27 AA, 2:38
28 Sister Harriet Sanborn and Sister Mary De Haus, O.P., *Response: 1877–1977* (Grand Rapids, 1977), p.9
29 MSD, *Extracts*, p.4
30 AA, 2:38. At this time the New York Community had 6 New Jersey Missions: St. Boniface (Paterson, 1872); St. Boniface (Jersey City, 1872); St. Paul (Greenville, Jersey City, 1873); St. Mary's (Glouster, 1873); St. Joseph's (Elilzabethport, 1875); St. Mary's (Totowa, 1875)
31 MSD, *300R*, pp.13–14
32 MSM, Globb, p.10
33 MSD, Original on file
34 MSD, *Extracts*, p.4
35 MSD, original on file. The number of trustees was changed to nine in 1912 when the title was changed to Sisters of St. Dominic of Caldwell, New Jersey. In 1970 the number returned to 7.

III. SOMETHING THAT WILL ENDURE

1 John J. Catoir, *A Brief History of the Catholic Church in New Jersey* (Privately Published, 1965), p.18.
2 Complete text can be found in Joseph Flynn, *The Catholic Church in New Jersey* (N.Y., Publishers' Printing Co., 1904), pp.504–506.
3 Catoir, p.19.
4 Carl Deveroux Hinrichson, *Bishops of Newark*, unpublished Ph.D. Dissertation (Washington, D.C., Catholic University, 1962), p.130.
5 *Ibid.*, p.486.
6 *Ibid.*, p.412
7 MSD, *300R*, pp.15–16.
8 Jerome Oetgen, *An American Abbott:* Boniface Wimmer O.S.B. (LaTrobe, Pa., Archabbey Press, 1976), pp.259–269.
9 George O. Kent, *Bismarck and His Times* (Evansville: South Illinois University Press, 1978), p.88.
10 MSM, *Diary of Thomasina Primmer O.P.*, pp.4–7

11 *Ibid.*, pp.1–3.

12 MSD, oral history.

13 Sister M. Edith, O.P., "The Reverend Mother M. Beda," *Torch* (Sept., 1933), pp.16–17, 26.

14 Theodore Roemer, O.F.M. Cap., *Ten Decades of Alms* (St. Louis: B. Herder Book Co., 1942), p.111.

15 *Ibid.*, p.137.

16 *Ibid.*, p.261.

17 MSD, *300R*, p.16.

18 MSD, *Annals II*, p.20.

19 Many German girls entered at age twelve and remained as postulants for a few years. No one could make profession until she was sixteen years old. Vows were pronounced once, and for life.

20 MSD, *Minutes of the Board of Consultors I* (Nov. 25, 1893), p.18.

21 James Leity, *Charity and Correction in New Jersey* (New Brunswick: Rutgers University Press, 1967), pp.121–122. For extensive material on the plight of the immigrants in Jersey City during this period see: Mary B. Sayles, "Housing Conditions in Jersey City," *Supplement to the Annals of the American Academy of Political and Social Sciences*, January, 1903.

22 Deaths from Consumption 1884–1900. Age of deceased in parentheses. Sisters Cherubin Glaser (28), Aquinas Dolan (23), Michael Gilling (30), Patricia Symes (21), Monica Gastl (36), Alberta Weber (19), Corona Lauterback (24), Emily Harrington (18), Ligouri Fleming (23), Walburger Eisenbut (21), Genevieve Cooney (18), Anna Daschinger (21), Constantia Rehm (28), De Sales Haligan (28), Cecilia Rendale (24), Borromeo Walleitner (23), Raymond Tegerty (24), Alvara Gillmeir (28), Athanacia Maier (27), Prisca Schmalz (33), Thomas Ziegler (23), Coletta Ederer (25), Ottila Hallerl (28), Hieronyma Ederer (31), Leona Young (31), Benigna Nidermaier (29). An additional 35 deaths occured 1900–1925.

23 A.A. 3.36, *Correspondence of Bishop Wigger*. Copy may be found in MSD.

24 This building had a long interesting history. In 1779 the Methodist Assemblage bought 90½ acres and by 1782 had built a parsonage. In 1823 it was used as Calvin S. Crane Boarding School. Reverend Brown Emerson of Connecticut used it as a residence from 1843–1847 when it was bought by Dr. Maynard who sold it to Sarah E. Beach. The renovated structure served as Beach Boarding House from 1864 until 1879 when it was sold to Mr. Hidden of the Newark Glass

Company along with 30½ acres on the other side of Bloomfield Avenue.

25 MSD, Sister Aloysius Amann, O.P., *Extracts*, p.7.

26 MSD, *300R*, pp.25–28. There is good reason to question the validity of the membership quoted as 150 (p.69). The official registry lists 83 professed and 35 who would be professed by 1895.

27 The ambivalent position of proper jurisdiction for women religious was explained by Rev. M.T. Smith, O.P., in Blum, pp.25–26: "Before the Constitution "Conditae a Christo" of Leo XIII, December 8, 1900 (Fontes N. 644), congregations of simple vows were not recognized as Religious in the strict sense of the term, and the guide and norms for the establishment of these congregations was Benedict XIV's Constitution "Quamvis‾Justo" of April 30, 1749 (Fontes N. 398). This constitution prescribed no mode of approval of religious institutes. In fact, it abrogated neither the law of Innocent III (Ch. 9, X, Tit. 36, Lib. III) in the IV Lateran Council forbidding Bishops to found or approve new Orders, nor that of Pius V forbidding Congregations of women with only simple vows. It derogated from Pius V's law inasmuch as it tolerated the existence of such communities and permitted the Bishops to tolerate them and treat them favorably, and it placed them entirely under the Bishop's jurisdiction.

Obviously there is no question here of any formal Episcopal Approbation. The right of the Bishop to approve religious congregations only developed from custom contrary to the written laws, which custom was recognized as valid from Benedict XIV's "Quamvis Justo." Vague and tenuous as the right thus acquired was, there were certainly no prescriptions as to precise forms of approbation or formal decrees of erection. Benedict XIII had recognized as sufficient (in his Bull "Pretiosus" of May 25, 1727, Bull. Rom. XXII—522-554) the fact the Bishop knew of the existence of these institutes and made no objection to them ("scientibus et tacentibus Ordinariis") (CLXXVII 38).

There were no more explicit rules regarding this matter laid down until Leo XIII's "Conditae a Christo" on December 8, 1900—long after the separation of Second Street from Brooklyn, and even after the formal approbation as a Third Order by Archbishop Corrigan. We must not expect to judge acts of 1869 in the light of and under the prescriptions of the law of 1900, or of the Code, and it does not follow that an element now prescribed for validity or liceity was necessary for either at that time. In fact, as Maroto says, the validity of foundations with merely equivalent approbation before the Code was certain, and the sanatio of 1922 was only ad cautelam.

...that a formal decree of erection was not essential to validity is borne out by a decree of the Sacred Congregation of Religious of Nov. 30, 1922, directing Ordinaries to draw up a decree of erection for every diocesan community which lacked one, which decree should have the effect of sanating any canonical defects in its foundation, should such sanation be necessary 'quatenus opus fuerit.' This last phrase shows, as Shafer points out, that it was a clarifying decree which removing uncertainty and implicitly approved congregations, made probable legitimacy thereafter certain."

28 Copy in MSD archives. Data concerning the foundation of the Board and the role of the spiritual director, *Minutes of the Board of Consultors, 1893–1918*, pp.1–3.

29 A.A. 3.38, *Correspondence of Bishop Wigger and the Dominican Sisters, 1887–1894.*

30 Mother M. Da Frose, O.P., *The Noble Heritage of the Congregation of the Immaculate Heart of Mary, Akron Ohio* (unpublished work, OLE archives: 1945), pp.117–119.

31 MSD, *Minutes*, p.12.

32 It is interesting to note that in each place the Sisters purchased their own convent and named it. (St. Boniface School—St. Dominic Convent; St. Venantius—Sacred Heart; St. Mary's—St. Catherine's). Perhaps this is indicative of a desire to become independent cloistered houses as numbers warranted it.

33 Da Frose, pp.117–119.

34 Copy in MSD.

35 MSD, *Minutes*, p.23.

36 Katherine Burton, *All the Way to Heaven* (Bronxville, 1958), p.50.

37 *Ibid.*, p.49.

38 *Ibid.*, p.54.

39 Blum, pp.28–29.

40 Blum, p.29.

41 A.A. 3.38, *Bishop Wigger: Religious Community Correspondence* (Dominican Sisters, 1884–1886).

42 *Ibid.*

43 *Ibid.*

44 *Ibid.*

45 Burton, p.58.

46 *Ibid.*, p.53.

47 Original in MSD.
48 MSD, *Minutes*, p.113.
49 *Ibid.*, p.115.
50 *Ibid.*, p.126.

IV. DIVIDE AND MULTIPLY

1 *Minutes* (1893–1918), p.171.
2 Marie Seuffert, the aunt of Mildred Seuffert, a staff member of Caldwell College, forwarded correspondence that reveals something of the local color of the village. "At the time I stayed at the Villa 1915 to 1917 I took private lessons every day at the Academy as I had to leave grammar school early due to the fact my Mother took sick and I was the only one able to take care of her. I had to make up two years of schooling before I could take the business course.... In those years we called the center of town the Village. It had a movie house and a little drug store where students from the Academy went for sundaes. We called them mysteries because the proprietor would put everything in them but would tell no one just how he made them. At the end of Bloomfield Avenue was the Monomonock Inn, a very exclusive place where elite events took place.
3 MSD, original on file.
4 The list included: one Iron Bedstead, a mattress, two pillows, two blankets, one comfortable, one white spread, 6 sheets, four night-gowns, six changes of underclothing, twelve pairs of Summer and Winter stockings, twelve handkerchiefs, six towels, six table napkins, a set of silverware, one black shawl, two black dresses and capes, two dark gingham aprons, six white aprons, three pairs of high button shoes, one pair of rubbers, six pairs of collars and cuffs, one piece of shaker flannel, one piece of white muslin.
5 See Appendix A. (profession 1913)
6 The ferry cost $.03 but the Sisters often did not have to pay.
7 Crawford, pp.318–19.
8 See Appendix B for names of the Novice and Postulant Mistresses. From 1881–1920 Novices and postulants lived together and had the same Mistress. For the next seven years the groups were placed under different Sisters. By 1955 when postulant classes were larger they were again separated.
9 Crawford, p.354, quotation from circular letter of Master General Martin Gillet, March 7, 1930.
10 The new code was promulgated by 1918.

11 MSD, *Board of Consultors Minutes* II (1918–1926), pp.8, 10.

12 In 1930 the custom of renewing vows annually for five years was introduced. The present *Constitutions* offers the professed the option of annual renewal, or renewal for two three-year periods, and final profession may be requested after three years.

13 This was the daily routine from the Chapter of 1912 until recent times.

14 MSD, *Minutes* I, p.197.

15 MSD, oral history. Though the Sisters were always conscious of the needs of orphans they never intended to adopt the care of orphans as an apostolic ministry. It is clear that funds collected for orphans were used to take care of the educational and residential expenses of needy children. Sisters Rita and Mannis entered the Community after spending ten years under the care of the Sisters.

16 Sister Clarice from the Akron Community told the author that Mother Mechtilde came to Lawrence and asked if any qualified eighth grade graduate wanted to come to the Mount as a scholarship student. Clarice came as a scholarship boarder and gradually Mother Mechtilde "helped her to see that she had a religious vocation."

17 MSD, copy of anonymous material on file.

18 MSD, *Necrology* 1939–1945, pp.34–36 for specific details.

19 MSD, letter received from Father Halliwell.

20 MSD, *Minutes* I, p.198.

21 The gimp was one yard of linen material. You doubled the piece and dipped it into cold starch. Then you placed it on a wooden triangle board to put in the creases after pleating (eight inches from the top) with your fingers. Then the completed piece was placed in the sun to dry. Sister Amabilis went on to say that the gimp was beautiful but the process was very time consuming and exasperating.

22 MSD, *Minutes* I, p.202. Though cloaks are no longer worn and the Hours are chanted in English, the *O Sacred Banquet* is still said if the prayers are celebrated in the presence of the Blessed Sacrament.

23 MSD, copy of letter from Apostolic delegate can be found in the *Hurley, Wisconsin file.*

24 MSD, copy in Hurley file.

25 *Ibid.*

26 MSD, original suggestions on file.

27 These regulations mirrored the contemporary sense of religious discipline and regulated relationships between members of the Community as well as those with "externes". Copy to be found in *Minutes of General Chapters 1915–1951.*

28 MSD, *Minutes* I, p.241.
29 MSD, *Minutes of General Chapters 1921*, p.4.
30 MSD, copy on file.
31 The information pertaining to the Ohio Missions is quoted from Mother M. Da Frose O.P., Chapters 5–8 unless otherwise noted. Only direct quotes will be acknowledged individually.
32 Da Frose, p.148.
33 OLE, *Minutes Book of Council*, p.6 quoted from unpublished work of Mother Rosario O.P.
34 OLE, oral history obtained from Sister Matilda, June 11, 1980.
35 Da Frose, p.164.
36 *Ibid.*, p.165.
37 *Ibid.*
38 *Ibid.*, p.168.
39 MSD, *Extracts*, p.18a.
40 Da Frose, p.169 and *Ibid.*, 18b.
41 *Ibid.*, pp.170–1. A simple ceremony was adopted by all Dominican Congregations in 1930.
42 It was decided to build a new school which cost $26,490.14.
43 MSD, letter on file. Rev. Fintan Gesser, O.S.B., *The Canon Law Governing Communities of Sisters* (St. Louis: B. Herder, 1956). pp.46–51 explains process of application.
44 MSD, *Extracts*, p.17.
45 MSD, *Minutes* III (1926–1943), p.27 (Aug. 2, 1925).
46 *Ibid*, p.37.
47 *Ibid*, p.35.
48 *Ibid*, p.44.
49 *Ibid*, p.43.
50 *Ibid*, p.50.
51 *Ibid*, p.47.
52 OLE, *Annals I*, p.4, quoted from Sr. Rosario's unpublished work, p.19.
53 Sixty seven members signed for affiliation.

FINAL PROFESSED

1. Sister M. Magdalene Lechner
2. Sister M. Pia Reim
3. Sister M. Yolanda Loesch
4. Sister M. Bernadette Lehner
5. Sister M. Luca Altschaffel
6. Sister M. Jordani Forster
7. Sister M. Ignatia Meindl
8. Sister M. Villani Miendl
9. Sister M. Scholastica Deter
10. Sister M. Ambrose Reichert

11. Sister M. de Ricci Barkley
12. Sister M. Venantia Lechner
13. Sister M. Beda Schmid
14. Sister M. Clarissa Attenberger
15. Sister M. Rosario Klimmer
16. Sister M. Regina Meyer
17. Sister M. Henrietta Weaver
18. Sister M. Justina Oberdoerster
19. Sister M. Jeannette Kimpflin
20. Sister M. George Fendt
21. Sister M. Cornelia Jacobs
22. Sister M. Matilda Bechter
23. Sister M. Petronilla Gosser
24. Sister M. Clare McCowen
25. Sister M. Josepha Werner
26. Sister M. Florentine Paridon
27. Sister M. Bernard Friess
28. Sister M. Dominic Bihler
29. Sister M. Clarita Bernard
30. Sister M. Victor Geis
31. Sister M. Austin Bernard
32. Sister M. Clarice Gansirt
33. Sister M. Paschal Dillon
34. Sister M. Romaine Sartory
35. Sister M. Constantia Schreiner
36. Sister M. Helen Pikunas
37. Sister M. Ralph Koeberle
38. Sister M. Mercia Boyle
39. Sister M. Bernice Roussert
40. Sister M. Stella Romito

TEMPORARY VOWS
41. Sister M. Ricardo Fanelly
42. Sister M. Bertha Klein
43. Sister M. Benita Kinsinger
44. Sister M. Dominica Pangburn
45. Sister M. Josephine Riffel
46. Sister M. Elizabeth Moine
47. Sister M. Cecilia Bauman
48. Sister M. Colette Tapp
49. Sister M. Theresa McGuckin
50. Sister M. Laurene Kleinwechter
51. Sister M. Margarita Walsh
52. Sister M. Rosalia Paulus
53. Sister M. Seraphina Summers
54. Sister M. Magdalena Karam
55. Sister M. Marcelline Oyster
56. Sister M. Miria Shutler
57. Sister M. Eucharia Zwick
58. Sister M. Dolorosa Muzik
59. Sister M. Lorita Gerbec
60. Sister M. Coletta Ruhlin

NOVICES
61. Sister M. Christine Lintol
62. Sister M. Agatha Miller
63. Sister M. Birginette Werner
64. Sister M. Margaret Rody
65. Sister M. Cecile Wagner
66. Sister M. Dolores Hohman
67. Sister M. Roselyn Weigand

54 MSD, *Minutes III*, p.53.
55 *Ibid*, p.54.
56 MSD, report of bursar on file: $75,592.86 (interest and taxes), $32,000 (assessments)
57 MSD, copy on file. The final agreement abrogates any payment of assessments so further investigation of the discrepancy that exists in available sources is unnecessary.
58 Da Frose, pp.177–178.
59 MSD, correspondence June through November 1930 on file.

60 MSD, *Minutes of General Chapter*, 1933, p.4.
61 MSD, eulogy on file.
62 *Ibid.*
63 OLE, oral history
64 MSD, Paul C. Perrotta, *Personal Tribute*
65 See Appendix B.
66 MSD, eulogy

V. NEW CREATION AMIDST DEPRESSION

1 In collaboration with William H.J. Kennedy, President of the Teacher's College in Boston, Massachusetts, Mother wrote a series of books on United States History (elementary grades: *America's Story* (1926), *The United States (1926; 1932); Old World Foundations of the United States* (1926); *America's Founders and Leaders* (1928); *Today and Yesterday* (1937) and *Before America Began* (1937), published by Benziger Brothers, New York.
2 Appendix C
3 Sr. Lucille Collins, O.P., *The Vision Is Tremendous* (Sparkill, N.Y.: Congregation of Our Lady of the Rosary, 1975), "Foreword" by Cardinal Cooke.
4 Da Frose, pp.124–127 provides additional details of this early mission.
5 MSD, Oral history, Sister Inez, September 1980
6 MSD, *Minutes* I, p.225.
7 Sister Inez, Ibid., From this time until 1931 the second floor of the Motherhouse was used as the Chaplain's quarters, the third floor was the Novitiate dormitory and the fourth, a classroom and community room for the novices and postulants.
8 The school stopped accepting boys from Grades 4–8 in 1920. By the 1940s it became a private girl's school but boys were once again registered for Kindergarten 1978–1980.
9 *Caldwell Progress* (August 18, 1939), pp.1, 5
10 MSD, complete text on file
11 MSD, complete text on file
12 MSD, complete text on file
13 MSD, financial statement indicates the promised and actualized payments May 1930 through October 1931.
14 MSD, copy in MSDA file.
15 MSD, copy on file.
16 MSD, Annual scrapbooks
17 MSD, copy of article from *West Essex News* (June 17, 1942) contained in annual scrapbook.

18 Senior class enrollment by years: 1943 (18), 1944 (25), 1945 (31), 1948 (50), 1949 (35), 1951 (48)

19 MSD, annual scrapbook

20 High school boarders resided in St. John's, Ryerson Avenue, until 1958 when the school adopted a fully commuter status.

21 *MSDA Student Handbook* (1980–81), p.3.

22 Monsignor Duffy acted as the administrator of the diocese from the death of Bishop O'Connor (May 1927) until the consecration of Bishop Walsh (March 2, 1928).

23 *Ibid*, pp.2.

24 MSD, *Minutes* II, p.207. *The Short History* states that Monsignor McClary suggested the name.

25 CC, contained in a synopsis called *Caldwell College At-A-Glance*, p.1–2.

26 CC, *Excerpts*, p.1.

27 *Ibid*, p.2.

28 CC, *History* 1939–1945 on file.

29 CC, complete form available.

30 CC, data included in letter sent to Reverend Daniel Lord, April 1947.

31 For a complete narrative concerning the history, ceremonial and significance of the College traditions consult, CC, Dolores Ernst, *The Traditions of Caldwell College*, paper researched for Siena Scholars.

32 MSD, oral history, Sister Joanna, November 1980.

33 CC, correspondence of Sister Raymond.

34 CC, *Ibid.*, May 16, 1944.

35 CC, copy of her report and all Middle States recommendations on file.

36 CC, compiled from miscellaneous sources in file.

37 Floyd Anderson, "Caldwell College, only Catholic College for Women in the Archdiocese of Newark", *The Advocate* (May 24, 1952), p.5.

38 *Ibid*.

39 Enrollment: 1958...297
                1962...650
Faculty: 1958 (Sisters 30, Priests 2, Lay Faculty 6; 1962 (Sisters 31, Priests 3, Lay Faculty 14)

40 CC, complete text on file

41 *Carillon* 1964

42 Complete text on file.

43 CC, for statistical information and development plans see Sr. Anne John, *Position Paper on Caldwell College*, presented as a report to the Community General Chapter 1975.

44 CC, *NASDTEC Report*, p.8

45 Copy of full text on file.

46 Annual report 1979–80, p.1

47 *Montclair Times* article found in School Scrapbook I, p.1.

48 All of the material is collated from the School Annals 1920–1939 unless otherwise noted.

49 Until the late 1960s Barclay Street in Downtown New York City was the location of many religious goods stores.

50 *Annals*, p.38.

51 *Ibid.*

52 MSD, *Minutes* V (1957–59), p.45

53 *Ibid*, p.94.

54 MSD, *Minutes* VI (1959–61), p.258

55 *Joy in the Arts*, (Spring, 1965), Foreword

56 Its history as an accredited high school begins in 1913.

57 SDA, *Trumpet* (October 1956), p.2

58 Jeanette Will, *"Dia Pollo Society,"* Yearbook 1909.

59 SDA Yearbook 1912.

60 MSD, *Minutes* I, p.190

61 The Hill is a colloqualism for Upper Jersey City or the Heights.

62 MSD, *Minutes* I, p.235.

63 Mary Fleckenstein, "Our New Home," *SDA Yearbook 1916*, pp. 29–30.

64 This Church is still the site for SDA graduations.

65 MSD, *Minutes* II, p.228

66 *Ibid.*, p.232

67 *Ibid.*, p.233

68 *Ibid.*, p.237

69 The "sanctity" of Madonna Hall was often violated by the daring student who looked both ways and zipped through in order to avoid going all the way downstairs or all the way upstairs to crossover to the Duncan Avenue side classrooms or the Principal's office.

70 No student "dared" to climb the beautiful red staircase leading to the Cloister.

71 Sr. Madonna Kelly, O.P., "Dominican Development is Moral and Intellectual," *The Trumpet* (October 1956), p.2.

72 The title comes from a quotation about St. Vincent Ferrer: "When his resonant voice rang out, it was like a penetrating blast from a silver trumpet."

73 It was feared that the 70s would witness a great demographic change in

the urban areas and watchful waiting seemed to be the best policy. Though enrollment did fluctuate: 445 (70–71); 423 (71–71); 418 (72–73); 390 (73–74), there has been a constant increase since them.

74 The facilities made expansion of athletics viable. The rates have increased over a three year period from $35 to $45 a year per student but everyone feels the money is justified in terms of the services rendered.

75 "Year of Experiment Begins", *The Trumpet* (May, 1978), p.1.

76 One hundred thirty-six young women applied for this program from its inception in 1928 through its closing in 1959. Of this number sixty-one actually entered religious life, and of these, all but one, entered the Caldwell Dominicans.

77 See Appendix C for Juniorate Mistresses 1929–1959.

78 The Scholasticate program was established for the profession class of 1931 but because of the apostolic needs of the schools the program was abandoned in 1934. The idea was resurrected again in 1959.

79 MSD, *Minutes* 1926–1943, p.89

80 The distinction in veil design remained the individuating factor until the early 70s when various experiments in dress made it necessary to design a pin, or pendant to indicate the particular congregation. The Caldwell design can be found on the back cover of this book.

81 See Appendix B.

82 Minutes, *Ibid*,

83 It must be noted that though the mission was in the South the volunteers did not have to be, and for the most part were not Sisters of weak health. The climate of the Bayou was damp and humid not conducive to lung care and the work was not part-time catechetics but full-time parochial education.

84 The author is indebted to Sister Patricia Ann who researched and transcribed much of the early history.

85 The Camp opened in 1921 and closed in 1960. Lasting friendships between the Franciscans and Dominicans and the children of Jersey City were formed at "Butler University", the pet-name for this experience in education.

86 In 1932 the swimming was done in a small canvas pool placed near the field past the playground (present site of Student Center). By 1934 a sand box, footbath and cement pool had been built on the site of the present Student Center Parking Lot. From 1935 until the camp closed in 1960 Sunnyfield pool in West Caldwell was used.

87 Sisters James and Bartholomew were the beloved perfects of the early

stages of the camp. Later Dominicans who directed the camp's summer experience for year-round residents and others were Sisters Walter, Helen George, and Incarnata. The revenue obtained was used to run the Camp and the surplus was used toward payment of the Motherhouse loans.

88 MSD, *Minutes* III, p.235.

89 Canon law requires that the Community apply to Rome to get approval for a third consecutive term.

90 MSD, *Minutes* III, p.139.

91 During the late 30s the Council had considered other uses for the building. Justin Routh O.P., the national director of the Holy Name Society had suggested the building be used for a Retreat Center, while Edward Hughes, O.P., the director of the Third Order Tertiaries had hoped to convert it into a house for professional Tertiaries who could then share a common life.

92 At this time the diocese is planning for the demolition of the building.

93 MSD, *Annals 1933*, p.7. Though the Motherhouse indebtedness was recognized as a total Community responsibility and revenues were forwarded as needed, it must be noted that many times local needs (viz. expansion of facilities at St. Dominic Academy or Lacordaire) were often unanswered in order to meet other financial obligations.

94 MSD, Eulogy on file.

VI. EXPANSION AND CONTINUOUS GROWTH

1 Even though Sister Veronica had declared herself ineligible because of ill health she was elected on the second ballot. She declined and a third ballot was taken.

2 MSD, *Minutes of the General Chapter* (1945), p.8.

3 This tradition continued and later took the form of selling a $10.00 chance book on a car raffle.

4

	1916	1947
Newark	400 per month	600
Trenton	300	450

5 The salary of religious women must enable them to provide for the physical needs (food, clothing, medicine, etc.) of the Sisters on the mission and to forward half of the monthly money to support the needs of the Motherhouse's unsalaried members, to maintain Community properties, and to reduce outstanding debts.

6 MSD, Minutes (1953–57), p.172.

7 Up until this time if your baptismal name had already been given to

another Sister, you were directed to take as your name in religion, your baptismal name and an additional one. From 1949 until the late 50s the single name tradition applied. Then the largeness of classes necessitated greater freedom in choosing a new name. After Vatican II many Sisters opted to return to the use of their baptismal (legal) names.

8 MSD, *Minutes of the General Chapter* (1951), p.7.

9 *Ibid.*, total decreased $243,797.89.

10 *Ibid.*, pp.9–10 for complete list.

11 Prior to this you could enter August 15 or February 2. By 1957 the date was again changed to September 8. At present the entrance date varies but is within the first week of September.

12 MSD, *Minutes* IV, p.16.

13 *Advocate* (Jan. 17, 1953), p.1.

14 *Ibid.*, p.3.

15 *Ibid.*, p.110.

16 *Ibid.*, p.165.

17 MSD, "Eulogy," p.5.

18 *Ibid.*, p.3.

19 See Appendix B.

20 MSD, "Eulogy," p.4.

21 MSD, *Annals* 1957–1963, p.5

22 aggiornamento—renewal that implies the adaptation of past traditions to a contemporary setting.

23 Since Caldwell's pre-entrance program was called the Juniorate (1928–1959) they use the term Scholasticate to avoid confusion.

24 Sister Bertrande Meyers, D.C., *Sisters for the 21st Century* (New York: Sheed and Ward, 1965), p.56.

25 *Ibid.*, p.127.

26 MSD, Minutes (1959–1961), p.200.

27 The program is explained in Chapter VII.

28 John Byrider, brother of Sister Charles, was instrumental in buying the house and equipping it adequately.

29 MSD, oral history, Mother Dolorita.

30 MSD, *Minutes* (1957–59), p.77.

31 The Guild under the direction of Sister Alouise and later Sister Margaret continued fund raising for the Infirmary by sponsoring social affairs. The annual St. Patrick's dinner dance is a part of the Caldwell tradition.

This Guild had a sister group called the St. Dominic Guild which was founded during the depression to assist the Sisters in getting food for their boarders and themselves. This West Essex group continued to contribute annually to the Infirmary. Their Spring Card Party is another tradition.

32 MSD, *Minutes* (1959–1961), p.160.

33 *Ibid.*, p.162.

34 MSD, the Counselling Service prospectus is on file.

35 MSD, *Minutes* (1959–1961), p.181.

36 *Ibid.*, p.202.

37 *Ibid.*, p.256.

38 MSD, Annals 1957–1963, pp.15–16.

39 For the documents, commentaries, and introductory remarks consult Walter M. Abbott, S.J. (Gen. Ed.), *The Documents of Vatican II*, (New York: America Press, 1966)

40 *Ibid.*, "Introduction," p.XVIII.

41 MSD, *Annals* 1963–1969, p.6

42 The Community membership in 1963 and 1969 was 574.

43 See Appendix B.

44 MSD, *Annals* 1963–1969, pp.26–28.

45 MSD, "A Necessary Point of View" (1968), p.1

46 *Ibid*, p.6.

47 The idea for the project was first recommended by Sister Vivien Jennings in a position paper, "Poverty and the Apostolate of Service," 1968.

48 MSD, Mother Dolorita. *Report to General Chapter 1969.* p.5.

VII. TOWARD RENEWAL

1 Most available works were on Dominican Spirituality and the history of the First Order with some treatment of contemplative and active women Dominicans. Most were authentic, highly documented, generally helpful in understanding the essentials, but largely from a masculine European perspective. The works of Mother Theodosia Drane and Hortense Kohler did provide some feminine dimension and in each succeeding decade additional material became available.

2 John Baptist Reeves, O.P., in *The Dominicans* (Dubuque, Priority Press, 1961), pp.13–14 asserts "that amongst the orders most important characteristics is a temper at once conservative and progressive. It clings tenaciously to all the traditions it embodies; yet it cannot endure that their development should stand still for a moment. In its own affairs, and in the works for which it was created by the Church, it has

always shown a remarkable genius for the continuous development of old institutions, suitable to the needs of each succeeding age, and without the least disfigurement or mutilation of any growth that has preceded."

The recent histories of women's communities and a survey of the processes and products of years of experimentation formulated in life-giving Constitutions testify that the Dominican character is at home among them.

3 MSD, *To Praise, To Bless, To Preach.* The Vocation of the Dominican Sister—A Timeless Challenge, (Caldwell, 1972) p.3.

4 For a little more background on the spirit, facts and directions of Women's Constitutions see Sister Clemente Dalvin, O.P. "Early Dominican Constitutions for Women" (Sinsinawa, Wisconsin: June 15, 1977)

In order to understand the Caldwell directions in a proper light one would have to do careful reading of the minutes, annals and Chapter reports from 1893 to the present which indicate a gradual desire, willingness and ability to absorb more control over the Community's destiny within prescribed norms. Sometimes dreams and plans were limited by ecclesiastical authority while at others, dreams and plans became a reality only through the encouragement and with the financial assistance of Diocesan administrators. *"In medio stat virtu—* is the norm for assessing the interaction.

5 There are six Standing Committees: Person and Community, Formation, Apostolate, Government, Finance, and Public Relations.

The Person and Community's areas of responsibility include: spiritual life (liturgy, retreats, renewal programs, recollection days, confessors, conferences, spiritual workshops, and religion/theology courses), social activities, vacations, retirement plan, health, and funeral arrangements. The Committee is composed of six elected members, one of whom is elected strictly for liturgy. A Dominican liturgist, an M.D., and a head nurse serve as Consultants to the Committee.

The Formation Committee's areas of responsibility include programs for all stages of Formation: vocation, recruitment, applicancy, postulancy, novitiate, and scholasticate. The membership of the Committee is made up of 1) a Director of Postulants, Novices, and Scholastics; 2) a Director of Academic Studies; 3) a Vocation Director; and 4) four elected Sisters, two of whom are local superiors. A priest, a psychologist, and an M.D. serve as Consultants.

The Apostolate Committe's areas of responsibility include: education (elementary, secondary, college, and religious), professional preparation of all Sisters, the apostolate to the poor, and other apostolic activities. The composition of the Apostolate Committee is carefully prescribed. Chaired by the Councillor for Apostolate, the Committee has four ex-officio members: the Academic Dean of Caldwell College; the Director of Academic Studies for Religious (an ex-officio member of the Standing Committee on Formation), who heads a sub-committee; the Coordinating Supervisor, who heads sub-committees for k–4, 5–8, and 9–12, and a sub-committee on special services; and the Religious Education Director, also in charge of a subcommittee. Additionally, the Apostolate Committee has four elected members: the Service Coordinator, who heads a subcommittee; and three other members. Consultants are chosen as needed.

The Government Committee's areas of responsibility include: superiors' workshops, guide in selections of superiors; guide for further experimentation, Directory up-date, definition of responsibilities of Community officials, the set up of Community voting procedure, and direct preparation for Chapters. Membership on the Committee is made up of two superiors and four non-superiors, all six of whom are elected. A Canon lawyer serves as Consultant.

The Finance Committee, headed by the Bursar General, is responsible for the organization of the community financial structure, individual house assessments, and reports and forms to be used by all bursars. The College Bursar is a member of the Committee, as are 5 elected members: one priory bursar, one convent bursar, and three other Sisters. A Certified Public Accountant and a financial advisor serve as Consultants.

The Secretary General chairs the Public Relations Committee which is responsible for two main areas: secretarial and public relations. Included in secretarial responsibilities are the Archives, a cross-file for Sisters, minutes of Council Meetings, correspondence of the Major Superior, and notices to the Community. Public Relations duties include the Office of Public Information, a quarterly newsletter, a monthly calendar, an annual Directory, a speaker's bureau, and vocation literature. The Committee is made up of four elected members. Consultants are a professional public relations agent and staff representatives of each major publication in New Jersey.

6 See Appendix C for specific councillors.

7 *Ibid*

8 The change was proposed because it seemed that the decreasing

number of Sisters dictated a corresponding decrease in the number of Sisters involved in Community leadership. It will be evaluated and can be changed if it does not meet Community need.

9 Anne Buckley, "She's used to Being Youngest", *The Advocate*, July 31, 1969. The title indicates that Sister Vivien was elected by postulation. She had just turned thrity-five and required a dispensation for Canon Law's 40-year age requirement. A telegram had been sent by Reverend Gerald Ruane (Chaplain) on June 30 and a second on July 2: *"Sister Vivien Jennings Dominican Caldwell received over two-thirds votes for Major Superior June 16th. Archbishop mailed the documents thereafter. Sister possesses highest qualifications, most dedicated religious___ answer to Jersey quickly as possible. (Ruane, Chaplain)".*

On July 26, 1969 the formal announcement of the dispensation and the result of the now licit and valid election was sent to the Community by Sister M. Angelica the Chapter Secretary.

10 Paraphrase of welcome address January 25, 1981, Centenary Mass at St. John's Church, Jersey City.

11 The report handles the many paradoxes which define the spirit and facts of the history of 1975–79.

12 *Sisters of St. Dominic Constitutions*, 1979, p.12.

13 All Congregations faced and are facing the same dilemmas. Though the changes eventually "look the same", each congregation had a unique path to trod.

14 MSD, copy of the survey and a comparison of the Caldwell and National percentages in specific answers provides a statistical explanation for our evolutionary approach to changes.

15 In the beginning many psalm books and hymnals were used and daily liturgists prepared specific themes—the Caldwell "paper chase." The one volume Liturgy of the Hours (the daily psalmody, readings and prayers of the universal church) is used by most houses and daily choral recitation with openness to local variations is the norm.

16 MSD, *1972 Chapter Report*, p.4. "Both young and old alike have made the observation to me (Sister Rita Margaret) that they came to religious life believing that they would have the atmosphere, the time, and the support of their sisters both in daily prayer and more intense times of recollection but that the real rhythm of the contemplative life is no longer available to them."

17 1975–77 Directions; 1977–79 the "Action for Independent Maturity program was adopted to the needs and interests of our Sisters.

18 Buckley.

19 *Constitutions,* p.17.

20 MSD, *Master Plan*, p.4. Sisters struggle to overcome "the boarding house mentality" associated with absence from commuity because of apostolic demands or individual spiritual, liturgical and recreational choices.

21 See Appendix C.

22 Affiliates, postulants and novices.

23 Junior professed sisters.

24 The Institute was the response of Sister Agnes Bernard, O.P. (Caldwell) and Sister Mary George R.S.M. (Plainfield) to diminishing numbers in congregational formation groups and the continuing need for quality spiritual and theological education. In the beginning members in the initial and scholasticate stages of formation from the Congregations represented in National Formation region 3 (New Jersey and eastern Pennsylvania) and especially the communities in the North Jersey sub-divison could take thrity-three credits (courses offered by highly qualified personnel), a three credit seminar and a comprehensive examination in order to achieve a certificate. The courses were accredited through Caldwell College and certificates were awarded. The program began in 1970 was formally disbanded in 1980.

25 All areas of formation will be explained at the end of the Chapter.

26 There were two postulants. This move to place postulant-formation in a mission followed a national trend. There were no postulants in 1978. In 1979 there was one postulant, and in 1980 there were two.

27 In 1975 there were two first and second year novices; 1976: two and two; 1977 three and three; 1978: two and two, 1979: one and zero.

28 In 1975 there were 21 scholastics; 1976, 14; 1977, 11; 1979, 11. In that time seven left the community at the expiration of vows and thirteen made final vows.

29 There have been four volunteers in that time: Kim Urban (Alabama), Fran Kujalowicz (Infirmary); Mary Frances Evans (Abaco); Karen Sciaraffa (Project Link.) Fran and Karen decided to enter after their year as a volunteer. Sister Jo Mascera is the present co-ordinator.

30 Every candidate receives the pages of the Journal which apply to her current status so that from the initial response through Final profession she can record her personal journey-story; be challenged by its Scriptural and personal questionnaires to deeper awareness, and make a daily recommitment.

A. *Affiliate:* one who is discerning a readiness to accept commitment to religious life according to the Caldwell Model. She may keep her present status (job, student) and live at home or in community. She makes no commitment.

B. *Postulant:* one who makes application to enter, lives in Community and prepares herself for novitiate. The time of the postulancy is left to the discernment of the individual and the decision of the Formation Team and Council.

C. *Novice:* one who enters a year of stillness to experience interior growth and a deepening knowledge of the vows, the Dominican spirit and apostolic focus and Community direction. The Novitiate includes apostolic experience and generally embraces a first year canonical presence and a second year apostolic mission-based experience before requesting first profession. A final month of presence is required immediately before profession.

D. *Scholastic:* one who matures through her mission-based common life and apostolic experiences and discerns readiness for final commitment. The Scholastic may make first profession for one or three years and may ask to make final profession any time after the first three years.

31 MSD, *Formation Focus*, "Final profession."
32 MSD, *Government Committee Statement*, 1972.
   Collegiality means co-responsibility in decision-making. The principle requires that all those affected by a decision should be involved in the making of that decision. Subsidiarity implies the process of delegating authority. The principal is simply that the authority to make a decision should be placed as close as possible to the point where the decision's impact will be felt.
33 MSD, *Constitutions*, p.18.
34 Sister Mary Luke Tobin, Position paper: "Government in Religious Community Today", March 1967, p.1.
35 The Community is divided into five age groups (those professed more than 50 years; 41–50 years; 31–40 years, 22–30 years; 21 or fewer years. Each group receives 18% of the delegation and 10% of the delegates are elected at large. Each Chapter will evaluate the apportionment and see if the various interest groups and apostolates remain adequately represented.
36 The number of houses choosing to elect has increased each year. Once the Sisters sensed that the legal statute and the local community discernment was a contemporary mode for the will of God to be

manifest, tensions concerning the option lessened and its use became more the norm.

During the 70s certain houses expanded the option to the election of superiors for 1/3 of the year so that more people could experience the role; in large houses several superiors were elected to provide better possibility for one-on-one or small group interaction.

37 MSD, Sister Catherine Bernadette file, "A Possible Approach," p.1.

38 At this Chapter terms were made four years instead of six. No one can be re-elected to the same position for more than two consecutive terms.

39 In Newark, The Sisters' Assembly has functioned as a forum for representatives to support efforts concerning social justice issues, understanding new ministerial roles in the Church, and other timely topics. They have periodically made recommendations to the ordinary and representatives have been requested to join diocesan committees. Sister Rita Margaret, Sister Maura Campbell and Sister Margie Jaros have served as Caldwell representatives while Sister Barbara Moore was its vice-president 1978–80 and Sister Alice Matthew its president 1979-80.

40 Though the experience was draining it certainly manifested the truth that each Caldwell Dominican had deep convictions and had learned how to articulate them.

41 Sister Vivien, *State of the Community Message 1972*, p.5.

42 The author is indebted to Edward Farrell who coined the pattern of co-founding and confounding in his work *Disciples and other Strangers*, "Disciple: Discovering a Kinship of Grace" (Denville, N.J.: Dimension Books, 1974), pp.32–43.

43 Sister Bertrand, O.P., *Report to the 1979 General Chapter*, Appendix II.

44 MSD, *Constitutions*, p.23.

45 *Ibid.*

46 Since we desired to set up a "foreign mission" expeditiously, language study seemed unrealistic.

47 Sister Bertrand, p.1.

48 *Ibid*, p.2.

49 MSD, Apostolate file describes the self study process in detail. Six of the schools scheduled for community withdrawal have obtained the services of another congregation.

50 *Constitutions,* p.47. As of 1980 the Community services 23 parish schools, two regional high schools, three community academies and

Caldwell College in four counties of New Jersey, and the dioceses of Newark, Paterson, Mobile (Alabama), Bridgeport (Connecticut), and Abaco (Bahamas). Of the 292 active sisters in 1979, 234 were involved in teaching school and administration, 26 in community service and 32 in religious education, diocesan vocation work and school supervision, pastoral or clinical ministry, health care and social justice research or advocacy roles.

51 Sister Vivien, p.4.
52 *Constitutions*, p.11.
53 Sister Edith Madgalen, *Financial Report to the General Chapter 1979*, p.1.
54 Census 1979: 122 unsalaried sisters; 30 partially salaried, total in community 387.
55 In 1969 the yearly salary was $1944.00; in 1973 $3,000 plus $300 for medical insurance and social security and as of 1979 $4716.80 plus $300.00. Similar negotiations are held to negotiate salaries of lay personnel.
56 Sister Edith Magdalen, cover letter.
57 *Dominican Charism*, position paper of the Dominican Leadership Conference 1975

APPENDIX A

Membership: Listed in *Vital Statistics Registry* by year of first profession. Italicized names indicate members who joined Akron Community by 1929. + indicates deceased members. Names in parenthesis indicate change of religious name after Vatican II. • indicates members who have left the Community.

1868: + Mother Catherine Muth
1874: + Sister Joanna Schuttinger
1875: + Mother Mechtilde Ostendarp
1876: + Sister Lucy McDonald, Sister Seraphica Lang
1877: + Sister Angelica Schlutter
1878: + Sister Alacoque Hartel
1879: + Sister Mary Philip Roche, Sister Basil Seidl
1880: + Sister Benvenuta Knight
1881: + Sister Josephine Vogel
1883: + Mother Avelline Quinn, Sister Dominica Kunz
1884: + Sister Augustine Lang
1885: + Sister Teresa Nixon
1886: + Sister Frances Reim, Sister Antoninus Schabenberger, Sister Hyacinth Hertrich, Sister Rose Kunz
1887: + Sister Gonzaga Strasser, *Sister Yolanda Loesch*, Sister Reginald Rosch, Sister Charitine Verhaegen; •Catherine Kiley

1888: + Sister Imelda Steinberger, Sister Cecilia Verhaegen, Sister Stanislaus Strasser, Sister Paula Geltermair, Sister Amanda Purcell, Sister Loretta Gmach, Sister Bernardine Kottermair

1889: + Sister Gertrude Birkmeyer, Sister Celestine Kienlein, *Sister Bernadette Lehner,* Sister Adalbert Strasser

1890: + Sister Casilda Johnson, *Sister Ignatia Meindl,* Sister Clementine Kottermair, Sister Camilla Brennan, Sister Chrysostoma Binder, *Sister Jordani Forster*

1891: + Sister Alexia Bischoff, Sister Antonia Wolf, *Sister Ambrose Reichert,* Sister Innocents Storzinger, Sister Veronica Murrer, Sister Barnaba Kenney; •Mary Scherm

1892: + Sister Agnes Amann, Sister Aquinata Stegmair, *Sister de Ricci Barkley*, Sister Stephen O'Connor, Sister Alphonsa Weber; •Helen Turner

1893: + Sister Columba Weigel

1895: + *Sister Magdalene Lechner*, Sister Clotilda Kransler, Sister Vincent Meyer, *Sister Beda Schmid*, Sister Alexandrine Kalb, Sister de Pazzi Reil, Sister Evangelist Huber, Sister Anselma Martin, Sister Albertine Schieder, Sister Stella Schroll, Sister Angela Fahrnholz, Sister Baptista Crimmins, Sister Xavier Flynn, Sister Thomasine Schmid, Sister Aloysius Amann, *Sister Clarissa Attenberger, Sister Rosaria Klimmer*, Sister Luitgardis Finsterholze, Sister Isadore Kinney, Sister Ferdinand Miller, Sister Alypia Kingston, Sister Edward Hausche, Sister Geraldine Owens

1896: + Sister Mercedes Sheehan, Sister Louise Buttner, Sister Navarette Kottermair; •Mary Wintermeier

1897: + Sister Concepta Lanigan, Sister Loyola Lyons, Sister Callista Neilan

1898: + Sister Isabella Sedlmaier, Sister Anastasia Albrecht

1899: + Sister Sebastian Schimmel, Mother Aquinas Cooney; •Margaret Collins

1900: + Sister Eugene Berrodin, Sister Assumpta Waickmann; •Nellie Stapleton

1901: + Sister Marcella Hughes, Sister Alberta Kinlan, Sister de Sales Dempsey, Sister Victoria Kraak; •Bertha Seindler

1902: + *Sister Regina Meyer*, Sister Arthur Haskins

1903: + Sister Cyrilla Guterl, Sister de Chantal Gilmartin, Sister Adalaide Bradley

The following lay Sisters took their official place in the Registry after
1903.

1884: + Sister Gabriel Storzinger
1885: + Sister Benedicta Brandt
1887: + Sister Armella Daschinger, Sister Annunciata Pfab
1888: + Sister Ann Connolly, Sister Ludivica Kottermair, Sister Barbara
        Nickodem
1889: + Sister Marcoline Corcoran, Sister Dorothea Doppel, *Sister
        Luca Altschaffel*, Sister Elizabeth Kreil
1890: + *Sister Villani Meindl*
1891: + Sister Florian Eglseder, Sister Damian Forster, Sister Thecla
        Danninger, Sister Michael McCabe; •Anna Frank
1892: + *Sister Scholastica Deter*, Sister Andrew Angerer
1893: + Sister Hilary Spitzer, Sister Nothburga Neuhauser, Sister Bor-
        gia Scherr, Sister Agatha Beischl, Sister Crescenz Bruner, *Sister
        Venantia Lehner*
1895: + Sister Margaret Kottermair, Sister Martha Bauer, Sister Zita
        Lavelle, Sister Bartholomew Schoner, Sister Humberta Schlo-
        der, Sister Virgine Schloder, Sister Sabina Ebner, Sister
        Matthew Ebner, Sister Dionysius Crimmins, Sister Rufina
        Lutz, Sister Alexander Smith, Sister Albina Kneidl
1896: + Sister Bertrand Rowald, Sister Placida Renkl
1900: + Sister de Aza Vielweib
1903: + Sister Leonard Ryan, Sister Eleanor Schneider, Sister Ferrer
        Conroy, Sister Monica Glennon, Sister Laura Berrodin, *Sister
        Justina Oberdoerster, Sister Henrietta Weaver;* •Pauline Gies,
        Clara Wybel, Margaret Quinn
1904: + Sister Perpetua Corcoran, Sister James Arkins, Sister Mannis
        Joyce, Sister Germaine Collins, Sister Marietta Anna, Mother
        Joseph Dunn, Sister Priscilla Rolling, Sister Ursula Hofmann,
        Sister Consuela Weber, Sister Charles Byrider, *Sister Jeannette
        Kimpflin*, Sister Alexine Brunette; •Elizabeth Holohan, Agnes
        Grimes
1906: + Sister Patricia Turner, Sister Hilda Connors, Sister Severina
        Hughes, Sister Thomas Holohan, Sister Edmund Callinan,
        Sister Felix Cummings, Sister Raymond Sandiford, *Sister
        George Fendt, Sister Cornelia Jacobs*; •Mary Mullins, Mary
        Dringler
1907:   *Sister Petronilla Grosser,* + Sister Gerard Esker, *Sister Matilda*

Baechter, Sister Rosalie Cavanagh, Sister Louis Mullen, Sister Corona Lawler, Sister Fidelis Motzer, Sister Ildephonse Leimbeck, Sister Felicitas Rogers, Sister Dolores Dunn, Sister Cyprian Curtis; ●Margaret McDonald, Emily Lavasseur, Frances Sheets

1908:   Sister Amabilis Callery, + Sister Benigna Deck, *Sister Clare McCowen*, Sister Julianna Maher, Sister Constance Dressler, Sister Servatia Madigan, Sister Martina Brentzell, Sister Victorine Loughlin; ●Marie Trudell, Catherine McNamara, Elizabeth Currier

1909: + Sister Pauline McCue, Sister Wilhelmina Peterson, *Sister Josepha Werner*, Sister Rita Joyce

1910: + Sister Caroline Grogan, Sister Flavia McGrath, Sister Benedicta Farrenkopf; ●Theresa Kramer, Margaret Maher

1911: + *Sister Florentine Peridon*, Sister Leocadia McNamara, Sister Beatrice Stapleton, Sister Raphael Powers, Sister Edwardine Murphy, Sister Celeste Daly, Sister Leona Moell, Sister Francis Rolling; ●Nora Hanrahan

1912:   *Sister Bernard Friess;* + Sister Sylvester McCarthy, Sister Blanche Grahek, *Sister Dominic Behler*, Sister Consolata Brown, Sister Carlotta Egan, Sister Lawrence Klein, Sister Virgilia Stratton; ●Veronica Bove, Grace Horning, Anna Kramer, Florence Brogan, Mary Steiner, Elizabeth Steiner, Anna Cunningham, Elizabeth Brennan

1913:   Sister Hildegarde Lill, Sister Georgiana Balzer, Sister Lucy Dugan, + Sister Alma Loesh, Sister Cleophas Greeter, Sister Genevieve McKaig, *Sister Clarita Bernard, Sister Victor Geis*, Sister Seraphine Nicolai, Sister Casimir Dunn, Sister Gregory Glanzman, Sister Clement Kiley

1914: + Sister Casilda Donnelly, Sister Florence Hart, Sister Gabriella Gallagher, Sister Robert Garland, Sister Evarista McCarthy, Sister Antoinette Kineke; ●Susan McKenna

1915:   Sister Mercedes Monahan, Sister Gerard Neff; + Sister Hyacinth Coss, *Sister Austin Bernard*, Sister Vincentia Qualey, Sister Valerian Motzer, Sister Rosemary Heimback, Sister Jane Connelly, Sister Miriam Bachmann, Sister Germaine Clarke, Sister Francis Moser, Sister Teresita Skiffington, Sister Eileen Coyle, Sister Viola Nagle; ●Agnes Donelan, Martha Collins, Maria McDermott, Catherine Smith

1916:   Sister Alberta Somoracki, Sister Amata Kosco, Sister Anita
        Schantz, Sister Gemma Perini, Sister Leonarda Knapp, Sister
        Marie Leifer, Sister Aedan Feury, *Sister Clarice Ganshirt*;
        + Sister Jerome Healey, Sister Mary John McKaig, Sister de
        Lourdes Cregier, Sister Zita Dodge, Sister Camilla Horan,
        Sister Mary Haflin, *Sister Paschal Dillon, Sister Romaine
        Sartory*; •Agnes Gavan, Blanche Smith
1917:   *Sister Constantia Schreiner, Sister Helena Pikunas;* + Sister
        Eucharia Boehner, Sister Grace Murray, Sister Charlotte Smith,
        Sister Maurice Matthews, Sister Petrina Denieff; •Anna
        Odrezze, Helen Langemann
1918:   Sister Borromeo McSorley, Sister Inez Roberts, Sister Gerald
        Corcoran, Sister Alice Conhartoski, Sister Concilia Considine;
        + Sister Jean Handley, Sister de Lima Fallon, Sister Anthony
        Seiz, Sister Conradine Moran, Sister Carmel Leifer, Sister
        Sienna Ferrin, Sister Augusta O'Sullivan, Sister Lucille Corbett,
        Sister Ruth Walsh, *Sister Ralph Koeberle*, Sister Laurentia
        Donahue; •Mary Schilling, Gertrude Woods
1919:   Sister Andrea Reusch, Sister Eugene Mahon, Sister Christopher
        McCann; + Sister Lavina Ennis, Sister Fortunata Linder, Sister
        Angela Bachmann, Sister Marguerite Coss, Sister Aquin Raher;
        •Coletta Moine, Agnes Shader
1920:   Sister Miriam Judge; + Sister Tomasita Nesbihal, Sister
        Dominice Kentz, Sister Veronique Flesch, Sister Antoinette
        Monti, Sister Rosalie Coss
1921:   Sister Margaret Mary Harder, Sister Anna Marie Gross, *Sister
        Mercia Boyle*; + Sister Patrick Hughes, Sister Kathleen Kelly,
        Sister Clare Marie Maguire, Sister Catherine Marie Martin,
        Sister James Marie Cummings, Sister Ferdinand Bowes, Sister
        Annunciation Burke, Sister Patrice Walsh, Sister Agonia
        Gallagher, Sister Ethel Marie Waegele, *Sister Bernice Roussert*;
        •Lucy Kozlarek
1922:   Sister Teresa Marie Healey, Sister Josita Devan, Sister de
        Lourdes Lynch; + Sister Bonaventure Moley, Sister Richard
        Howley, Sister Callista Weber, Sister Catherine Fitzgerald,
        Sister Monica Hart, *Sister Stella Romito*
1923:   Sister Immaculata Boyle, Sister Pierre Engel, Sister Seraphine
        Janicek, Sister Alicia Giles, Sister Benigna O'Brien, Sister
        Bernarda Riehl; + Sister Cornelius Mullen, Sister Charlotte

Gross, Sister Corita O'Mara, Sister Joan Hession, Sister Francis Beirne, Sister Adele Delaney, Sister Estelle Esser, Sister Helena Carbon, Sister Berchmans Flynn

1924: Sister Joanna Tracy, Sister Ancille Hunger, Sister Roberta Ansbro, Sister Leo O'Neill, *Sister Ricardo Fanelly*, Sister Georgita Milbauer; + Sister Catherine de Ricci Golding, Sister Norine Keeshan, Sister Rosita Krompinger, Sister Flavia McKee, *Sister Bertha Klein, Sister Bonita Kinsinger*, Sister Elaine Cummings, Sister Cletus Barrett, Sister Agnita Conlon

1925: Sister Norbert O'Neill, *Sister Josephine Riffle*, Sister Celine McGuire, Sister Corine Burns, Sister Marita Donnelly, *Sister Dominica Pangburn*, Sister Mildred Larkin; + Sister Lucina Hyland, Sister Angeline Pescherine, Sister Ruth Durr, Sister Annette McCormic, *Sister Elizabeth Moine*; ●*Rose Bauman*, Harriet Rooney

1926: Sister Edmund O'Neill, Sister Florence Dunn, Sister Marion Carlin, Sister Carlotta Barry, *Sister Colette Tapp*, Mother Dolorita Ansbro; + Sister Aurelia Ferrin, Sister Hubert Gantley, Sister Rosaire Knerr, Sister Demetria Kelly, *Sister Theresa McGuckin, Sister Bernardine Beyrer; Sister Lawrene Kleinwechter*, Sister Noelene Daly; ●Marion Bocker, Mary O'Brien, Muriel Linder

1927: Sister Mary Paul Moley, Sister Herbert Dreyer, Sister Alexia Cullen, Sister Alouise (Marie Curtis), Sister Carmelita Hausser, Sister Rosemond Murphy, Sister Claude Halsch, Sister Caritas Ashe, Sister Suso Griffin, Sister Maria Maresca, *Sister Rosalia Paulus*, Sister Marjorie Guilfoyle, Sister Eucharista Kempner; + Sister Ceslaus Lacey, Sister Annunciata Phillips, Sister Dorette Wallace, *Sister Margarita Walsh, Sister Seraphine Summers*; ●Margaret Flynn, Eleanor Quinn, Regina Routh, Clare Titus, Elizabeth Connolly, Angeline Barwood, Marcella Quinlan

1928: Sister Virginia McNally, Sister Incarnata Luke, Sister de Lima Noonan, Sister Lillian Flanagan, Sister Therese Affuso, Sister Marcella Lynch, Sister Frederick Engel, *Sister Coletta Ruhlin*, Sister Letitia Clare, Sister Vincetta de Angelo; + *Sister Magdalena Karam, Sister Miria Schutter, Sister Marcelline Oyster, Sister Eucharia Zwick, Sister Dolorosa Muzik, Sister Lorita Gerbec*, Sister Harietta McGinniss, Sister Michaeleen Whelan; ●Catherine Herold, Lucille Linder

1929:   Sister Georgina Christiano, Sister Madonna Kelly, Sister
        Eugenia Fenton, Sister Dolorine Broshnahan, Sister Walter
        Proudfoot, Sister Rosina McTague, Sister Patricius Feury,
        Sister Maura Campbell, Sister Eleanor Fay, Sister Madeline
        Sorge, Sister Julian Coskren; + Sister Francesca Hackett, Sister
        Helena Flanagan; •Ethel McManus

1930:   Sister Clara Holleran, Sister Barbara Smith, Sister Emily
        Pileggi, Sister Immacula Winberry, Sister Pius Sirois, Sister
        Margaret Ames, Sister Teresa Higgins, Sister Jordan Costello;
        + Sister Diana Korten, Sister Muriel Griffin; •Catherine
        McCormick

1931:   Sister Josephine Kilkelly, Sister Matthias Casey, Sister
        Bernadette Dirig, Sister Mary George Dury, Sister Faith
        Deisler, Sister Emmanuel Blanche, Sister Marcella Henry
        Hoffman, Sister Catherine Louise Burke, Sister Anna Daniel
        Coleman, Sister Josephine Clare Rinn; + Sister Regina
        McEntee; •Marion Bott, Elizabeth Nowicki

1932:   Sister Mary Magdalen O'Connor, Sister Winifred Kilkelly,
        Sister Agnes Mary Schmid, Sister Mary Roland Thompson,
        Sister Veronica Mary McMahon, Sister Mary Elizabeth
        Shackett, Sister Rita Thomas Luddy; + Sister Agnes Joseph
        Peters, Sister Margaret Veronica Welsh, Sister Dorothy Marie
        Shiel; •Anna Bertossi

1933:   Sister Margaret Imelda Dooley, Sister Clare Louise Kinchel-
        lagh, Sister Catherine Patricia Condon, Sister Rita Joan
        Wagner, Sister Helen Marie Horrigan, Sister Julia Marie
        Moore, Sister Mary Dorothy Broderick, Sister Mary Cecilia
        Quirk, Sister Helen Veronica Leahy, Sister Helen George Ponto,
        Sister Marie Frances Kling, Sister Eleanor Patricia King;
        + Sister Margaret Clare Foley

1934:   Sister Louis Marie Heizler, Sister Gertrude Marie Lennon,
        Sister Anne Catherine Kron, Sister Margaret Anne Fahy, Sister
        Florence Marie Hofmann, Sister Mary Agatha Broshnahan,
        Sister Irene Marie Richards, Sister Catherine Frances Patterson,
        Sister Margaret Eucharia Farrell; •Catherine Lacey

1935:   Sister Grace Marie Murray, Sister Anne Kathleen Mc Mahon,
        Sister Rita Marie McGlynn, Sister Rita Joseph Hofmann;
        + Sister Loretta Claire Dunn; •Catherine Rooney, Josephine
        Cummins

1936:   Sister Catherine Denis (Mary Catherine Shultz); + Sister

Margaret Francis Scheidel, Sister Dorothy Joseph Russell

1937: Sister Geraldine Marie Kegel, Sister Janet Peal, Sister Gertrude Agnes Thompson; + Sister Agnes Winifred Otis, Sister Anne Dolores Sprouls, Sister Margaret Maureen McDonald, Sister Catherine Cecilia Machette; •Rita Donaky, Margaret Brander, Mary O'Leary

1938: Sister Helen Anne Murphy, Sister Mary Josepha Comer, Sister Lucille Marie Whittington, Sister Mary Harriett Gutteridge, Sister Maria Gabriel Brackett, Sister Rita Margaret Chambers, Sister Helen Ruth Taylor; + Sister Loretta Anne King; •Mary Lena Levesque, Julia Rommel

1939: Sister Veronica Joseph Sprouls, Sister Mary Robert Liddell, Sister Agnes Genevieve Bowman, Sister Helena Margaret Griffin, Sister Eileen Marie McGuinness; + Sister Marianna Pawlikowski, Sister Rita Catherine Sullivan, Sister Margaret Teresa O'Neil, Sister Mary Edna Newton, Sister Eileen Imelda Lynch; •Dorothy O'Neill

1940: Sister Catherine Bernadette Hughes, Sister Jane Frances Cuthbertson, Sister Anne Francis Moon, Sister Gerardine Mueller, Sister Grace John Cuffe, Sister Mary Amelia Cetera; + Sister Alice Edward McCarthy; •Margaret Nolan, Yolanda Toppeta, Elizabeth Greeley

1941: Sister Margaret Virginia Blum, Sister Bernadette Agnes Proudfoot, Sister Rita Frances Dowd, Sister Mary Martha Ley, Sister Maureen Elizabeth Breslin, Sister Patricia Ann Finnerty; + Sister Josephine Anne O'Keefe; •Louise Hanley, Rita Mitchell, Juanita Skinner, Edwardina Cassidy, Margaret Soltis

1942: Sister Doris Ann Bowles, Sister Grace Eileen Hewitt, Sister Loretta Marie Kruger, Sister Mary Kathleen Malarky, Sister Mary Dominic Tweedus, Sister Charles Marie Booy, Sister Evelyn Francis Klett, Sister Rose Marie Whelan, Sister Marietta Anne Harding, Sister Margaret George Miller; + Sister Elizabeth Mary Brush; •Mildred Denein, Elizabeth Henkel

1943: Sister Margaret William McDonald, Sister Margaret Ellen Rooney, Sister Mary Evelyn Mulcahy, Sister Helen Marguerite Leddy, Sister Elizabeth Marie Mason, Sister Ann Thomas Haberle, Sister Frances Michael Murphy, Sister Ann Dominic Vano, Sister Eileen Raymond (Eileen Byrne); •Marie King

1944: Sister Ann Maureen Castelot, Sister Marie Therese Gleeson, Sister Robert Marie Eberenz, Sister Joseph Marie Gessner,

Sister Georgine Marie Conrad, Sister Agnes Bernard Duggan, Sister James Marie Hannon, + Sister Grace Thomas (Grace Engels); •Alice Kelly, Mary Hogan

1945:   Sister Margaret Louise Conery, Sister Genevieve Marie Long, Sister Magdalene Marie Duffy

1946:   Sister Alice Matthew Thees, Sister Virginia Pierre Feury, Sister Jean Therese Thompson, Sister Bernadette Michael Makely, Sister Catherine Thèrêse Jewell, Sister Elizabeth Francis Brisson, Sister Theresa Irene Doherty, Sister Kathleen Margaret O'Connell; •Agnes Duff, Theresa Rizzitta

1947:   Sister Vincent Marie (Shirley Krisam), Sister Carmel Dominic (Carmel Livolsi), Sister Inez Raymond (Inez Marie D'Bonaventura), Sister Elizabeth Michael Boyle, Sister Catherine Christopher Sullivan, Sister Julia Catherine (Julia Marie Solden), Sister Anne John O'Loughlin; •Claire McCarthy, Marie Shallis, Eleanor Dale, Dolores Hogan, Louise Huray

1948:   Sister Edith Magdalen Visic, Sister Jeanne Veronica Duszynaki, Sister Maureen James Fahey, Sister Helen Francis Coakley, Sister Rose Martin Ping, Sister Jeanne Adrienne Kierce, Sister Leo Marie (Marie Murphy), Sister Margaret Charles De Rosa; + Sister Maureen Anne (Mary Freiss); •Elvira Pavia, Patricia Carroll, Mary McSparron

1949:   Sister Francis Gerald Wirth, Sister Lauretta Timothy Healy, Sister Margaret Thomas McGovern; + Sister Mary Bernard Dolan; •Josephine La Salandra, Rose Ann De Aiso, Mary Ann O'Hare, Elvira Bonanni, Margaret Stack, Marguerite Ryan, Joan Smith

1950:   Sister Mary Helen Raba, Sister Grace Margaret Haggart, Sister Catherine Gerard Kirchner, Sister Margaret Lucille Peterson, Sister Agnes Louise Freynet, Sister Mary Ann O'Connor, Sister Emma Patricia Murphy; •Margaret Coppinger, Claire Wauters, Lois Schroeder, Antoinette Di Lonardo, Catherine Hunter, Ruth Nesbihal, Madeline Di Gioacchino

1951:   Sister Mary Thomas Aussem, Sister Mary Kevin (Ann Byrne), Sister Mary Albert (Bettyann Schultz), Sister Mary Martin (Ann Murtha), Sister Diane (Barbara Jukins), Sister Christine Coakley, Sister Mary Rose Fallon, Sister Mary John Kearney, Sister Joanne Ryan, Sister Brien Lee; + Sister Imelda (Kathleen Driscoll); •Irene Marston, Gloria Tenton, Eileen Murphy, Elaine Larsson, Gloria Fama, Carmen Fragoso, Marion Meney

1952:   Sister Stephen (Rita Calabrese), Sister Alexis Stewart, Sister
        Dolores Procassini, Sister Jeanne Passek, Sister Gilbert Frey,
        Sister Mary Agnes Gore, Sister Bertrand Austin; •Mary
        Oberlies, Loyola Stuckey, Jane Durr, Joan Sporer, Margaret
        McDonald, Rosemary McNeil, Eileen Mulligan, Margaret
        Pelechis, Kathleen Kelty

1953:   Sister Augustine O'Donnell, Sister Catherine de Ricci (Cather-
        ine Killeen), Sister Michel Rodgers, Sister Mary Claire Weber,
        Sister Kenneth (Mary McAlary), Sister Lenore De Coster, Sister
        Vincent (Joan Doyle), Sister Stella Patvin; •Florence Carpenter,
        Eileen Brady, Mary Kearns, Patricia Walsh, Laura Finucan,
        Arlene Osterman, Patricia McDermitt

1954:   Sister Rene Waseleski, Sister Mary Andrew Kennedy, Sister
        Angelica Del Fattore, Sister Leonard (Nancy Bourk), Sister
        Vivien Jennings; + Sister Mark (Grace Cassidy), Sister Edward
        (Barbara Dempsey); •Suzanne Faulkner, Patricia O'Brien, Joan
        Flanagan, Gladys Ryan, Evelyn Ryan, Eileen Coughlin, Sally
        McGrath, Margaret McAlary

1955:   Sister Shaun Sheflott, Sister Mary Judith Lynch, Sister Mary
        Daniel O'Keeffe, Sister Rosalie Prew, Sister Dolorosa (Ann
        Marie Lennon), Sister Adrienne Fallon, Sister Terrance
        (Patricia McKearney), Sister Coleen (Catherine Daly), Sister
        Joyce Vincent, Sister Marilyn Chupilo, Sister Ferrer (Maureen
        Murnane), Sister Pauline Caddle; •Catherine O'Connor, Mary
        Egan, Margaret O'Leary, Dorothy Reilly, Marie Mazza, Irene
        Cunnane, Eileen Kelly, Mary Ann Kennedy, Alice Romano,
        Madeline Castora, Mary Sanborn, Anne Marie Murphy, Cath-
        erine Romano

1956:   Sister Michaelann (Jacqueline Scanlon), Sister Alacoque
        (Margaret Mary Meyer), Sister Noel (Mary McGuinness), Sister
        Veritas Picardi, Sister Danelle McCarthy, Sister Loyola
        (Catherine Reilly), Sister Patrice Werner, Sister Gerarda Panek,
        Sister de Montfort Kinchellagh; + Sister Timothy (Shirley
        Maechler); •Patricia Tickey, Valerie Simpson, Dolores Ryan,
        Helen De Blase, Barbara Streisguth, Ann Holland, Julia
        Santiago, Diane Donovan, Patricia McCarthy, Frances Mallon,
        Catherine Kelly, Joan Doerbeck, Agnes De Vestern

1957:   Sister Jeanne Marie Prince, Sister Mary Immaculate McGov-
        ern, Sister Thomas Marie Morris, Sister Maurice (Joan
        Spingler), Sister Mary Charles (Barbara Moore), Sister Xavier

(Carol Van Billiard), Sister Elise Redmerski, Sister Brigid Brady, Sister Jonathan (Mary Ann Brezina); •Marjorie Carter, Mary Francis Walter, Patricia Kelly, Florence Maclachlan, Ida Costello, Dolores Nagle, Mary Modlin, Alice Seamon, Janice Webb, Patricia Lynn, Mary Ann Prendergast, Helen Frances Enright, Cecelia Duerr, Ann Marie Schmitt, Catherine Offringa, Ann Murray

1958:   Sister Clarita Mayer, Sister Seton Marie (Miriam Kiernan), Sister Mary Luke Dworshak, Sister Nicholas (Judith Foloky), Sister Mary Roger (Honora Werner), Sister Michael Marie (Justine Pinto); •Muriel McArdle, Dorothy Obropta, Janet Reilly, Barbara McNeill, Louise Hegarty, Genevieve Ferraer, Mary Ann Leonard, Mary Louise Pugh, Josephine Melici, Nancy Lyman, Marie Varley, Blanche Gwendolyn Dowd, Maureen Garrison, Patricia Howard, Joan Vargoscik, Joan Richardson, Catherine Kress, Mary Anne Greco, Dorothy Noble, Maryann Filosa, Joan Ferger

1959:   Sister Anne Brendan (Anne Sullivan), Sister Anne Claire (Lois Kikkert), Sister Mary Consolata (Jane Albert), Sister Mary William (Patricia Mahoney), Sister Daniel Marie (Alice Uhl), Sister Mary Victorine (Barbara Catherine Krug), Sister Catherine Brian Tierney, Sister Ann Manus (Patricia O'Donnell), Sister Miriam Therese Mac Gillis, Sister Ann Monica Seeman; •Sara Jane Beckley, Joan D'Alessio, Elizabeth Jesonis, Eileen McElligott, Mary Lou Sherry, Margaret Murtha, Patricia Turvey, Judith Barrett, Lucille Momot, Lorraine Grill, Lyn Skeuse, Bernadette Pankowicz

1960:   Sister Mary Regis McCann, Sister Francis Margaret Smith, Sister Stephen Louise (Miriam Cannavale), Sister Anne Leonard (Mary Agnes Sullivan), Sister Joseph Dorothy (Donna Marie O'Brien), Sister Jeanne Catherine Sheridan, Sister Marie Patrick Boyle, Sister John Margaret (Lois Curry), Sister Jane Marie Smith; •Jeannine Nazarro, Carmella Zocchi, Gary Ann Dunn, Moira Sharkey, Michaeleen Green, Faith Andres, Marilyn Hegarty, Rosemary Arena, June Mahalik, Barbara Staffa, Lois Connor, Maureen McCabe, Barbara Simms, Jacqueline Patton, Lynn O'Brien, Patricia Gallagher, Marylou Bourgers, Frances Rettino, Virginia Gail Giuseffi

1961:   Sister Joan Marie Sheehan, Sister Rose Michael (Josephine Mascera), Sister Alice Edward Classick, Sister Michael Maurice

Leahy, Sister M. Victoria (Lillian Tovo), Sister Mary Francis (Arlene Antczak), Sister De Sales (Anne Halpin), Sister Daniel Anne (Eleanor Uhl), Sister Marie Paul Schessler, Sister Patricia Mary (Patricia Hogan); •Patricia Parkerton, Nancy Pierro, Mary Jane O'Brien, Ruth Hatch, Barbara Hagan, Carolyn Kennedy, Margaret Tevlin, Donna Hirsch, Kathleen Detlet, Jacqueline Knoetgen, Teresa Suruda, Theresa Vertucci, Stephanie Bernarducci

1962:   Sister Ann Marie Rimmer, Sister Helen John (Catherine Waters), Sister Elaine Marie (Elaine Keenan), Sister Marie Gerard (Jeanne Goyette), Sister Rita William (Mary Fallon), Sister Regina Marie (Mary Reid), Sister Grace William (Gracemarie Cirino), Sister Margaret Joseph (Margaret Jaros), Sister Catherine Mary (Patricia Costello); •Shirley Marry, Kathleen Kelly, Julia Jacques, Marie Louise De Benedittis, Kathleen Ruf, Sharon Burke, Marion Fama, Louise Vodjack, Mary Lytle, Angelina Rispoli, Geraldine Convery, Carol Treger, Patricia Davis, Julia Bersey, Mary Hanlan, Catherine Bouton

1963:   Sister Teresita (Diane Papp), Sister M. Paula (Suzanne Janis), Sister M. Lawrence (Patricia Crowley), Sister M. James (Ellen McMahon), Sister M. Arthur (Geraldine Yerg), Sister M. Thomasine (Alice McCoy); •Joan Smith, Leona Ryan, Dorothy Aste, Grace Moore, Patricia Lewis, Joan Burns, Mildred Spader, Patricia Palmer, Anne Busby, Margaret Lenehan

1964:   Sister Raymond (Suzanne McCaffrey); •Heather Sharkey, Margaret O'Malley, Roseanne Naples, Kathryn Kifner, Mary Pytel, Kathleen McMahon, Maureen Kennedy, Eileen McGinty, Veronica Tuohy, Kathleen Hall

1965:   Sister Francis Mary (Patricia Brennan), Sister Claire Marie (Barbara Cowan), Sister Xavier Mary (Elsie Bernauer), Sister Ellen Mary (Eileen Ivory); •Kathleen Duffy, Roseanne Cerra, Elizabeth Eick, Cynthia Little, Carol Ping, Patricia Sullivan, Kathleen McCarthy, Anne Marie Minnefor

1966:   Sister Bernadette Mary Raia, Sister Kenneth Marie (Judith Russell); •Jeanette Strand, Ann Marie Simini, Eleanor O'Connor, Ann Crisci, Patricia Ruhnke, Alyce Famula, Joyce Murphy, Joan Del Fattore, Mary Dalessio

1967:   Sister Mary Joseph Bircsak, Sister Barbara Ann (Deborah Lynch), Sister Peter Mary (Rosemary Gleeson); •Dorothy Barnes, Barbara Brandes, Dolores Lew, Rosemary Ortolano, Eleanore Miragliotta, Barbara Witt, Bernadette McKenna,

Judith Ann Picarelli, Janet Anne Sparra, Judith Bierne, Mary
Virginia Dougherty, Jane Sweeney, Dolores McGreevy, Mary
Ann Sauer, Joanne Gongla, Susann Shea, Gertrude Parker

1968:   Sister Judith Ann (Judith Rudolph), Sister Colleen Marie
(Colleen Gray), Sister Gertrude Mary Dunham, •Barbara
Liebold, Marian Daly, Linda Van Pelt, Mary Eileen Welsh,
Mary Jo Pompeo, Susan Ivory, Marianne Nazaretta, Maureen
Bonner

1969:   Sister Donna Ciangio, Sister Patricia Brian (Patricia Tavis);
+ Sister Terrence Marie (Theresa Puccio); •Therese Mamel,
Nancy Becker, Rita Williams, Patricia Eula, Marian Sulenski,
Alberta Vasarkovy, Elaine Cote, Maurica Doyle, Margaret
Willeford, Celeste Sullivan

1970:   There was no profession in 1970. The candidates who entered in
1968 made profession in January or June of 1971

1971:   Sister Joanne Marie Beirne, Sister Kathleen Lynch, Sister Marie
Elizabeth (Mary Elizabeth Magno), Sister Ann O'Rourke, Sister
Pamela Ann (Pamela Higgins), Sister Margaret Marie
(Margaret Ann Ryan); •Mary Jane O'Connor, Jane Ellen
Selinske, Mary Denise Walsh, Barbara Capriglione, Mary
Berlin, Margaret Mary Moorehead, Teresa Bruno

1972:   Sister Joanne Brennan, Sister Patricia Stringer, Sister Frances
Sullivan; •Mary Connors, Donna Fahy, Sally Foley, Nancy
Kasyan, Michele Metzler, Dianne Sarama, Jean Michelin

1973:   Sister Patricia Tully; •Kathy Leo

1974:   •Brenda Seibert, Judith Chapdelaine

1975:   Sister Marie Mueller, Sister Dorothy Mae Saunders; •Margaret
Mary Faulkner, Mary Edwards

1976:   Sister Luella Ramm, Sister Beverly Cardino

1977:   •Maryclaire McMahon

1978:   Sister Patricia Daly, Sister Carol Dempsey; •Margie Fox

1979:   Sister Mary Lou Bauman, Sister Lena Picillo; •Deborah
Sturdevent

1980:   Sister Jayne Sadowski; •Linda Dowling

1980:   Novice—•Frances Kujalowics

1980:   Postulants—Barbara Ann Dolan, Karen Anne Schiaraffa

For these and all those who entered as postulants and left before
receiving the habit, whose names are not recorded, we praise the Lord and
ask for an increase of members and a renewal of the Spirit for all those
who have been a part of the fabric of this history.

APPENDIX B

Chronology of Community Educational Commitments

Mother Catherine

Sept. 1872 St. Boniface, Jersey City (Sisters withdrawn, June 1973)

Sept. 1878 St. Dominic Academy (Moved to Bergen Avenue as High School, 1913)

Sept. 1884 St. Dominic, Roseland Avenue, Caldwell (Transferred to the Mount, 1893)

May 1887 St. Mary, Rahway

Sept. 1887 St. John the Baptist, Jersey City

Sept. 1887 St. Mark, Rahway (Closed 1912)

Sept. 1887 Our Lady of Mt. Carmel. Boonton

Nov. 1888 St. Venantius, Orange (Sisters withdrawn, June, 1976)

Sept. 1889 Assumption, Lawrence, Mass. (Sisters withdrawn, June, 1971)

Sept. 1889 St. Ann, Newark

Sept. 1893 Mount St. Dominic Academy Grade School, Caldwell (Closed 1980)

Sept. 1893 Mount St. Dominic Academy High School, Caldwell; Junior High added Sept. 1980

Mother Mechtilde

Sept. 1895 St. Mary Magdalene, Newark (Closed June, 1920)

Sept. 1901 St. Mary, Dover (Wharton) (Sisters withdrawn, June, 1979)
Sept. 1902 St. Joseph, Union City (Sisters withdrawn, June, 1977)
Sept. 1907 St. Aloysius, Caldwell
Aug. 1909 St. Brigid, North Bergen (Sisters withdrawn, June, 1978)
Sept. 1910 St. Virgil, Morris Plains
Mother Avelline
Sept. 1913 St. Aedan, Jersey City
Sept. 1915 S.S. Peter and Paul, Hoboken
Sept. 1916 St. Mary, Rutherford
Sept. 1919 St. Catherine, Elizabeth (Sisters withdrawn, June, 1979)
Sept. 1920 Lacordaire, Upper Montclair
June 1923 Blessed Sacrament, Bridgeport, Conn. (1974: St. Mary, St. Cryil Methodius and Blessed Sacrament merge as East Bridgeport School System; 1976: St. Cyril and Methodius withdrawn; presently school is called Blessed Sacrament/Saint Mary)
Sept. 1924 Our Lady of the Lake, Verona (Sisters withdrawn, June, 1973)
Sept. 1924 St. Francis Xavier, Newark (Sisters withdrawn, June, 1950)
Sept. 1924 Sacred Heart, Dover (Sisters withdrawn, June, 1977)
Sept. 1927 St. Elizabeth, Linden
June 1927 Holy Spirit, Asbury Park (Sisters withdrawn, June, 1979)
Twenty locations in Ohio were begun during the same timespan. Of these, ten were closed between 1887 and 1911.
Mother Joseph
Sept. 1931 St. Michael, Union
Sept. 1939 Caldwell College, Caldwell
Sept. 1940 St. Margaret, Bayou La-Batre, Alabama (High School division closed 1959)
Sept. 1943 St. Catherine, Mobile, Alabama (Sisters withdrawn, June, 1976)
Nov. 1944 St. Peter Claver (mission), Asbury Park (Sisters withdrawn, 1957)
Mother Aquinas
Sept. 1949 Bayley Ellard Regional High School, Morristown (Dominicans withdrawn 1959)
Sept. 1950 St. Paul the Apostle, Irvington
Sept. 1950 St. John the Apostle, Clark
Sept. 1952 St. Philomena, Livingston
Sept. 1953 St. Teresa, Paterson (Sisters withdrawn, June, 1977)

Sept. 1953 Ascension, New Milford

Sept. 1953 St. Cassian, Upper Montclair

Sept. 1953 Christ the King, Hillside (Sisters withdrawn, June, 1973)

Sept. 1954 St. Philip the Apostle, Clifton (Sisters withdrawn, June, 1979)

Sept. 1954 St. Theresa, Kenilworth (Sisters withdrawn, June, 1977)

Sept. 1954 Our Lady of Peace, New Providence

Sept. 1956 Sacred Heart, Lyndhurst

Sept. 1956 St. Joseph, West Orange (Sisters withdrawn, June, 1976)

Mother Dolorita

Sept. 1958 St. Catherine of Siena, Cedar Grove

Sept. 1958 Our Lady of Sorrows, Garfield (Principal only as of June, 1973)

Sept. 1958 Nativity, Midland Park (Principal only as of June, 1973; Sisters withdrawn, June, 1975)

Sept. 1958 St. Peter the Apostle, Parsippany

Sept. 1961 Our Lady of Lourdes, Mountainside (Sisters withdrawn, June 1971)

Sept. 1961 Our Lady of the Blessed Sacrament, Roseland (Sisters withdrawn, June, 1971)

Sept. 1962 Union Catholic Girls High School, Scotch Plains (Merged with Union Catholic Boys High School, 1979)

Sept. 1963 St. Agnes, Clark (Sisters withdrawn, June, 1979)

Sept. 1963 St. Raphael, Livingston (Sisters withdrawn, June, 1973)

Sept. 1965 St. Thomas More, Fairfield (Principal only as of June, 1973; withdrawn, 1979. Director or Religious Education retained)

Sept. 1965 Holy Spirit, Union (Principal only as of June, 1975; withdrawn 1977)

Sept. 1967 Paul VI High School, Clifton (Principal only as of 1979)

Sister Vivien

Sept. 1969 Project Link, Newark

Sept. 1969 St. Francis De Sales, Abaco, Bahamas

Sept. 1971 St. Antoninus, Newark (Adopted from Charities. Closed June, 1974)

Sept. 1971 Our Lady of the Blessed Sacrament, East Orange (Adopted from Charities; principal only; withdrawn, June, 1978)

APPENDIX C

Chronology of Community Leadership

GENERALATE

1881–1894 Mother Catherine and consultors (1893): Sisters Mechtilde, Joanna, Seraphica, Alacoque, Josephine, Avelline, Dominica

1894–1912 Mother Mechtilde and Sisters Avelline, Joanna, Augustine, Josephine, Hyacinth, Dominica, Basil (1900–1903), Pia (1904–1912), Philip (1903–1912)

1912–1915 Mother Avelline and same consultors as above, with addition of Sister Irene and Mother Mechtilde ex-officio

1915–1921 Reverend Mother Avelline and Council: Sisters Alacoque, Irene, Joseph (S.G.), Clementine; Bursar, Sister Imelda

1921–1927 Reverend Mother Avelline and Council: Sisters Veronica, Mechtilde (replaced by Sister Augustine in 1925), Joseph, Mary Philip (S.G.); Bursar, Sister Isadore

1927–1933 Reverend Mother Joseph and Council: Sisters Avelline, Veronica, Aloysius (S.G.), Clarissa (replaced by Sister Perpetua, July 1929); Bursar, Sister Rose

1933–1939 Reverend Mother Joseph and Council: Sisters Veronica, Mother Avelline, Perpetua, Aloysius (S.G.): Bursar, Sister Rose

1939–1945 Reverend Mother Joseph and Council: Sisters Veronica, Concepta, Servatia (S.G.), Mother Avelline; Bursar, Sister Thomas

1945–1951 Mother M. Aquinas and Council: Sisters Concepta, Felix, Servatia (S.G.), Victoria; Bursar, Sister Marie

1951–1957 Mother M. Aquinas and Council: Sisters M. Dolorita, Germaine, Norine (replaced by Sister Anita, 1953), Servatia (S.G.); Bursar, Sister Adele

1957–1963 Mother M. Dolorita and Council: Sisters Alouise, Mary Dorothy, Marie (S.G.), Mercedes; Bursar, Sister Borromeo

1963–1969 Mother M. Dolorita and Council: Sisters Germaine, Miriam, Marie (S.G.), Mercedes; Bursar, Sister Borromeo

1969–1975 Sister Vivien Jennings (Major Superior) and Council: Sisters Rita Margaret (Person and Community), Catherine Bernadette (Government), Agnes Bernard (Formation), Bertrand (Apostolate), Margaret Thomas (Secretary General and Public Relations), Edith Magdalen (Bursar and Finance)

1975–1979 Sister Vivien Jennings and Council: Sisters Margaret Thomas (Person and Community), Alice Uhl (Government), Patricia Mahoney (Formation), Bertrand (Apostolate), Lenore de Coster (Secretary General and Public Relations), Edith Magdalen (Bursar and Finance)

1979   Sister Margaret Thomas (Major Superior), Sister Patricia Mahoney (Person and Community, on-going Formation), de Montfort (Apostolate), Helen Marguerite (Finance). Appointed: Sister Rita Joseph (Secretary General), Sister Alice Matthew (Treasurer), and Sister Gerarda Panek (Public Relations)

FORMATION PERSONNEL

Novitiate (1881 ff)

Mother Catherine
Mother Mechtilde
Sister Alacoque Hartel
Sister Hyacinth Hertrich
Sister Assumpta Waikman
Sister Rose Kunz

Sister Concepta Lonigan
Sister Fidelis Motzer
Sister Flavia McKee
Sister Incarnata Luke
Sister Mary John Kearney
Sister Mary Immaculate McGovern

Sister Veronica Murrer   Sister Joan Doyle
Sister Aquinas Cooney   Sister Angelina Rispoli
          Sister Catherine Christopher Sullivan

Postulate (1920–1927; 1955 ff)
Sister Josephine Vogel   Sister Arlene Antczak
Sister Maura Campbell   Sister Patricia Mahoney
Sister Corine Burns   Sister Patricia Crowley
Sister Genevieve Marie Long   Sister Frances Sullivan

Juniorate (1928–1959)   *Scholasticate* (1959 ff)
Sister Clarissa   Sister Maura Campbell
Sister Amabilis   Sister Mary McGuinnes
Sister Inez   Sister Emma Patricia
Sister Anna Daniel   Sister Patricia Mahoney
Sister Herbert   Sister Catherine Christopher
Sister Immaculata
Sister Mary Agatha
Sister Helen Ruth

Vocation Directresses (from 1971–1977 the Novice
Mistress served as Vocation Directress)
(1952ff)
Sister Frances Beirne   Sister Frances Sullivan
Sister Mildred Larkin   Sister Patricia Stringer
Sister Genine Reilly   Sister Carmel Livolsi (diocesan
Sister Leona Ryan   office)

Dominican Apostolic Volunteers (1975 ff)
Sister Maureen McCabe and Sister Josephine Mascera
Personnel Directresses
Sister Catherine Bernadette, Sister Patricia Costello and Sister Margaret
Lucille

School Supervision
Sister Felix   Sister Germaine (Secondary)
Sister Perpetua   Sister Walter (Secondary)
Sister Mercedes   Sister Celine (Music)
Sister Margaret
Sister Frederick
Sister de Montfort

Diocesan
Sister Catherine Killeen (Newark)
Sister Christine Coakley (Newark)
Sister Mary Judith Lynch (Paterson)
Sister Doris Ann Bowles (Archdiocesan Superintendent)

The Community grarefully acknowledges the spiritual leadership provided by the diocesan priests who served as chaplains and the Dominican Fathers who ministered as weekly and extraordinary confessors as well as retreat masters.